Developing Inclusi

In this groundbreaking book, one of the world's leading authorities on ways of developing equitable education systems addresses the greatest challenge facing education systems around the world, that of developing schools that are effective in educating all children. Using evidence from research carried over the last 25 years in many countries, Mel Ainscow explains pathways to be followed in order to turn the global aspiration for inclusion and equity into policy and practices in the field.

Making extensive use of examples from different parts of the world, *Developing Inclusive Schools* provides:

- Practical guidance for teachers regarding ways of making their lessons inclusive;
- Accounts of how this thinking has been implemented in schools;
- Advice for school leaders on how to create an inclusive culture within their organisations;
- Examples of how inclusion and equity have influenced national policies in different contexts;
- Explanations of the implications for policy makers, researchers and teacher educators.

Developing Inclusive Schools will be of huge significance to researchers, educators and practitioners in the fields of education policy and politics, inclusion and special education around the world.

Mel Ainscow is Emeritus Professor, University of Manchester; Professor of Education, University of Glasgow; and Adjunct Professor at Queensland University of Technology. A long-term consultant to UNESCO, he is internationally recognised as an authority on the promotion of inclusion and equity in education.

'Mel Ainscow draws on a lifetime of passionate and unrelenting commitment to inclusion, equity and professional collaboration to write a book that is one for the ages. He shows how we can and should achieve inclusion by adhering to a small number of general principles but with total respect for the unique nature of every country, culture and context in which these principles are applied. This is the masterwork of inclusion in education'.

Andy Hargreaves, *Boston College and University of Ottawa*

'An inspirational must-read for anyone concerned with equity in education, this book maps the struggles, the learning and the insights of a leading thinker in the field'.

Lani Florian, *University of Edinburgh*

'Mel Ainscow has carried out the best and most thorough work I know on grounded system change. He has the examples, he has led the work, he has worked with practitioners, policy makers, communities and students. Read *Developing Inclusive Schools* carefully and fully: it contains a treasure trove of insights'.

Michael Fullan, *OISE/University of Toronto*

'*Developing Inclusive Schools* is a milestone in understanding how inclusive education developments have evolved during the last three decades. It not only maps and addresses challenges, dilemmas and tensions, but paves the way forward towards more inclusive education systems across the world'.

Renato Opertti, *UNESCO-IBE (International Bureau of Education)*

Developing Inclusive Schools

Pathways to Success

Mel Ainscow

Routledge
Taylor & Francis Group

LONDON AND NEW YORK

Designed cover image: © Getty Images

First published 2024
by Routledge
4 Park Square, Milton Park, Abingdon, Oxon OX14 4RN

and by Routledge
605 Third Avenue, New York, NY 10158

Routledge is an imprint of the Taylor & Francis Group, an informa business

© 2024 Mel Ainscow

British Library Cataloguing-in-Publication Data
A catalogue record for this book is available from the British Library

Library of Congress Cataloging-in-Publication Data
Names: Ainscow, Mel, author.
Title: Developing inclusive schools : pathways to success / Mel Ainscow.
Description: New York : Routledge, 2024. | Includes bibliographical references and index.
Identifiers: LCCN 2023051589 (print) | LCCN 2023051590 (ebook) | ISBN 9781032571423 (hbk) | ISBN 9781032571430 (pbk) | ISBN 9781003438014 (ebk)
Subjects: LCSH: Inclusive education--Cross-cultural studies. | Mainstreaming in education--Cross-cultural studies. | Educational equalization--Cross-cultural studies. | Special education--Cross-cultural studies. | Education and state--Cross-cultural studies. | Educational change--Cross-cultural studies.
Classification: LCC LC1200 .A558 2024 (print) | LCC LC1200 (ebook) | DDC 371.9/046--dc23/eng/20240123
LC record available at https://lccn.loc.gov/2023051589
LC ebook record available at https://lccn.loc.gov/2023051590

ISBN: 978-1-032-57142-3 (hbk)
ISBN: 978-1-032-57143-0 (pbk)
ISBN: 978-1-003-43801-4 (ebk)

DOI: 10.4324/9781003438014

Typeset in Galliard
by KnowledgeWorks Global Ltd.

Contents

Preface

When I started thinking about writing this book, my idea was to produce a second, updated edition of *Understanding the Development of Inclusive Schools*, which was first published in 1999. Having taken advice from various colleagues, including Alison Foyle at Routledge, I decided that it had to be a new book.

As the book developed, I came to see it as a sequel to the earlier volume. It reports my efforts to put the suggestions I made over 25 years ago into practice. In doing so, it revisits many of my earlier publications, reworking and refining ideas and reflecting further on examples of practice in the field.

A few months ago, one of my colleagues commented that much of my work involved telling stories. Initially I thought that this was intended as a criticism, but I have come to realise that it is something to celebrate. As this book illustrates, stories can be a powerful way of challenging thinking and encouraging reflection, sometimes leading to action.

Running through these accounts is my own story. Over the years, my work has been related to a variety of headline themes, starting from special education, through to integration, on to inclusive education and then educational equity. Bearing this formulation in mind, the book reflects the evolution of my ideas regarding how to foster inclusion and fairness within education systems (see Ainscow 2016a, for a detailed account of this process). In particular, my thinking has moved in the following directions:

- From a narrow focus on special education to a much wider concern with processes, I have called *school improvement with attitude*;
- From efforts to achieve integration for particular groups of learners towards the development of inclusive forms of education that focus on the *presence, participation and achievement* of all children and young people;
- From an analysis of the characteristics of individual learners to the analysis of *barriers and resources* that exist within particular learning contexts;
- From an emphasis on the development of individual schools towards efforts to achieve system-level reform through a focus on *levers for change*.

A pattern emerges from the accounts I provide. This involves periods of uncertainly as my thinking was challenged by new experiences and different contexts, through a process I have described as *making the familiar unfamiliar.* What also becomes evident is the way that working with colleagues has helped me to cope with these disturbances, such that they often became critical incidents that led to developments in my ideas.

Given the range of projects reported in this book, it is inevitable that lots of colleagues have been involved, far too many to name here. In some instances, their names are mentioned in the references I list. Many of these are colleagues at the Universities of Manchester and Glasgow and at Queensland University of Technology. And, of course, I owe a debt of gratitude to the many teachers, students and policymakers with whom I have cooperated.

Finally, I owe a particular thanks to Alan Dyson and Kiki Messiou who each read and commented on earlier drafts of the text. As on many other occasions over the last 25 years, their challenging comments, perceptive advice and professional guidance were of enormous importance.

Mel Ainscow
Manchester
September 2023

1 Taking an inclusive turn

In the concluding paragraph of my 1999 book, *Understanding the Development of Inclusive Schools*, I commented on the evaluation I had carried out with colleagues of an initiative to reform kindergarten education in Anhui Province, China. I explained that we had concluded that the project had been successful, not least in drawing the attention of teachers in the schools to new possibilities for reaching out to children in their local communities who had previously been excluded. Over the gateway to one of the kindergartens was a motto that seemed to be guiding their efforts. It read, *All for the children, for all the children*. What I witnessed in many of the classrooms reflected the commitment of the teachers to this principle.

With this principle in mind, this book focuses on what is arguably the greatest challenge facing education systems around the world, that of finding ways of including all children and young people in schools. In economically poorer countries this is mainly about the millions of children who are not able to attend formal education (UNESCO 2020). Meanwhile, in wealthier countries, such as my own, many young people leave school with no worthwhile qualifications, whilst others are placed in special provision away from mainstream education and some choose to drop out since the lessons seem irrelevant (OECD 2012). Across these diverse contexts, learners from economically disadvantaged backgrounds are particularly vulnerable to marginalisation, as are those with disabilities and others from minority groups.

Faced with these challenges, there is evidence of an increased interest internationally in the idea of making schools more inclusive and education systems more equitable (Ainscow 2020a). However, the field remains confused as to the actions needed in order to address this challenge. In the chapters that follow, I set out to provide some clarity on what needs to be done to move schools and, indeed, educational systems forward. In particular, I describe my search for pathways to success.

In this introductory chapter I begin by explaining the basis of my argument, linking this to the ideas I presented in my 1999 book *Understanding the Development of Inclusive Schools*.

DOI: 10.4324/9781003438014-1

An inclusive turn

Whilst recent years have seen an increased interest in the idea of inclusive education, the field remains confused as to what this implies. Indeed, I recall hearing the Australian academic Roger Slee comment that the idea has travelled so much that it has become *jet lagged*.

In many countries, inclusive education is still thought of as an approach to serving children with disabilities within general education settings. However, internationally, it is increasingly seen more broadly as a reform that supports and welcomes diversity amongst all learners (UNESCO 2020). As such, it presumes that the aim of inclusive education is to eliminate social exclusion that is a consequence of attitudes and responses to diversity in race, social class, ethnicity, religion, gender and abilities.

Traditionally, the main response to difficulties experienced by learners has been through forms of special education. In recent years, this field has gone through a crisis of thinking about its guiding assumptions. As a result, the appropriateness of separate systems of education has been challenged, both from a human rights perspective and from the point of view of effectiveness (Tomlinson 2017). More specifically, it is argued that the continued use of what is sometimes referred to as a *medical model* of assessment – within which educational difficulties are explained in terms of a child's deficits – prevents progress in the field, not least because it distracts attention from questions about why schools fail to teach so many children successfully.

With this agenda as my overall focus, I have argued that what is needed is an *inclusive turn* (Ainscow 2006). This represents a radical new approach to the way that difficulties in education are defined and addressed. As I will explain, this change is difficult to introduce, not least because the traditional perspectives and practices associated with the field of special education continue to dominate thinking in the field, encouraged by what Sally Tomlinson (2012) refers to as *an expanded and expensive SEN industry*.

Throughout this book, I argue that an inclusive turn is more likely in contexts where there is a culture of collaboration that encourages and supports problem-solving. This involves those within a particular context in working together to address barriers to education experienced by some learners. It also necessitates supportive relationships between teachers, learners, families and others involved in the lives of young people.

A sequel

This book should be seen as a sequel to *Understanding the Development of Inclusive Schools*, which was published 25 years ago. In writing that earlier book, my aim was to stimulate and challenge those concerned with school effectiveness and improvement to consider how far their work really has taken account of the learning of *all* children. At the same time, I set out to challenge those involved in the field of special education to reconsider their roles in the light of this different perspective.

The ideas that I explored and the suggestions I made in that earlier book were, at the time, radical. They arose as a result of reflections on experience of working with teachers and schools over previous years, in the United Kingdom and overseas. In particular they had arisen from my involvement in two large-scale projects. The first of these was a school improvement project, Improving the Quality of Education for All (IQEA), which involved a small team of university academics collaborating with English schools during what proved to be an unprecedented period of national educational reform. The experiences of this project led us to rethink many of our assumptions as to how school improvement can be achieved, noting in particular the way local histories and circumstances bear upon the improvement efforts of individual schools (Hopkins, Ainscow and West 1994).

The second project was a UNESCO teacher education initiative to do with the development of more integrated forms of schooling. This project, called *Special Needs in the Classroom*, originally involved research in eight countries (i.e. Canada, Chile, India, Jordan, Kenya, Malta, Spain and Zimbabwe) and subsequently led to dissemination activities of various kinds in over 50 countries (Ainscow 1994).

During the early phases of the UNESCO project, it was assumed that materials and methods would be developed that could be distributed in a straightforward way for use in different parts of the world. Gradually those of us leading the project came to realise, as others involved in international development activities in education had done (e.g. Fuller and Clark 1994), that schooling is so closely tied to local conditions and cultures that the importation of practices from elsewhere is fraught with difficulties. In other words, learning from other people – particularly those who live their lives in faraway places – is by no means straightforward!

The experiences of these two initiatives had major implications for the development of the thinking and practice I described in the 1999 book. In particular, they led me to reflect on how we can develop understandings that will be useful in encouraging the development of schools that will be successful in fostering the participation and learning of all students within a community. This pointed to questions such as: how do we make use of the diversity of experience and knowledge that exists within any given context to support the improvement of educational arrangements? At the same time, how can we learn from the experiences of others in ways that can support the development of practice? If so, what is the nature of the learning that might occur?

Learning from differences

In addressing these questions, the 1999 book reflected on my own experiences of working alongside practitioners to illustrate ways in which an engagement with differences can stimulate new thinking about the issue of reaching out to all learners. Throughout the text, I used examples based on observations made in schools and classrooms in various parts of the world in order to show how such experiences had stimulated a reconsideration of my thinking about practice in my own country. This led me to argue that the power of comparison for the development of practice comes not from lifting approaches and moving them from place to place but from using the stimulus of more exotic environments to reconsider thinking and practice in familiar settings (Delamont 1992). It is about making what is strange familiar and what is familiar strange, as when seeing your own town in a new light when showing a visitor round. Features that are normally ignored become clearer, possibilities that have been overlooked are reconsidered and things that have become taken for granted are subject to new scrutiny.

The shifts in my thinking that took place as a result of these two projects involved a reconceptualisation of how some children come to be marginalised within or even excluded from schools. This shift drew attention to many possibilities for the development of schools that might easily have been overlooked. It also helped me to realise that a concern with local context has to be at the heart of any development activities, whether these are concerned with classrooms, schools or overall education systems.

In this way I also became aware of the importance of existing practice as the essential starting point for our efforts. Indeed, as my colleagues and I looked more closely at what was going on in the classrooms in which we worked, we realised that very often much of the expertise that was needed in order to reach out to all learners was already there. As a result, the strategy becomes less about importing ideas from elsewhere and more to do with finding ways of making better use of local knowledge. Put simply, our experience is that schools know more than they use! Therefore, the task becomes essentially one of helping teachers, and those supporting them, to analyse their own practices as a basis for collaboration and experimentation.

Definitions

In *Understanding the Development of Inclusive Schools*, I argued that the agenda of educational improvement should be concerned with overcoming contextual barriers that may be experienced by any student. However, the tendency at the time was (and still is today) to think of inclusive education as being concerned only with students with disabilities and others categorised as having *special educational needs*. Furthermore, inclusion is often seen as simply involving the movement of students from special to mainstream contexts, with the implication that they are *included* once they are there.

In contrast, I see inclusion as a never-ending process, rather than a simple change of state, and as dependent on continuous pedagogical and organisational developments within mainstream schools. The implication is that every school is inclusive to some extent and that all schools have to continue a never-ending process of finding ways of reaching new students who bring with them new challenges.

In taking this thinking forward, it is important to emphasise the positive benefits of inclusion for parents and children rather than seeing inclusion as an ideological principle to be accepted as an article of faith. Specifically, it is helpful to emphasise the distinction between needs, rights and opportunities. All children have needs (e.g. for appropriate teaching), but they also have the right to participate fully in a common social institution (a local mainstream school) that offers a range of opportunities for them. The current system in many countries often forces parents to choose between ensuring that their child's needs are met (which often implies placement in special provision of some form) and ensuring that they have the same rights and opportunities as other children (which implies mainstream school placement). The aim therefore should be to create a system where these choices become unnecessary.

A narrow view of inclusion has particularly limited validity in economically poorer nations, though, as I show in later chapters, experiences in such countries may cause reflection on the appropriate focus of policy in wealthier countries. It is clear that in any country, a lack of facilities, the need for curriculum reform, insufficient or inappropriate teacher education, poor school attendance, problems of family poverty, cultural dislocation, the conditions giving rise to street children, problems of disease and differences between the language of instruction and the home language may be as important as issues of disability in affecting participation in schools.

All of this moves the issue of inclusion to the centre of discussions about the improvement of schooling. Rather than being a somewhat marginal theme, concerned with how a relatively small group of students might be attached to mainstream schools, it lays the foundations for an approach that can lead to the transformation of the system itself. Of course, none of this is easy, not least in that it requires the active support of everybody involved in the business of schooling, some of whom may be reluctant to address the challenges that I present.

In this respect my work has a particular message for those, like me, who have previously made their careers in the special education field. We have to be clear about our purposes and self-critical about the approaches we use. Too often our contributions have unintentionally acted as barriers to the development of more inclusive forms of schooling.

Ingredients

Bearing these concerns in mind, my 1999 book went on to explain how an engagement with less familiar contexts can stimulate a process of critical reflection, thus enabling previous experiences to be reconsidered and new possibilities for improvement to be recognised. In my own case this drew attention to a series of propositions that have continued to guide my school improvement efforts.

To be clear, these ideas do not represent a recipe that can be lifted and applied in any context. Rather they should be seen as a series of *ingredients* that can guide the development of schools in order that they can become more effective in reaching out to all learners.

I went on to explain these ingredients as follows:

Ingredient 1.   Use existing practices and knowledge as starting points for development

It took me a long time to appreciate that existing practice represents the best starting point for development activities, not least because of my previous experience and training in the field of special education. Specifically, it took me many years to recognise that the ways in which earlier attempts to develop integrated arrangements for students defined as having special needs had often, unintentionally, undermined our efforts. As we tried to integrate such students into mainstream schools, we imported practices derived from earlier experience in special provision. What we learned was that many of these approaches were simply not feasible in primary and secondary schools. At the same time, their use tended to encourage new forms of segregation, albeit within mainstream school settings.

Here, I am thinking in particular of the individualised responses based on assessments and programmes of support for individuals of the sort that have been the predominant orientation within the special education world. For many years this was very much the orientation that shaped my own work (e.g. Ainscow and Muncey 1989; Ainscow and Tweddle 1979, 1984). Gradually, however, experience taught me that such approaches do not fit with the ways in which mainstream teachers plan and go about their work. For all sorts of sensible and understandable reasons, the planning frame of such teachers has to be that of the whole class. Apart from any other considerations, the sheer numbers of children in the class and the intensity of the teacher's day make this inevitable.

Consequently, when integration efforts are dependent upon the importation of practices from special education, they usually lead to difficulties. Indeed, they are likely to involve yet new forms of segregation, albeit within mainstream settings (Fulcher 1989), through the use of what Slee (1996) calls *dividing practices*. For example, in some countries, we have seen the proliferation of often untrained classroom assistants who work with some of the most vulnerable children and their individual programmes in mainstream schools. When such support is withdrawn, teachers feel that they can no longer cope. Meanwhile, the legal requirement for individualised education plans in some countries has encouraged colleagues in schools to feel that even more children will require such responses, thus creating massive budget problems.

The gradual recognition that schools for all will not be achieved by transplanting special education thinking and practice into mainstream contexts opened my mind to new possibilities that I had previously failed to recognise. Many of these relate to the need to move away from the individualised planning frame, referred to above, to a perspective that emphasises a concern for and an engagement with the whole class. Thus, as an Italian teacher explained many years ago, what is needed are strategies that *personalise* rather than individualise learning.

In the 1999 book I argued that an understanding of what these strategies might involve can be gained from the study of practice, particularly the practice of class teachers in primary schools and subject teachers in secondary schools. As my awareness of the value of such studies developed, so my interest in observing and trying to understand practice grew. This led me to argue that a scrutiny of the practice of what we sometimes call *ordinary teachers* provides the best starting point for understanding how classrooms can be made more inclusive.

Ingredient 2.   See difference as opportunities for learning rather than problems to be fixed

In *Understanding the Development of Inclusive Schools*, I argued that attempts to reach out to all learners will be influenced by the ways in which student differences are perceived. At the risk of oversimplifying what is undoubtedly a complicated issue, I suggested two possibilities. On the one hand differences may be seen in a normative way. This means that students are defined in terms of certain taken-for-granted criteria of normality, against which some come to be seen as being abnormal. Within such an orientation those who do not fit into existing arrangements are seen as needing attention elsewhere or, at least, assimilation into the status quo. Alternatively, perceptions may be guided by a view that all students are unique, with their own experiences, interests and aptitudes. Associated with this second, transformative orientation is a belief that schools have to be developed in ways that can take advantage of this diversity which is, therefore, seen as a stimulus for learning and development.

Here some of the traditional practices of many Western countries, including my own, have discouraged movement towards a transformative approach. Specifically, the tradition has been to perceive some students' differences as requiring a technical response of some kind (Heshusius 1989; Iano 1986). This leads to a concern with finding the *right* response, i.e. different teaching methods or materials for students who do not respond to existing arrangements. Implicit in this formulation is a view that schools are rational organisations offering an appropriate range of opportunities, that those students who experience difficulties do so because of their limitations or disadvantages and that *they*, therefore, are in need of some form of special intervention (Skrtic 1991). It is my argument that through such assumptions, leading to a search for effective responses to those children perceived as being *different*, vast opportunities for developments in practice and improvements in schools are overlooked.

I accept, of course, that it is important to identify useful and promising strategies. However, I believe that it is erroneous to assume that systematic replication of particular methods in themselves will generate successful learning, especially when we are considering populations that historically have been marginalised or even excluded from schools. This led me to argue that an emphasis on a search for *quick-fix* methods often serves to obscure attention from more significant questions such as, why do we fail to teach some students successfully?

Consequently, I argued that it is necessary to shift away from a narrow and mechanistic view of teaching to one that is broader in scope and takes into account wider contextual factors. In particular it is important to resist the temptation of what Bartolome (1994) refers to as the *methods fetish* in order to create learning environments that are informed by both action and reflection. In this way, by freeing themselves from the uncritical adoption of so-called effective strategies, teachers can begin the reflective process that will allow them to recreate and reinvent teaching methods and materials, taking into account contextual realities that can either limit or expand possibilities for improvements in learning.

It is important to remember, too, that schools, like other social institutions, are influenced by perceptions of socioeconomic status, race, language and gender. This being the case, I argued that it is essential to question how such perceptions influence classroom interactions. In this way the emphasis on methods must be broadened to reveal deeply entrenched deficit views of *difference*, which define certain types of students as *lacking something* (Trent, Artiles and Englert 1998). Specifically, we have to be vigilant in scrutinising how such deficit assumptions may be influencing perceptions of certain students.

Teaching methods are neither devised nor implemented in a vacuum. Design, selection and use of particular teaching approaches and strategies arise from perceptions about learning and learners. In this respect even the most pedagogically advanced methods are likely to be ineffective in the hands of those who implicitly or explicitly subscribe to a belief system that regards some students, at best, as disadvantaged and in need of fixing, or, worse, as deficient and, therefore, beyond fixing.

This so-called deficit model has been subject to massive criticism over many years (e.g. Ballard 1997; Dyson 1990; Fulcher 1989; Oliver 1988; Trent, Artiles and Englert 1998). This has helped to encourage a shift of thinking that moves explanations of educational failure away from a concentration on the characteristics of individual children and their families towards a consideration of the process of schooling. However, despite good intentions deficit thinking is still deeply ingrained and too often leads many to believe that some students have to be dealt with in a separate way. In a sense it confirms the view that some students are *them* rather than part of *us* (Booth and Ainscow 1998).

This further encourages the marginalisation of some students, whilst at the same time distracting attention away from the possibility that their presence can help to stimulate the development of practices that might well benefit all students. In other words, I argued, those who do not respond to existing arrangements should be regarded as *hidden voices* who, under certain conditions, can encourage the improvement of schools. In this way, differences can be seen as opportunities for learning rather than as problems to be fixed.

Ingredient 3.   Scrutinise barriers to student participation

The approach to inclusion that I suggested in my 1999 book involves *a process of increasing the participation of students in, and reducing their exclusion from, school curricula, cultures and communities.* In this way the notions of inclusion and exclusion are linked together because the process of increasing participation of students entails the reduction of pressures to exclude. This link also encourages us to look at the various constellations of pressures acting on different groups of students and acting on the same students from different sources.

For these reasons, I suggested that yet another starting point for the development of practice within a school has to be with a close scrutiny of how existing practices and organisational arrangements may be acting as barriers to the *presence, participation and learning* of some learners. This means that attention has to be given to helping practitioners to develop a reflective attitude to their work such that they are continually encouraged to explore ways of overcoming such contextual barriers. With this in mind, the approaches discussed in my earlier book placed considerable emphasis on the need to observe the process of schooling and to listen carefully to the views of those involved.

In adopting this same perspective in the chapters that follow, many illustrations of what form this can take are provided, as well as examples of methods for analysing contexts that have been found to be helpful. As I will explain, all of this is part of a form of action research that I call collaborative inquiry, a phrase that I adopted from the work of other scholars (i.e. Reason and Bradbury 2001).

Ingredient 4.   Make effective use of available resources to support learning

I explained in my earlier book that a feature of lessons that seem to be effective in encouraging student participation is the way available resources, particularly human resources, are used to support learning. In particular, I emphasised the importance of a range of resources that is available in all classrooms and yet is often poorly used – that of the students themselves.

Within any classroom the students represent a rich source of experiences, inspiration, challenge and support which, if utilised, can inject an enormous supply of additional energy into the tasks and activities that are set. However, all of this is dependent upon the skills of the teacher in harnessing this energy. This is, in part, a matter of attitude, depending upon a recognition that students have the capacity to contribute to one another's learning, recognising also that, in fact, learning is to a large degree a social process.

This thinking can help teachers to develop the skills necessary to organise classrooms that encourage this social process of learning. Here we can learn much from some of the economically poorer countries of the South, where limitations of resources have sometimes led to a recognition of the potential of *peer power*, through the development of *child-to-child* programmes (Hawes 1988). Meanwhile, in Western countries, the idea of cooperative group work has led to the development of teaching specifications that have enormous potential to create richer learning environments (e.g. Johnson and Johnson 1989).

Ingredient 5.   Develop a language of practice amongst teachers

Much of the earlier work with schools that I described in my 1999 book involved attempts to strengthen the capacity of schools to handle change. This led me to look closely at schools where improvement efforts had led to changes in practice to see what lessons might be learned from their experiences.

In stating that, however, I was not suggesting that our engagement with such a school would help to devise blueprints that can point the way forward for all schools. What I have learnt as a result of many years of working in schools to support the introduction of a variety of innovations is that they are complex and idiosyncratic places. What seems to help development in one school may have no impact or even a negative effect in another.

So, whilst we can, I believe, learn through vicarious experiences, this learning has to be respected for its own qualities. Essentially it is a form of learning that provides a stimulus to reflect on existing experience and current understandings rather than a means of providing prescriptions that can be transposed to other environments. Consistent with this view, throughout the chapters that follow, I provide many examples of classroom encounters and school processes that have provided me with such a stimulus.

Ingredient 6.   Create conditions in schools that encourage a degree of risk-taking

My interest in studying practice took me beyond just a consideration of the work of individual teachers. Much of my early research convinced me of the importance of the school context in creating a climate within which more effective practices can be developed. The nature of such positive contexts can take many forms, and, therefore, attempts at generalisations are very difficult. Nevertheless, my monitoring of developments in particular schools, over time, suggests certain patterns that are at least worthy of consideration.

In particular, these experiences led me to define a series of organisational conditions that seem to facilitate the risk-taking that seems to be associated with movements towards more inclusive practices. More specifically they indicate that such movement is not about making marginal adjustments to existing arrangements but rather about asking fundamental questions about the way the organisation is currently structured, focusing on aspects such as patterns of leadership, processes of planning and policies for staff development. In this way the development of inclusive schools comes to be seen as a process of school improvement (Ainscow 1995).

My impression is that when schools are successful in moving their practice forward, this tends to have a more general impact on how teachers perceive themselves and their work. In this way a school begins to take on some of the features of what Senge (1989) calls a learning organisation, i.e. *an organisation that is continually expanding its capacity to create its future* (p. 14). Or, to borrow a useful phrase from Rosenholtz (1989), it becomes *a moving school,* one that is continually seeking to develop and refine its responses to the challenges it meets.

I argued that, as schools move in such directions, the cultural changes that occur can also impact on the ways in which teachers perceive students in their classes whose progress is a matter of concern. What may happen is that as the overall climate in a school improves, such children are gradually seen in a more positive light. Rather than simply presenting problems that have to be overcome or, possibly, referred elsewhere for separate attention, such students may be perceived as providing feedback on existing classroom arrangements. Indeed, they may be seen as sources of understanding as to how these arrangements might be improved in ways that would be of benefit to all students. If this is the case, as I have already suggested, the children sometimes referred to as having special needs represent hidden voices that could inform and guide improvement activities in the future. In this sense, as my colleague Susan Hart suggested, special needs are special in that they provide insights into possibilities for development that might otherwise pass unnoticed (Hart 1992).

It is important to recognise, of course, that the cultural changes necessary to achieve schools that are able to hear and respond to the *hidden voices* are in many cases a profound one. Traditional school cultures, supported by rigid organisational arrangements, teacher isolation and high levels of specialisms amongst staff who are geared to predetermined tasks, are often in trouble when faced with unexpected circumstances. On the other hand, the presence of children who are not suited to the existing *menu* of the school provides some encouragement to explore a more collegiate culture within which teachers are supported in experimenting with new teaching responses. In this way problem-solving activities may gradually become the reality-defining, taken-for-granted functions that are the culture of the inclusive school, i.e. a school that is attempting to reach out to all students in the community.

Conclusion

In this chapter I have summarised the ideas that I presented in my 1999 book, *Understanding the Development of Inclusive Schools*, as overlapping and interconnected by the idea that attempts to reach out to all learners within a school have to include the adults as well as the students. I argue that schools make progress towards more inclusive arrangements through a process of growth that leads to the development of conditions within which every member of the school community is encouraged to be a learner.

Twenty-five years later, the approaches to the promotion of inclusive schools recommended in this book build on and take forward these same ideas. As such, they are less about the introduction of particular techniques, or new organisational arrangements, and much more about processes of social learning within particular contexts.

I argue that the use of evidence as a means of stimulating experimentation and collaboration should be seen as a central strategy. As Copland (2003) suggests, inquiry can be the *engine* to enable the distribution of leadership that is needed in order to foster participation in learning and the *glue* that can bind a community together around a common purpose.

All of this has major implications for leadership practice within schools and across education systems. In particular, it calls for efforts to encourage coordinated and sustained efforts around the idea that changing outcomes for vulnerable groups of students is unlikely to be achieved unless there are changes in the thinking of adults. Consequently, the starting point must be with policy makers and practitioners: in effect, enlarging their capacity to imagine what might be achieved and increasing their sense of accountability for bringing this about. This may also involve tackling taken-for-granted assumptions, most often relating to expectations about certain groups of students, their capabilities and behaviours.

Chapter summaries

The chapters that follow explore the implications of this thinking for policy and practice in the field. In summary, they are as follows:

Chapter 2, Searching for pathways, presents a radical challenge to thinking in the field regarding the idea of inclusive education. Contrasting this with the predominant approach – that of serving children with disabilities within general education settings – it is argued that the aim of inclusive education must be to eliminate social exclusion that is a consequence of attitudes and responses to diversity in race, social class, ethnicity, religion, gender and ability. As such, it represents a major challenge to existing thinking regarding the development of education systems. A roadmap for promoting an inclusive dialogue within schools is provided by the *Index for Inclusion*, a review instrument developed originally for use in England but now available in many countries. The chapter goes on to describe the changes that have occurred with regard to global thinking since 1990. In so doing, it indicates the ways in which my ideas have influenced these international policy moves. I then go on to describe a series of studies carried out since the publication of my 1999 book that inform the rationale presented in subsequent chapters. All of these studies involved groups of university researchers in supporting, recording and analysing collaborative inquiries as they occurred in project schools.

Chapter 3, Developing schools for all, explains my attempts to contribute *directly* to thinking and practice in relation to inclusive developments in schools. For many years I have worked closely with educational practitioners, in my own country and overseas, as they have attempted to move towards more inclusive ways of working. Acting as a critical friend, I see my task as helping them to learn from their experiences and, in so doing, to point to patterns and examples of practice that might be instructive to others who are addressing similar agendas. In this sense my aim is not to propose recipes that can be applied universally but rather to suggest ingredients that might be worthy of further consideration within particular contexts. In this chapter I use examples from the field in order to explain the nature and potential of this approach.

Chapter 4, Promoting inclusive practices, explores how partnerships be-tween practitioners and researchers can facilitate developments in practice. This involves an engagement with evidence generated through a range of methods, much of which involve listening to the voices of those involved in processes of education, particularly the views of students. I argue that such evidence can make the familiar unfamiliar in ways that challenge as-sumptions, encourage the sharing of ideas and stimulate joint efforts to develop more inclusive practices. However, none of this provides a simple way forward. To gain the potential benefits, it is necessary to address the challenges involved in using processes of collaborative inquiry within the busy contexts of schools and in contexts where many other barriers exist.

In **Chapter 5, Using collaborative inquiry**, I provide practical guidance on methods for promoting inclusive developments in schools. It is important to stress that this guidance does not take the form of a blueprint to be fol-lowed rigidly. Rather, it is intended to be adapted by those leading develop-ments in particular contexts. Examples are used to illustrate how different forms of evidence can be used to identify and address barriers experienced by learners. Particular emphasis is placed on the importance of observation and engaging with the views of learners. The implications for relationships are also examined, including the roles of those who have leadership tasks.

Chapter 6, Leading inclusive school development, stresses the importance of contextual factors in helping to promote inclusive thinking and prac-tices. In particular, it focuses on the importance of the deeper levels of basic assumptions and beliefs that are shared by members of an organisa-tion, operating unconsciously to define how they view themselves and their working contexts. I argue that progress in relation to inclusion depends on the extent to which these values include the acceptance and celebration of difference, and a commitment to offering educational opportunities to all students, coupled with the extent to which they are shared across a school staff. Guidance is provided as to how relevant leadership practices can be developed.

Widening the agenda, **Chapter 7, Changing education systems,** argues that the extent to which schools can move in an inclusive direction is much influenced by external factors, not least those associated with national poli-cies as they are implemented at the local area level. With this in mind, the chapter uses experience of working with policy makers in attempts to move thinking and practice forward in relation to inclusion in schools. Reflecting on these experiences, the chapter suggests a series of propositions that can be used to promote equity more widely across education systems in ways that will facilitate the development of inclusive schools. The sorts of fac-tors that make it difficult to implement these ideas are explained, including the current emphasis on the so-called *what works* approach to educational improvement.

Chapter 8, Addressing barriers, looks more closely at the concerns raised in the previous chapter about the difficulties involved in the introduction of efforts to promote inclusion and equity within education systems. Using examples from England, Wales, Cyprus, Uruguay and Scotland, it suggests that there are many sources of inequity in education, related to political, economic, social, cultural and institutional factors, and that these factors vary both within and across countries. This means that whilst lessons can undoubtedly be learned from the accounts provided, they must be interpreted and applied with care. Reflecting on these experiences, the chapter explains that barriers facing students can arise from pressures on schools created by national policies, assessment and accountability measures. In addition, the attitudes and actions of practitioners in the light of these factors sometimes act as further barriers to the presence, participation and achievements of learners.

Chapter 9, Facing new challenges, focuses on new developments that are influencing education policies in various countries. To illustrate the possibilities and challenges that these create, the chapter focuses on developments in England, where recent years have seen efforts by successive governments to improve the education system. These have involved an increased emphasis on the idea of allowing schools greater autonomy within a policy context based on market forces as the main improvement strategy. This approach to educational development is a growing international trend that has major implications for the promotion of equity. It is argued that, whilst school autonomy can be a positive force, it requires coordination at the local level and the introduction of accountability arrangements that provide space for experimentation as well as resources to promote the professional development of teachers.

Finally, **Chapter 10, Reaching out to all learners,** reflects further on what I have learnt over the last 25 years about how to develop inclusive schools. Keeping in mind the importance of context when thinking about educational developments, this leads me to focus on finding local pathways that help identify and addressing barriers that are limiting the presence, progress and achievement of learners. As I argue throughout this book, this requires a collective will amongst stakeholders, using evidence to stimulate and guide their efforts. With this in mind, I reflect on national developments in the Netherlands and Portugal, each of which presents interesting and instructive patterns of development. Reflecting on these experiences, and others described throughout the book, the chapter provides a guiding framework that can be used to identify pathways that can help promote inclusion and equity within particular education systems. The chapter concludes by considering the implications for the roles of research and researchers in helping to move thinking and practice forward.

Telling stories

Throughout the chapters that follow, stories from the field are told to illustrate the arguments being developed. These accounts reflect the importance of explicitly articulating and sharing what Warren, Park and Tieken (2016, p. 252) call our *stories of self* – *stories that articulate the deeply embedded values that shape our identities and purpose as researchers.*

At the same time, the stories are influenced by a narrative inquiry methodology (Clandinin 2019), in that they are intended to provide readers with a sense of what it is like for those in the field who become involved in attempts to engage with evidence to stimulate improvements in practice and policy. In this way, I have it in mind to make the familiar unfamiliar, not least by providing accounts from across different national contexts.

The stories take two forms:

- **Vignettes** – these shorter anecdotes are used to illustrate the arguments developed in the text and
- **Accounts of practice** – these longer examples are intended to provide readers with a richer sense of the circumstances and events being described.

Many of the examples I provide took place in the United Kingdom. When they come from other parts of the world, this is made clear.

In considering these examples it is important to take account of the circumstances in which they take place. As I stress throughout this book, as far as educational developments are concerned, *contexts matter*. With this in mind, I am concerned to avoid the mistake made by some commentators who, in seeking to present arguments that have global significance, fall into the trap of oversimplifying educational processes and practices by ignoring problems of interpretation and translation. At the same time, I am conscious that, as a visitor to these contexts, my own understandings are always partial and, in some instances, may even be mistaken.

2   Searching for pathways

Laos is one of the economically poorest countries in the world. Certainly, in the classrooms that I visited there were few material resources. Nevertheless, one of the lessons I observed in a primary school in the capital city, Vientiane, pointed to some important ways forward for promoting inclusive learning.

The teacher spent the first ten minutes of the lesson talking to the children about a topic to do with nature. His presentation was illustrated by a drawing he had done, which was pinned to the blackboard. After ten minutes or so the children moved into groups of three to five and began discussions.

My interpreter explained that the teacher had set a question for them to address arising from his initial presentation. It was apparent from the speed with which all of this happened that the class were used to working in this way. What was also noticeable was the change in the classroom atmosphere. The children who had previously seemed rather passive – listening or maybe not listening – were now much more engaged in the agenda of the lesson.

Mobilising resources

A feature of lessons like this one that seems to be effective in encouraging student participation is the way available resources, particularly human resources, are used to support learning. In particular I am referring to a range of resources that is available in all classrooms and yet is often poorly used, that of children and young people themselves. Within any classroom, the students represent a rich source of experiences, inspiration, challenge and support which, if utilised, can inject an enormous supply of additional energy into the tasks and activities that are set.

However, all of this is dependent upon the skills of the teacher in harnessing this energy. This is, in part, a matter of attitude, depending upon a recognition that students have the capacity to contribute to one another's learning; recognising also that, in fact, learning is to a large degree a social process. It can be facilitated by helping teachers to develop the skills necessary to organise classrooms that encourage this social process of learning.

Experiences like this informed the approach that I introduced in *Understanding the Development of Inclusive Schools*. In describing these as involving

DOI: 10.4324/9781003438014-2

an inclusive turn, I have subsequently explained that this involves a radical challenge to thinking in the field regarding the idea of inclusive education. This perspective contrasts with the predominant approach, that of serving children with disabilities within general education settings. It argues that the aim of inclusive education is to eliminate social exclusion that is a consequence of attitudes and responses to diversity in race, social class, ethnicity, religion, gender and ability. As such, it represents a challenge to existing thinking regarding the development of education systems.

In this chapter, I explain the pathways that I have explored since the publication of my 1999 book. Before introducing these experiences, however, I begin by summarising changes that have occurred with regard to global thinking that have implications for efforts to encourage inclusive educational developments. In so doing, I indicate the ways in which my ideas have influenced these moves.

Education for all

Since 1990, the United Nation's Education for All (EFA) movement has worked to make quality basic education available to all learners. The EFA Declaration set out an overall vision, which is about being proactive in identifying the barriers some learners encounter in attempting to access educational opportunities (UNESCO 1990). This also involves the identification of resources available at national and community levels and bringing them to bear on overcoming those barriers.

This vision was reaffirmed by the World Education Forum meeting in Dakar, 2000, held to review the progress made in the previous decade. The Forum declared that EFA must take particular account of the needs of the poor and the disadvantaged, including working children, remote rural dwellers and nomads, ethnic and linguistic minorities, young people affected by conflict, HIV/AIDS, hunger and poor health and those with special learning needs (UNESCO 2000).

Moving forward, a major impetus for inclusive education was given by the World Conference on Special Needs Education in 1994. I was closely involved in the planning of this event, during which more than 300 participants, representing 92 governments and 25 international organisations, met in Salamanca, Spain. The overall purpose of the conference was to further the objective of Education for All by considering the fundamental policy shifts required to promote the approach of inclusive education, namely enabling schools to serve all children, particularly those defined as having special educational needs (UNESCO 1994).

Although the immediate focus of the Salamanca conference was on what was termed special needs education, its conclusion was that:

> *Special needs education – an issue of equal concern to countries of the North and of the South – cannot advance in isolation. It has to form part of an*

overall educational strategy and, indeed, of new social and economic poli-
cies. It calls for major reform of the ordinary school.

(p. iii–iv)

The aim, then, is to reform education systems. This can only happen, it is
argued, if mainstream schools become capable of educating all children in
their local communities. In a much-quoted extract, the Salamanca Statement
concluded that:

Regular schools with [an] inclusive orientation are the most effective means
of combating discriminatory attitudes, creating welcoming communities,
building an inclusive society and achieving education for all; moreover,
they provide an effective education to the majority of children and improve
the efficiency and ultimately the cost-effectiveness of the entire education
system.

(p. ix)

As this key passage indicates, the move towards inclusive schools can be justified on a number of grounds. There is an *educational justification*: the requirement for inclusive schools to educate all children together means that
they have to develop ways of teaching that respond to individual differences
and that therefore benefit all children; a *social justification*: inclusive schools
are able to change attitudes to difference by educating all children together
and form the basis for a just and non-discriminatory society; and an *economic
justification*: it is likely to be less costly to establish and maintain schools which
educate all children together than to set up a complex system of different types
of school specialising in particular groups of children.

Broadening the agenda

Further impetus to the movement towards inclusive education was provided
by the 48th session of the IBE-UNESCO International Conference on Education held in 2008, with its theme *Inclusive Education: The Way of the Future*
The long-term objective of this event was to support UNESCO member states
in providing the social and political conditions which every person needs in
order to exercise their human right to access, take an active part in and learn
from educational opportunities (Opertti, Walker and Zhang 2014). Once
again, I was involved in the planning of this event, during which ministers and
government officials from around the world, plus representatives of voluntary
organisations, discussed the importance of broadening the concept of inclusion to focus on all children, under the assumption that every learner matters
equally and has the right to receive effective educational opportunities.

Moving forward, the year 2016 was particularly important in relation to the
future of the EFA movement and, indeed, the legacy of Salamanca. Commit-
ments were made in the form of 17 Sustainable Development Goals adopted

by all United Nations Member States. Sustainable Development Goal 4 aims to *ensure inclusive and equitable quality education for* all (UNESCO 2015). This led to the publication of the Education 2030 Framework for Action, which emphasises inclusion and equity as laying the foundations for quality education.

The importance of including disabled children is an essential strand within this new international policy agenda. This was stressed in the United Nations' Convention on the Rights of Persons with Disabilities (United Nations 2008), which states:

> *The right to inclusive education encompasses a transformation in culture, policy and practice in all educational environments to accommodate the differing requirements and identities of individual students, together with a commitment to remove the barriers that impede that possibility.*
>
> (*General Comment No 4*)

The Convention defines non-inclusion, or segregation, as the education of students with disabilities in separate environments (i.e. in separate special schools or in special education units located with regular schools). It commits to ending segregation within educational settings by ensuring inclusive class-room teaching in accessible learning environments with appropriate support. In essence, this means that education systems must provide a personalised educational response, rather than expecting students to fit the system.

The introduction of the concept of equity into these international policy debates was significant in that it pointed to the importance of fairness, leading to the need to address all forms of exclusion and marginalisation, disparities and inequalities in access, participation and learning processes and outcomes. In this way, it was made clear that the international EFA agenda really has to be about *all*.

This book is concerned with putting this thinking into action. It is also concerned with the roles that research and researchers might play within such efforts. In doing so, it starts from an understanding of educational inequities as *wicked problems*, being difficult to define because of their many interacting and shifting components, and which require *solutions* to be debated, worked through, tested and reformulated in the field (Termeer, Dewulf and Biesbroek 2019).

Relevant resources

A new commitment reinforcing inclusion and equity in education was ex-pressed at an International Forum, co-organised by UNESCO and the Min-istry of Education of Colombia in September 2019 to celebrate the 25th anniversary of the Salamanca Declaration (UNESCO 2019). As underlined by the theme *Every learner matters*, the Forum was an opportunity to revive the broadened notion of inclusion as a general guiding principle to strengthen equal access to quality learning opportunities for all learners. This formulation was explained in the pre-conference discussion paper I authored.[1]

In support of these global developments, I led the development of the following resources for UNESCO:

- **Guide for Ensuring Inclusion and Equity in Education**[2](2017), which offers practical support to member states to help review how well equity and inclusion currently figure in existing policies, decides what actions need to be taken to improve policies and monitor progress as actions are taken. This document introduced a principle that has subsequently been influential and is central to the thinking put forward in this book: *Every learner matters and matters equally.*
- **Towards Inclusion and Equity in Education: Status, Trends and Challenges**[3] (2019), produced as a result of UNESCO's International Forum, held in Cali in September 2019, to give new impetus to inclusion in the context of the 2030 Agenda for Sustainable Development.
- **The UNESCO International Bureau of Education resource pack,** *Reaching Out to All Learners,*[4] the second edition of which was published in March 2022. I led the development of these materials, working with a team of international experts. The resource pack is intended to influence and support inclusive thinking and practices at all levels of an education system. It is designed to be relevant to teachers, school leaders, district-level administrators, teacher educators and national policy makers. The materials are currently being disseminated globally by IBE-UNESCO, with my support, through cooperation with governments and other international organisations.

Continuing challenges

Despite all these important developments, a recent Global Monitoring Report points out that an estimated 258 million children and young people are still not in school (UNESCO 2020). Meanwhile, the OECD (2021) reports that the poorest learners, living in the poorest areas, systematically achieve less well than their wealthier peers, with these patterns found across higher and lower income countries. It also finds that race, gender and a host of other factors, intersect and deepen these entrenched economic and spatial inequities

Furthermore, the UNESCO Institute for Statistics data show that more than 617 million children and adolescents are not achieving minimum proficiency levels in reading and mathematics (UIS 2019). It is also important to note that only half of the world's children receive pre-primary education, a failure that limits children's futures and deepens inequities in later learning (UNICEF 2019). Significantly, the disadvantaged are least served by quality early childhood care and education, although they benefit most from such interventions. There are also high rates of student dropout globally, particularly at the secondary level, as well as challenges experienced by many marginalised groups during the transition to higher education (UNESCO 2015).

In developing countries, low access to higher education for young people living in socio-economically disadvantaged contexts, and/or who are vulnerable for various reasons, is one of the most dramatic gaps in opportunities. This holds back the overall development of these nations.

In addition, it is vital to recognise that large gender gaps continue to exist with regard to access, learning achievement and continuation in education in many settings, most often at the expense of girls, although in some parts of the world boys are at a greater disadvantage. There is evidence, too, that education systems often perpetuate rather than challenge gender inequalities (UNGEI 2012).

Whilst these concerns are most acute in the developing world, there are similar concerns in many wealthier countries, as noted by the OECD (2018), which reports that across its member countries, almost one in five students do not reach a basic minimum level of skills to function in today's societies. It also states that students from low socio-economic background are twice as likely to be low performers, implying that personal or social circumstances are obstacles to achieving their educational potential.

This global situation presents a moral imperative for policy makers, educators and researchers to act in ways that can move education systems in more equitable directions. If they are to make progress, so too is the need for them to work in ways which are more closely connected with each other and with the communities they are seeking to support (Gutierrez and Lipman 2016; Lawson and Van Veen (2016); Rickinson and Edwards 2021; Warren et al. 2018).

Promising developments

Like all major policy changes, progress in relation to inclusion and equity requires an effective strategy for implementation. As explained in the previous chapter, this requires new thinking that focuses attention on the *barriers* experienced by some children that lead them to become marginalised as a result of contextual factors, such as inappropriate curricula and forms of assessment, and inadequate teacher preparation and support. The implication is that addressing such barriers is the most important means of developing forms of education that are effective for all children. In this way, the focus on inclusion and equity becomes a way of achieving the overall improvement of education systems.

The situation across the world in relation to this challenging policy agenda is complex, with some countries making great strides, whilst others continue to have segregated provision of various forms of education for some groups of learners. There are, however, countries where there has been encouraging progress, such as:

- For more than 30 years, **New Brunswick in Canada** has pioneered the concept of inclusive education through legislation, local authority policies and professional guidelines (AuCoin, Porter and Baker-Korotkov 2020)

More recently, New Brunswick adopted a policy which defines the critical elements of an inclusive education system that supports students in common learning environments and provides supports for teachers. It sets clear requirements for school practice including procedures for the development of personalised learning plans, inclusive graduation, as well as strict guidelines when a variation of the common learning environment may be required.

- The **Italian** government passed a law in 1977 that closed all special schools, units and other non-inclusive forms of provision (Ianes, Demo and Dell'Anna 2020). This legislation is still in force, and more recent amendments have further strengthened the inclusive nature of the education system. Not only did this close segregated educational facilities but, starting with preschools, it also removed the possibility of exclusion from school as a corrective sanction. Whilst practice varies from place to place, there is no doubt that the principle of inclusion is widely accepted. There is, however, recent concern about an increase in students being withdrawn for periods outside the regular classroom for additional support.

- An inclusive education policy has led to significant progress in **Sierra Leone**, with more children enrolled in schools than ever before, particularly girls.[5] In early 2021, Sierra Leone approved its first-ever policy on inclusive education, the National Policy on Radical inclusion in Schools. This policy seeks to increase enrolment, retention and successful transition of all students in pre-primary, primary and senior secondary education regardless of disability, gender, pregnancy or parenting status, geographic location and socio-economic background.

- Having enacted legislation making disability discrimination within education unlawful, **Portugal** has gone much further in enacting an explicit legal framework for the inclusion of students with and without disabilities in education (Alves, Campos Pinto and Pinto 2020). Recent legislation requires that the provision of support for all students be determined, managed and provided at the regular school level, with local multidisciplinary teams responsible for determining what support is necessary to ensure all students (regardless of labels, categorisation or a determination of disability) have access and the means to participate effectively in education, with a view to their full inclusion in society. It is also significant that Portugal has developed progressive assessment practices to support the achievement of all learners. As the Portuguese education system moved forward in relation to inclusion over the last two decades, the country has also seen impressive developments in terms of equity (OECD 2022). As explained in Chapter 10, it is one of the few countries with a positive trajectory of improvement in all of the subjects assessed by OECD's Programme for International Student Assessment (PISA).

- In **Finland**, a country which regularly out-performs most other countries in terms of educational outcomes, education is viewed as a right and not as a privilege. The country's success is partly explained by the progress of the lowest performing quintile of students who out-perform those in other countries (Sabel et al. 2011). This has increasingly involved an emphasis on support for vulnerable students within mainstream schools, as opposed to in segregated provision. There is a particular focus on the prevention of learning difficulties in Finland, and a high level of resources are directed at this in primary schools. For example, all Finnish schools are assigned specialists to support any student who requires additional help.

Further encouragement regarding inclusion and equity is provided by the *Report Card* prepared for UNICEF by the Innocenti Centre (2018) which concludes:

> *Tackling educational inequality does not mean sacrificing high standards. Countries with higher average achievement tend to have lower levels of inequality.... Bringing the worst performing students up does not mean pulling the best-performing students down.*
>
> *(p. 3)*

This report focuses on educational inequalities in 41 of the world's richest countries, all of which are members of the Organisation for Economic Co-operation and Development and/or the European Union. It argues that there is no systematic relationship between country income and indicators of equality in education. For example, it is notable that some of the economically poorer countries in the comparison, such as Latvia and Lithuania, achieve near-universal access to preschool learning and curb inequality in reading performance among both primary and secondary school students more successfully than countries that have far greater resources. The Report Card concludes that Finland, Latvia and Portugal have the most equal education systems.

In drawing attention to these examples of policy development, it must be stressed that they should not be seen as being perfect. Rather, they are countries where there are interesting developments from which to learn. They are also varied with respect to the approach being taken and what they have achieved. Consequently, whilst lessons can undoubtedly be learned from these developments, they must be replicated with care. There are many sources of inequity in education related to political, economic, social, cultural and institutional factors, and these vary across countries. This means that what works in one country may not work elsewhere. An emphasis on system change strategies being contextually sensitive is one of the pervading themes of the recommendations made in this book.

Other global trends

In some countries, increasing pressures to improve the rankings of education systems on global league tables is creating new barriers to progress in relation to inclusion and equity. This arises because of an increased emphasis on school autonomy, competition between schools and parental choice (Meyland-Smith and Evans 2009). The schools involved have different titles, such as charter schools in the United States, free schools in Sweden, academies in England and independent public schools in parts of Australia. Implicit in these independent state-funded schools is an assumption that greater autonomy will allow space for the development of organisational arrangements, practices and forms of management and leadership that will be more effective in promoting the learning of all students, particularly those from economically disadvantaged and minority backgrounds.

In Chapter 9, I explain in more detail how this global trend is a matter of considerable debate, and there are varied views as to the extent to which it is leading to the desired outcomes. In particular, there is a concern that the development of education systems based on autonomy, coupled with high-stakes accountability and increased competition between schools, will further disadvantage learners from low-income and minority families (Salokangas and Ainscow 2017). For example, parental choice and competition between schools have widened the gap between schools that are seen to be more successful and those that are perceived to be less so in countries as varied as Chile, England, Sweden and the United States.

Meanwhile, the Government in New Zealand published a policy document based on the findings of a review of national policy carried out by an independent task force (Ministry of Education 2019). This concludes that a key reason for the country's poor equity and achievement outcomes is that, since reforms introduced in 1989, schools have predominantly operated as autonomous, self-managing entities, loosely connected to each other and with a distant relationship with the centre. This autonomy has left schools to operate largely on their own and without sufficient support. The document outlines the Government's strategy for the reform of the schooling system. This will involve a move towards a networked system that is more responsive to the needs of all learners, an approach I recommend later in this book.

In relation to these concerns, the OECD (2012) reports the success of certain education systems that rank highly on measures of both quality and equity. As a result, it argues:

> *The evidence is conclusive: equity in education pays off. The highest performing education systems across OECD countries are those that combine high quality and equity. In such education systems, the vast majority of students can attain high level skills and knowledge that depend on their ability and drive, more than on their socio-economic background.*

> (p. 14)

The implication, then, is that it is possible for countries to develop education systems that are both equitable and excellent. The question is: how can this be achieved? Broadly stated, this is the agenda I address in this book.

Development and research

The development of the approach I am recommending began with the *Improving the Quality of Education for All (IQEA)* project that I reported in my 1999 book. Initially this involved a small group of researchers from the University of Cambridge working with schools in and around London (Ainscow and Hopkins 1992). Subsequently, IQEA led to developments in other parts of the world (see Ainscow 1999; Clark et al. 1999; Hopkins 2007; Hopkins et al. 1994; West and Ainscow 2010 for more detailed accounts of some of these projects). All of these activities involved teams of researchers working in partnership with networks of schools to identify ways in which the learning of all members of a school community – students, parents and staff – could be enhanced.

Work with schools in the IQEA projects was based upon a contract that attempted to define the parameters for our involvement, and the obligations those involved owed to one another. It emphasised that all staff be consulted; that an in-school team of coordinators be appointed to carry the work forward; that a critical mass of staff were to be actively involved; and that sufficient time would be made available for necessary classroom and staff development activities. Meanwhile, we committed ourselves to supporting the school's developments, usually in the first place for one year. Often the arrangement continued, however, and, in some instances, we were involved for periods as long as seven years. We provided training for the school coordinators, made regular school visits and contributed to school-based staff development activities. In addition, we attempted to work with the schools in recording and analysing their experiences in a way that also provided data relevant to our own ongoing research agendas.

As a result of such engagements with schools involved in the IQEA project, we evolved a style of collaboration that was to influence later initiatives, which we referred to as *working with, rather than working on* (Ainscow and Southworth 1996). This phrase attempted to sum up an approach that deliberately allowed each project school considerable autonomy to determine its own priorities for development and, indeed, its methods for achieving these priorities. In attempting to work in this way, we found ourselves confronted with staggering complexity and by a bewildering array of policy and strategy options. It was our belief that only through a regular engagement with these complexities could a greater understanding of school change be achieved.

These ideas were taken forward and developed through a series of further studies, including:

- *Understanding and Developing Inclusive Practices in Schools.* This collaborative action research study, which occurred between 2000 and 2004, involved a network of 25 urban schools in three English local education authorities and three partner universities. Within the network schools, we saw how the use of evidence to study practice can help to foster the development of more inclusive forms of teaching (see: Ainscow, Booth and Dyson 2004; Dyson et al. 2003; Howes et al. 2004, 2005).

- *The Stockborough Equity Research Network.* Between 2006 and 2011, we had a chance to explore these ideas in more detail through our involvement in another network of schools in England (see Ainscow et al. 2012a, 2012b). This initiative was located in a local authority characterised by socio-economic disadvantage and social and ethnic segregation, which we called *Stockborough*. It involved staff inquiry groups in the participating schools, usually consisting of five or six members representing different perspectives within their school communities.
- *Ethical Leadership: A collaborative investigation of equity-driven evidence-based school reform.* This study involved a research network of schools, spread across the geographically spread State of Queensland, Australia, and a team of eight university researchers. Together, we explored how ethical leadership could promote ways of interpreting and using various forms of evidence to promote learning and equity (see: Harris et al. 2017, 2020; Spina et al. 2019).
- *Inclusive Inquiry.* Carried out between 2012 and 2020 in five European countries, this research focused specifically on how students can themselves contribute to the development of inclusive teaching and learning. It involved the development of a strategy in which children and young people become researchers who learn how to use research techniques to gather the views of their classmates, as well as observe lessons (see Ainscow and Messiou 2017; Messiou et al. 2016; Messiou and Ainscow 2015, 2020).

All of these studies involved teams of university researchers in supporting, recording and analysing collaborative inquiries as they occurred in project schools. As a result, we came to define this as a process of knowledge generation that occurs when researcher and practitioner knowledge meet in particular sites and is aimed at producing new knowledge about ways in which broad values might better be realised in future practice.

A family of approaches

These studies adopted different terms to describe the methodologies they adopted, such as collaborative inquiry, practitioner action research, action learning and lesson study. Recently Yurkofsky et al. (2020) labelled approaches such as these collectively as *continuous improvement* methods, noting that they share four characteristics:

- Grounding improvement efforts in local problems or needs;
- Empowering practitioners to take an active role in research and improvement;
- Engaging in iteration, which involves a cyclical process of action, assessment, reflection and adjustment; and
- Striving to encourage change across schools and systems, not just individual classrooms.

These approaches can be seen as being part of a *family* within the overall tradition of action research (Reason and Bradbury 2001) that developed out of the action research tradition of Kurt Lewin (1946) and the work of many other academics (e.g., Elliott 1991; Kemmis and McTaggart 1988; Schön 1983; Stenhouse 1975). They emphasise an engagement in inquiry to inform and improve practice, and the intentional combining of knowing and doing for achieving positive social change (Kemmis 2010).

Since the focus of the inquiry is usually defined by the engagement of the participants, careful consideration is required in determining who is included, and how and who will speak for whom, and who sets the research agenda. Therefore, negotiating power issues and the relationships between collaborating practitioners, stakeholders and academics *requires ethical probity where each party recognizes, understands and respects mutual responsibilities* (Campbell and Groundwater-Smith 2007, p. 2).

The preoccupation with equity means that it also requires a particular concern to give voice to those who may be powerless or unheard in decision-making processes (Groundwater-Smith 2011). Moreover, actively engaging participants in inquiry *problematises the question of who is researcher and who is researched, raising issues around anonymity, the 'ownership' of findings and dissemination* (Locke, Alcorn and O'Neill 2013, p. 107).

Related considerations concern decision-making around how outcomes will be evaluated in order to determine whether the inquiry processes have led to positive change. Questions to be considered include:

- What forms of evidence were used to determine the outcomes for those who have participated in the process and those who are the intended beneficiaries of the change efforts that were the focus of the project?
- How far did processes improve the social and professional practices in the contexts in which they were conducted?
- How will the outcomes from the inquiry be used?

Collaborative inquiry processes, although not set on achieving consensus, do provide opportunities for negotiation of multiple perspectives around shared agendas, rather than producing evidence from a single viewpoint or source. A helpful strategy in this respect is what Wasser and Bresler (1996) refer to as *group interpretive processes* as a means of analysing and interpreting evidence. This involves an engagement with the different perspectives of practitioners, students and university researchers in ways that are intended to encourage critical reflection, collaborative learning and mutual critique. In these contexts, the varied theoretical perspectives of members of the research teams provide a valuable means of questioning taken-for-granted assumptions and helping practitioners to reconsider neglected possibilities for moving practice forward.

The issue of trustworthiness is a particular challenge to collaborative research of this sort, which involves such a high degree of participation among stakeholders. Commenting on this issue, Schön (1987) argues that without a serious effort to make clear what is meant by rigour, participatory research *becomes an open sesame to woolly-headedness, a never-never land where anything goes* (p. 10). He goes on to suggest that appropriate rigour in the study of practice should focus on validity (e.g. how do we know what we claim to know?) and utility (e.g. how useful is the research to practitioners?).

With this in mind, the studies I refer to in this book all made use of three forms of triangulation, supporting observations and reports from a number of viewpoints. These involved comparing and contrasting evidence about the same actions and activities from different people (e.g. teachers, support staff and students); scrutinising events from different angles by making use of a variety of methods for collecting information; and using outsiders as observers.

Influenced by the ideas of Karl Popper, Schön goes on to argue that the fundamental test for validity in participatory inquiry is through *competitive resistance to refutation*. This involves juxtaposing alternate plausible accounts of the phenomenon in question. Schön notes: *In the absence of an alternate hypothesis, one is likely to be overwhelmed by the obviousness of what one already knows* (p. 348).

Guided by this advice, members of our research teams usually discussed with their practitioner partners, and with one another, written accounts of the work carried out in the schools, including alternative explanations as to what lessons could be drawn from these experiences. In this way, the aim was to draw conclusions that were both valid and relevant.

Inclusion and equity as principles

These various projects pointed to the importance of terminology when trying to move schools in an inclusive direction. In particular, terms such as *equity* and *inclusion* can be confusing since they may mean different things to different people. This is a particular problem when trying to move forward with other people – not least in schools, where everybody is so busy. If there is not a shared understanding of the intended direction of travel, progress will be difficult. There is, therefore, a need for agreed definitions of these concepts.

As noted earlier, inclusive education is increasingly seen as a principle that supports and welcomes diversity amongst all learners. It presumes that the aim of this is to eliminate social exclusion that is a consequence of attitudes and responses to diversity in race, social class, ethnicity, religion, gender and ability. As such, it starts from the belief that education is a basic human right and the foundation for a more just society. Hence, there is an emphasis on equity, which implies a concern with fairness. In the UNESCO *Guide for Ensuring Inclusion and Equity in Education* (2017) that I helped to develop with a group of international experts, we sum this up as follows: *Every learner matters and matters equally.*

Using this principle to develop policies and practices in many countries suggests that it is helpful to use a definition of inclusive education that involves the following elements:

Inclusion is a process. That is to say, inclusion has to be seen as a never-ending search to find better ways of responding to diversity. It is about learning how to live with differences and learning how to learn from differences. In this way differences come to be seen more positively as a stimulus for fostering learning, amongst children and adults.

Inclusion is concerned with the identification and removal of barriers. Here barriers may take different forms, some of which are to do with existing policies, the way schools are organised, relationships and the forms of teaching provided. Consequently, it is necessary to collect, collate and evaluate evidence about these factors in order to plan for improvements in policy and practice. This involves using evidence of various kinds to stimulate creativity and problem-solving.

Inclusion is about the presence, participation and achievement of all students. Here *presence* is concerned with where children are educated, and how reliably and punctually they attend; *participation* relates to the quality of their experiences whilst they are there and, therefore, must incorporate the views of the learners themselves; and *achievement* is about the outcomes of learning across the curriculum, not merely test or examination results.

Inclusion involves a particular emphasis on those groups of learners who may be at risk of marginalisation, exclusion or underachievement. This indicates the moral responsibility to ensure that those groups that are statistically most at risk are carefully monitored, and that, where necessary, steps are taken to ensure their presence, participation and achievement within the education system. At the same time, it is necessary to be vigilant in watching out for learners who may be overlooked.

We have found that a well-orchestrated debate about these elements can lead to a wider understanding of the principle of inclusion (Ainscow, Booth and Dyson 2006). Furthermore, such a debate, though by its nature slow and, possibly, never-ending, can have leverage with respect to fostering the conditions within which schools can feel encouraged to move in a more inclusive direction. These debates must involve all stakeholders within communities, including families, political and religious leaders, and the media. They should also involve those within national and local district education offices. Over recent years, in countries such as Australia, Colombia, Mexico, Oman, Peru, Sweden and Uruguay, I have used the indicators provided by the *UNESCO Guide for Ensuring Inclusion and Equity in Education* (2017) to facilitate such discussions.

Use of evidence

In order to address questions about inclusion and equity in education systems, it is important to know who is included, who is segregated and who is excluded from schooling. Without some form of statistical analysis in relation to these concerns, there can be no accountability. However, when data collection efforts are only focused on particular categories of learners, there is a risk of promoting deficit views of those students who share certain characteristics or come from similar backgrounds. This also distracts attention from more fundamental questions, such as: *Why are we failing some learners? What are the barriers experienced by some of our students?*

Previously I have argued that evidence is the *life-blood* of inclusive development (Ainscow 2005, 2012). Therefore, deciding what kinds of evidence to collect and how to use it requires care, since, within education systems, *what gets measured gets done*. This is widely recognised as a double-edged sword precisely because it is such a potent lever for change. On the one hand, data are required in order to monitor the progress of children, evaluate the impact of interventions, review the effectiveness of policies and processes, plan new initiatives and so on. On the other hand, if effectiveness is evaluated on the basis of narrow, even inappropriate, performance indicators, then the impact can be deeply damaging. Whilst appearing to promote the causes of accountability and transparency, the use of data can, in practice: conceal more than they reveal; invite misinterpretation; and, worse of all, have a perverse effect on the behaviour of professionals. The challenge is, therefore, to harness the potential of evidence as a lever for change, whilst avoiding these potential problems.

The starting point for making decisions about the evidence to collect at the system level should be with an agreed definition of inclusion. In other words, we must *measure what we value*, rather than is often the case, *valuing what we can measure*. In line with the suggestions made earlier, then, evidence collected within an education system needs to relate to the *presence, participation and achievement* of all students, with an emphasis placed on those groups of learners regarded to be *at risk of marginalisation, exclusion or underachievement.*

This means that, in an education system based on the principles of inclusion and equity, all students should be assessed on an ongoing basis in relation to their progress through the curriculum. This allows teachers to respond to a wide range of individual learners, bearing in mind that each learner is unique. It means that teachers and other professionals must be well informed about their students' characteristics and attainments, while also assessing broader qualities, such as their capacity for cooperation. However, the ability to identify each student's level of performance, or to enumerate certain students' particular difficulties, is not enough. Teachers in inclusive systems need to gauge the effectiveness of their teaching for all of their students and should know what they need to do to enable each student to learn as well as possible.

An engagement with evidence is particularly crucial at the level of the school, where it can provide the stimulus for professional learning aimed at the development of inclusive thinking and practice. The starting point for developing inclusive practices is with the sharing of existing approaches through collaboration amongst staff, leading to experimentation with new practices that will reach out to all students (Ainscow 2016b). This requires the development of a common language with which colleagues can talk to one another and, indeed, to themselves, about detailed aspects of their practice. Without such a language, teachers find it very difficult to experiment with new possibilities (Huberman 1993).

The Index for Inclusion

A framework that offers a roadmap for promoting an inclusive dialogue within schools is provided by the *Index for Inclusion*,[6] a review instrument we developed originally for use in England over 20 years ago but is now available in many countries. The Index is intended to help draw on the knowledge and views of teachers, students, parents/carers and community representatives about barriers to participation that exist within the existing *cultures, policies and practices* of schools in order to identify priorities for change. In connecting inclusion with the detail of policy and practice, the Index encourages those who use it to build their own view of inclusion, related to their experience and values, as they work out which policies and practices they wish to promote or discourage. In Chapter 3, I go on to explain the significance of the rationale of the Index for the programme of development and research project reported in this book.

The Index was developed through a project carried out on behalf of the Centre for Studies on Inclusive Education, over a three-year period (see account in Ainscow 1999). This involved a team of teachers, parents, governors, researchers and a representative of disability groups with wide experience in attempts to develop more inclusive ways of working. They carried out two phases of action research, in partnership with a total of 22 schools, in six different local authorities.

The Index for Inclusion involves schools in a process of inclusive school development, drawing on the views of staff, governors, students, parents/carers and other community members. It is concerned with improving educational attainments through inclusive practices and thus provides an attempt to redress a balance in those schools that have concentrated on raising attainment at the expense of the development of a supportive school community for staff and students.

The process of working with the Index is itself designed to contribute to the inclusive development of schools. It encourages staff to share and build on their existing knowledge about what impedes learning and participation. It also assists them in a detailed examination of the possibilities for increasing learning and participation in all aspects of their school for all their students. This is not seen as an additional initiative for schools but rather as a systematic way of engaging in school development planning, setting priorities for change, implementing developments and reviewing progress.

It is important to understand that the view of inclusion presented in the Index is a broad one, which goes well beyond many of the formulations that have been previously used. It is concerned with minimising barriers to learning and participation, whoever experiences them and wherever they are located within the cultures, policies and practices of a school. It involves an emphasis on mobilising under-used resources among staff, students, governors, parents and other members of the school's communities. In this context diversity is seen as a rich resource for supporting the development of teaching and learning.

Using the Index

The Index materials guide the exploration of a school along three interconnected dimensions: creating inclusive cultures, producing inclusive policies and evolving inclusive practices (Figure 2.1). They cover all aspects of school life, from collaboration and values, to induction and learning support policies, to classroom practices and resource planning.

The dimensions were chosen to direct thinking about school change and represent relatively distinct areas of school activity. In the past, too little attention has been given to the potential of school cultures to support or undermine developments in teaching and learning. It is through inclusive school cultures that those changes in policies and practices, achieved by a school community, can be sustained and passed on to new staff and students. However, our experience indicates that sustainable development depends on change occurring in all the dimensions.

The materials contain a branching tree structure that encourages progressively more detailed examination of all aspects of a school. The three dimensions are expressed in terms of a series of indicators, and the meaning of each of these is clarified by a series of questions. Figure 2.2 provides an example of the indicators.

The indicators are statements of inclusive aspiration against which existing arrangements in a school can be compared in order to set priorities for development. The detailed questions are then intended to ensure that the materials can challenge the thinking in any school, whatever its current state of development. Together, the dimensions, indicators and questions provide a progressively more detailed map to guide the exploration of the current position of a school and to plot future possibilities.

The three dimensions of the *Index*

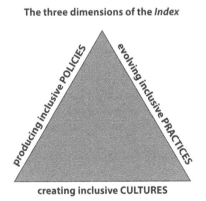

Figure 2.1 The three dimensions of the Index for Inclusion.

Indicator C1.1 Teaching is planned with the learning of all
students in mind

• **Lessons encourage the participation of all students**

• **Lessons develop an understanding of difference**

• **Students are actively involved in their own learning**

• **Students learn collaboratively**

• **Assessment contributes to the achievements of all
students**

Figure 2.2 An example of the indicators in the Index for Inclusion.

Using the Index to explore pathways

Considerable work has gone on in relation to the use of the Index for school development purposes, including projects I have been involved in within England, as well as countries as diverse as Australia, Brazil, India, Norway, Portugal, Romania and South Africa.

Some vignettes provide illustrations of how the Index was used in relation to particular circumstances. They illustrate how those within schools chose to select relevant areas of the Index and adjust the materials, including their wording, in order to make them appropriate.

VIGNETTE 2.1   Developing inclusive practices

The coordinating group in an English primary school carried out a survey of the views of students, staff and parents, using the indicators as the basis of a rating scale. From the analysis of these data it was decided to concentrate on the development of aspects of classroom practice, focusing specifically on the following indicators:

• Lessons are responsive to student diversity
• Lessons are made accessible to all students
• Children are actively involved in their own learning
• Children's differences are used as resources for teaching and learning

Over the period of a school year, efforts were made to use these indicators during lesson planning. Eventually it was decided that something more specific was needed in order to stimulate developments in practice. The head-teacher was able to mobilise some extra resources so that pairs of teachers could be freed to work in one another's classrooms. Using the four indicators as the basis of a mutual observation schedule, the teachers made a record of what they saw as golden moments. These were examples of classroom interactions that illustrated how the indicators could be turned into action.

Eventually, after every teacher in the school had been involved in these observation activities, a staff meeting was held during which each pair of colleagues talked about their experiences. A document was produced as a result of these discussions which summarised what had been learnt. It focused on issues such as the use of questions and how to respond to disruptive behaviour. In commenting on the document, however, the headteacher explained that it was a poor record of what had been discussed during the meeting. She commented, *You would have to have been there to appreciate the richness of the professional learning that was going on.*

It seems that through shared experiences within classrooms, the teachers in this school were stimulated to reflect on one another's styles of teaching. The story suggests that groups of teachers can use elements of the Index to focus investigations into their practice in ways that enable discussions to focus on important details that are often overlooked. We see a similar pattern in Vignette 2.2

VIGNETTE 2.2   Strengthening support

In a large urban secondary school in Portugal a team of eight teachers, including the principal, carried out surveys of staff, students and parents. As a result of analysing their findings, they recommended to their colleagues that efforts needed to be made to address what they saw as three interconnected priority areas in order to make their school more inclusive. These areas were summarised as follows:

Priority 1: During lessons students are encouraged to work together.

1.1 Do lesson activities require students to collaborate?
1.2 Do teachers ask students to discuss the content of lessons?
1.3 Do teachers help students to learn the skills of working together?

Priority 2: Students support one another.

2.1 Do students talk to each other about their learning tasks?
2.2 Do students feel that their classmates help them?
2.3 Are any students ignored by other members of their class?

Priority 3: Staff development policies support teachers in responding to student diversity.

3.1 Are there meetings where teachers can share their ideas?
3.2 Do teachers have opportunities to observe one another's practices?
3.3 Do teachers feel that they are supported in dealing with difficulties?

Over a period of a year the whole school used these indicators and questions as a framework for moving practice forward. They also provided a means of collecting more detailed evidence through mutual classroom observations, including the use of group analysis of video recordings.

Possibly the most powerful strategy they used involved a series of interviews with groups of students. These were carried out by an advisory team from outside the school. The school coordinating team spent a whole day analysing transcripts from these interviews. They went on to use extracts as the basis of staff development activities in the school. Some extracts were also used on posters that were displayed in the staff room. These invited teachers to write their reactions to comments made by the students.

The Index for Inclusion was also used in Romania, in the context of a UNICEF-funded project known as The Development of Inclusive School Environments in the Community. In this context, considerable use was made of visual recording systems in order to encourage participatory inquiry processes in reviewing processes and outcomes of action research in the schools. These approaches worked particularly well in terms of helping colleagues within networks of schools to share their experiences and perceptions, and to summarise their learning.

VIGNETTE 2.3   Engaging with evidence

Each school in the Romanian project focused on a small number of indicators chosen by their coordinating groups (e.g. *Students are valued equally; The school has an efficient policy for decreasing student absences*). They were then encouraged to collect and analyse various forms of evidence in relation to these indicators. For example, the idea of *mindmaps* was used to help school groups to carry out an audit of evidence in order to review progress. This technique was demonstrated on the blackboard, and groups were asked to be creative in finding visual ways of illustrating their ideas. Each indicator was written in a circle on a poster. These were spaced apart.

Groups then noted any evidence they had that suggested progress towards this indicator. No guidance was given as to what was meant by *evidence* so as to encourage creative thinking. It was suggested that the relative *strength* of evidence should be indicated in some way and that efforts should be made to illustrate how particular evidence might relate to more than one indicator. The posters were then displayed on the wall, and colleagues were asked to go and look at the work of other schools. Here it was emphasised that schools might borrow ideas from one another. Finally, school groups discussed the following questions: *What other evidence do we need to evaluate our work?* and *Do we need to change our indicators for the next phase of action research?*

The Romanian schools also used *timelines* in order to construct both group and individual records of processes used in their schools (Ainscow et al. 1995). During the first stage, groups designed a 12-month timeline on a large sheet of paper, noting key events in their schools. This was introduced using an example drawn on the blackboard. Once the overall timeline was designed, each group member was asked to draw a summary version of their own on a small piece of paper. Then pairs of participants were formed from different schools. Before the individuals talked to each other they were asked to record their personal *highs and lows* along their school timeline. Again, this was illustrated with an example on the blackboard. No discussion was allowed whilst individuals completed this step. Then, each person talked to their partner about their personal experience and feelings during the year. It was stressed that active listening was required, only interrupting if it was necessary to seek clarification. Each person had five minutes to explain their timeline.

The next stage involved school groups entering their *highs and lows* lines on the school poster version of the timeline. Here attention was placed on the need to recognise that school learning involved personal learning. It was also noted that differences can be a useful resource for facilitating a deeper understanding of change processes. The final stage in the activity involved the school groups in summarising the outcomes of these processes by completing two sentences, as follows: *We make progress when ...*, and *Things are difficult when ...*. During a plenary session, each school group read out their two completed sentences.

Learning from difference

In using the Index for Inclusion in schools such as these we saw how this sometimes led to a degree of collusion amongst those involved, such that unwelcome ideas or evidence may be overlooked. Consequently, in later initiatives we worked with partner schools in order to explore ways of introducing a more critical dimension to the process.

Most significantly, we saw how certain types of evidence can be used to encourage those within a school to question their practices and, indeed, the assumptions behind these practices. In these contexts, the following approaches proved to be promising:

- Mutual observation of classroom practices, followed by structured discussion of what happened;
- Group discussion of a video recording of one colleague teaching;
- Discussion of statistical evidence regarding test results, attendance registers or exclusion records;

- Data from interviews with students; and
- Staff development exercises based on case study material or interview data.

This led us to document how such approaches can encourage discussions within schools that are both supportive and yet challenging. In particular, we saw how they can sometimes *make the familiar unfamiliar* in order to stimulate self-questioning, creativity and action.

So, for example, in some schools, the discussions challenged existing assumptions as to the nature of educational difficulties experienced by students. Specifically, we saw questioning of the assumption that some students' characteristics are such that they require a different form of teaching from that offered to the majority of students. Such an orientation led to a concern with finding the *right* response, i.e. different teaching methods or materials for students who do not respond to existing arrangements. Implicit in this formulation is a view that schools are rational organisations offering an appropriate range of opportunities; that those students who experience difficulties do so because of their limitations or disadvantages; and that they, therefore, are in need of some form of special intervention (Skrtic 1991). Our concern was that, sometimes, such assumptions sometimes led to a search for effective responses to those children perceived as being *different*. As a result, opportunities for developments in practice may be overlooked.

I should add that all of this was challenging to the thinking of everybody involved, not least to those of us from universities. Our assumptions were also challenged; we too had to find ways of dealing with and, hopefully, learn from one another's perspectives. We also found that we had more learning to do in order to develop our skills in challenging our teacher colleagues in a supportive way.

Conclusion

In tracing some of my efforts to find pathways for developing inclusive schools, this chapter has summarised global developments over the last three decades that have helped to move thinking forward. Informed by a series of international events and policy documents that were influenced by the thinking I presented in my 1999 book, *Understanding the Development of Inclusive Schools*, this led to a broadening of the concept of inclusion. Described as involving an inclusive turn, this formulation is informed by the principle that every learner matters equally and has the right to receive effective educational opportunities.

This perspective informs the Education 2030 Framework for Action, which emphasises inclusion and equity as laying the foundations for quality education. This policy framework also stresses the need to address all forms of exclusion and marginalisation, disparities and inequalities in access, participation and learning processes and outcomes. In this way, it is made clear that the international education agenda really has to be about *all*.

Set within these major changes in global thinking, the chapter has introduced the programme of development and research that I have carried out with colleagues over the last 25 years. This involves attempts to develop an education system based on the principles of inclusion and equity.

An engagement with evidence is particularly crucial at the level of the school, where it can provide the stimulus for a starting point for developing inclusive practices with the sharing of existing approaches through collaboration amongst staff, leading to experimentation with new practices that will reach out to all students. This requires the development of a common language with which colleagues can talk to one another and, indeed, to themselves, about detailed aspects of their practice. Without such a language, teachers find it very difficult to experiment with new possibilities.

In the next chapter I explain how this thinking has subsequently informed further efforts to find effective pathways for developing inclusive schools in a range of contexts.

Notes

1 https://en.unesco.org/sites/default/files/2019-forum-inclusion-discussion-paper-en.pdf
2 https://unesdoc.unesco.org/ark:/48223/pf0000248254
3 https://unesdoc.unesco.org/ark:/48223/pf0000374246
4 https://unesdoc.unesco.org/ark:/48223/pf0000243279
5 https://education-profiles.org/sub-saharan-africa/sierra-leone/~inclusion
6 https://www.eenet.org.uk/resources/docs/Index%20English.pdf

3 Developing schools for all

Visiting a primary school classroom in Inner Mongolia, China, I was shocked to find that there were approximately 70 children sitting in rows of desks packed into a long, rather bleak-looking room. The teacher stood at one end of the room on a narrow stage in front of a blackboard.

Lessons were 40 minutes long, and, although each was taught by a different teacher, they mostly followed a common pattern. Typically, this involved a process by which the teacher talks or reads and, frequently, uses questions to stimulate choral or individual responses from the class. Throughout the lessons the pace was fast and the engagement of students appeared to be intense. Afterwards, a teacher explained how she tries to help those who experience difficulties by directing many more questions to them and by encouraging their classmates to go over the lesson content with them during the breaktimes.

Learning from experiences

What, then, does an English observer make of such an experience? Does it suggest patterns of practice that might be relevant to teachers in my country where, despite much smaller classes, it is not uncommon to find some children whose participation in lessons is marginal to say the least? Why are these Chinese students so quiet and obedient throughout a day of lessons that appear so repetitive?

It would be so easy to jump to simple conclusions that might appear to offer strategies that could be exported to other parts of the world. On the other hand, there are so many factors to consider. It is apparent, for example, that other influences help to shape the events observed in this classroom. I am told that teachers are held in high esteem in Chinese society, although this may be changing as a result of recent economic reforms. It also seems that children are often under considerable pressure from their families to achieve success at school. Indeed, in some parts of Asia there are signs in fast food restaurants which say *No studying*, presumably to discourage students from crowded home environments who are seeking space to pursue their schoolwork. Such community attitudes are but a part of a range of influences that help to shape the interactions that occur in local schools but which are difficult for the foreign visitor to determine.

DOI: 10.4324/9781003438014-3

Having said that, the Chinese story does point to the importance of teachers planning their lessons with all members of the class in mind. Here we bring into focus a central dilemma that confronts any teacher faced with their class. It is this: *how do I work with the whole class and, at the same time, reach out to each member as an individual?*

In the years since the right to educational opportunity was extended to all members of the community in many Western countries, it has become increasingly apparent that traditional forms of schooling are no longer adequate for the task. Faced with increased diversity, including the presence of students whose cultural experience or even language may be different from their own, and others who may find difficulties in learning within conventional arrangements, teachers have had to think about how they should respond.

A stance

Keeping this challenge in mind, this chapter traces my efforts to apply and, in so doing, refine the thinking I presented in my 1999 book *Understanding the Development of Inclusive Schools*. A pattern emerges from the accounts I present. This involves periods of uncertainty as my thinking is challenged by new experiences and different contexts, through a process I have described as *making the familiar unfamiliar*. What also becomes evident is the way that working with colleagues has helped me to cope with these disturbances, such that they often became critical incidents that led to developments in my ideas.

As explained in Chapter 1, in considering these examples, it is important to take account of the circumstances in which they took place. At the same time, I am concerned to avoid the mistake made by many commentators who, in seeking to present arguments that have global significance, fall into the trap of oversimplifying educational processes and practices by ignoring problems of interpretation and translation. At the same time, I am conscious that, as a visitor to these contexts, my own understandings are always partial.

For many years I have worked closely with educational practitioners and policy makers, in my own country and overseas, as they have attempted to move towards more inclusive ways of working. Acting as a critical friend, I see my task as helping them to learn from their experiences and, in so doing, to identify patterns and examples of practice that might be instructive to others who are addressing similar agendas. In this sense my aim is not to propose recipes that can be applied universally but rather to suggest ingredients that might be worthy of further consideration within particular contexts. In this chapter I explain the nature and potential of this thinking.

The approach I describe uses processes of collaborative inquiry to stimulate *school improvement with attitude* (Ainscow, Booth and Dyson 2006). At its best, this approach provides space and opportunities for developing new understandings and generating new practices. However, I argue that such possibilities can only be utilised if potential barriers in the wider context are understood and overcome. In particular, the projects I present in this chapter illustrate how national educational policies, though well intended, can some-times present hurdles that have to be addressed.

An ecology of equity

In order to take this thinking forward, Alan Dyson and I set up the Centre for Equity in Education at The University of Manchester. Established in the early 2000s, it ran as a distinct entity from 2005 to 2016, with its work being taken forward subsequently in the Manchester Institute of Education. The Centre was established with a remit to create opportunities to think about equity in ways which can respond to the needs of all learners; engage with, and be responsive to, the complex, localised contexts in which education takes place; and enable policy makers, practitioners, wider stakeholders and researchers to work together to develop new interventions that can give meaning to the values of equity in these complex and contrasting contexts (Kerr and Ainscow 2023).

As we worked with schools, my colleagues and I became aware of the com-plexities all of this involved. This led us to think about the processes at work as being linked within what my colleague Alan Dyson described as an *ecology of equity* (Ainscow et al. 2012a). By this, we meant that the extent to which students' experiences and outcomes are equitable is not dependent only on the educational practices of their teachers or even their schools. Instead, it depends on a whole range of interacting processes that reach into the school from outside. These include the demographics of the areas served by schools, the histories and cultures of the populations who send (or fail to send) their children to the school and the economic realities faced by those populations.

Beyond this, they involve the underlying socio-economic processes that make some areas poor and others affluent and that draw migrant groups into some places rather than others. They are also influenced by the wider poli-tics of the teaching profession, of decision-making at the district level and of national policy-making and the impacts of schools on one another over is-sues such as exclusion and parental choice. In addition, they reflect models of school governance, the ways in which local school hierarchies are established and maintained and how school actions are constrained and enabled by their positions in those hierarchies.

It is important to recognise the complexities of interactions between the different elements in this ecology and their implications for achieving more equitable school systems:

- **Within schools.** These are issues that arise from school and teacher prac-tices. They include the ways in which students are taught and engaged with learning; the ways in which teaching groups are organised and the different kinds of opportunities that result from this organisation; the kinds of social relations and personal support that are characteristic of the school; the ways in which the school responds to diversity in terms of attainment, gender, ethnicity and social background; and the kinds of relationships the school builds with families and local communities.

- **Between school.** These are issues that arise from the characteristics of the local school system. They include the ways in which different types of schools emerge locally; the ways in which these schools acquire different statuses so that hierarchies emerge in terms of performance and preference; the ways in which schools compete or collaborate; the processes of integration and segregation which concentrate students with similar backgrounds in different schools; the distribution of educational opportunities across schools; and the extent to which students in every school can access similar opportunities.

- **Beyond school**. This far-reaching arena includes the wider policy context within which schools operate; the family processes and resources which shape how children learn and develop; the interests and understandings of the professionals working in schools; and the demographics, economics, cultures and histories of the areas served by schools. Beyond this, it includes the underlying social and economic processes at national and in many respects at global levels out of which local conditions arise.

Looking at in this way, it is clear that there is much that individual schools can do to tackle issues within their organisations and that such actions are likely to have a profound impact on student experiences and perhaps have some influence on inequities arising elsewhere. However, it is equally clear that these strategies do not lead to schools tackling between- and beyond-school issues directly. No school strategy can, for example, make a poor area more affluent or increase the resources available to students' families, any more than it could create a stable student population, or tackle the global processes underlying migration patterns. However, there are issues of access, or of the allocation of students to schools, that might be tackled if schools work together on a common agenda.

A strategic model

The involvement of so many partners in the studies I present in this chapter involved many organisational challenges. In particular, there was a need to ensure that the work in the participating schools followed a similar pattern, whilst at the same time allowing discretion in order to relate activities to local circumstances. Similarly, we needed a means by which the university teams involved in the projects could generate evidence in relation to a common research agenda.

With these challenges in mind, a strategic model was developed (Ainscow et al. 2006). Its purpose was to clarify the positions and relationships within the partnerships we were establishing between practitioners and local policy makers on the one hand and researchers on the other (see Figure 3.1). We saw these as involving two interlinked strands of research carried out by practitioners and researchers.

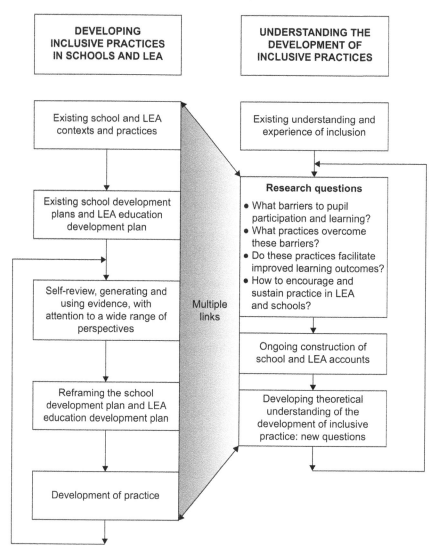

Mapping the research strategy
- Two linked research cycles -

DEVELOPING INCLUSIVE PRACTICES IN SCHOOLS AND LEA

UNDERSTANDING THE DEVELOPMENT OF INCLUSIVE PRACTICES

Existing school and LEA contexts and practices

Existing understanding and experience of inclusion

Existing school development plans and LEA education development plan

Research questions
- What barriers to pupil participation and learning?
- What practices overcome these barriers?
- Do these practices facilitate improved learning outcomes?
- How to encourage and sustain practice in LEA and schools?

Self-review, generating and using evidence, with attention to a wide range of perspectives

Multiple links

Ongoing construction of school and LEA accounts

Reframing the school development plan and LEA education development plan

Developing theoretical understanding of the development of inclusive practice: new questions

Development of practice

Figure 3.1 The strategic model).

Source: Ainscow, Chapman and Hadfield (2020).

The first of these strands is driven by the agendas of the partner schools. It sets out to use existing knowledge within these contexts, supplemented by further research evidence, as the means of fostering developments in the field. The second strand attempts to scrutinise these developments in order to address the overall agenda of the network, using existing theory and previous research as a basis for pursuing deeper understandings. Between the two strands is a set of *boundaries* that have to be crossed in order that the two driving agendas can be synchronised.

Through various projects, we have subsequently refined this model (Ainscow, Chapman and Hadfield 2020). We have also learned more about the difficulties that can occur as researchers attempt to negotiate these boundaries with practitioners. However, the major omission in our initial model was not detail about the practicalities of managing researcher-practitioner relationships but a failure to think through the nature of the knowledge each possessed and the ways in which such knowledge might be shared and used by each group. The matter was particularly confusing since we encouraged practitioners to undertake their own research, while we as researchers sometimes involved ourselves in discussions about the details of practice and policy.

Our perspective on educational development proved to be helpful in clarifying these issues. This does not differentiate between research-based and practice-based knowledge, much less between researcher and practitioner knowledge. It does, however, differentiate between the sorts of *understandings* which sustain ongoing practice and the *interruptions* which can *disturb* such understandings. Moreover, it became clear that, somehow, the interruptions have to come from *outside* current understandings, not in the sense that they must be generated beyond the classroom or school but that they must start from different assumptions. We saw how interruptions in this sense can take many forms, such as encounters with students who do not respond well to established approaches to teaching and learning, or with teachers who do things differently, or with schools with varied value systems.

We also saw how research evidence can sometimes create the capacity for practitioners to step outside their current understandings. This is not because research-based knowledge is in some sense superior to practice-based knowledge – and certainly not because researchers somehow know more than practitioners. Rather, it is because research-based knowledge and practice-based knowledge are built from different assumptions and according to different rules. There is always the potential, therefore, that they will lead to different understandings. In many cases, it seems likely and proper that research will aim at providing evidence for practice and policy. In other words, the understandings generated by each will be similar and the findings of research will readily become practitioner knowledge. However, we found that research-based and practice-based knowledge can sometimes stand in a critical relationship with one another.

Bearing these arguments in mind, in what follows, I explore possibilities for linking within-school, between-school and beyond-school strategies in order to develop more equitable improvement approaches. In order to develop my argument, I reflect on four initiatives in particular.

Improving the quality of education for all

As explained in Chapter 2, my involvement in collaborative forms of research began towards the end of the 1980s at the University of Cambridge with

Improving the Quality of Education for All (IQEA), which I established with David Hopkins. Over the following years, many other colleagues became involved as the initiative grew, both in the United Kingdom and overseas (for more detailed accounts of some of these projects, see Ainscow 1999; Ainscow and Hopkins 1992; Clarke, Ainscow and West 2006; Hopkins 2007; Hopkins, Ainscow and West 1994; West and Ainscow 2010). These developments all involved teams of researchers working in partnership with schools to identify ways in which the learning of students, parents and staff could be enhanced.

Our monitoring of developments in the schools involved in IQEA led us to conclude that such inquiry-based analyses can be a powerful means of stimulating schools' deliberations as they design their own improvement strategies. We also found that they were useful in identifying strategies appropriate to each school's own stage of development. In the case of schools seen as relatively low-performing, the initial emphasis was usually placed on gathering evidence that could be used to strengthen system procedures, usually through the tightening of management and leadership arrangements (West, Ainscow and Stanford 2005). For schools that were working more effectively, the focus was likely to be on continuing improvement, not least by looking at within-school variation. We also found that there is always scope for the strengthening of teachers' classroom practices, as no school works equally well for all of its students.

These findings from IQEA about the potential of inquiry-based approaches influenced the development of another project set in England that focused more specifically on the development of inclusive schools.

Understanding and developing inclusive practices in schools

This initiative began in 2000 when members of our group at the University of Manchester's Centre for Equity in Education won a grant from the Economic and Social Research Council (ESRC) Teaching and Learning Research Programme that enabled us to push forward our ideas about inquiry-based approaches to the development of schools. The initiative, which took the form of a three-year collaborative action research project, involved 25 urban schools, their associated local education authorities and three partner universities (i.e. Canterbury Christ Church, Manchester and Newcastle). Together we explored ways of developing more inclusive practices in the schools.

We saw inclusion as a value and set of practices about which something was already known. Moreover, as established authors and researchers in the field, we had played our part in generating this prior knowledge (e.g. Ainscow 1999; Booth 1995; Clark et al. 1999; Dyson and Millward 2000). We also knew from our own work and from others in this field that acceptance of the value and practices of inclusion was frequently resisted by practitioners who saw themselves as having other priorities and as working within constraints that made inclusive practice impossible. This was particularly the case in the then-English policy context where a *relentless focus on standards*, as defined by test scores, was being imposed on schools by the central government.

We therefore needed a means of releasing practitioners from the constraints of national policy and enabling them to change their value positions and assumptions. Drawing on the framework provided by the Index for Inclusion, we saw the use of evidence as offering this means. We made the assumption that, when practitioners were confronted by evidence about their own practices, they would, with appropriate encouragement from their critical friends, begin to recognise the non-inclusive elements of those practices and find ways of making them more inclusive. Fortunately, this is what did most often happen.

Our analysis revealed how social learning processes within schools influenced people's actions and, indeed, the thinking that informed their actions (Ainscow, Nicolaidou and West 2003). Often this was stimulated by various forms of evidence that created a sense of interruption to existing ways of thinking and working. Particularly powerful techniques in this respect involved the use of mutual observation, sometimes through video recordings, and evidence collected from students about teaching and learning arrangements within a school. Under certain conditions such approaches provided interruptions that stimulated self-questioning, creativity and action. In so doing, they sometimes led to a reframing of perceived problems that, in turn, drew attention to overlooked possibilities for addressing barriers to participation and learning.

We concluded, however, that none of this provided a straightforward mechanism for the development of more inclusive practices. We found that any space for reflection that was created as a result of engaging with evidence may sometimes be filled according to conflicting agendas. Indeed, we documented detailed examples of how deeply held beliefs within schools prevented the experimentation that is necessary in order to foster the development of more inclusive ways of working (Ainscow and Kaplan 2005).

The outcomes of this study have been widely reported in the scholarly literature (e.g. Ainscow, Booth and Dyson 2006; Ainscow et al. 2006; Dyson, Gallannaugh and Millward 2003; Howes et al. 2004, 2005). In terms of the development of a methodology for enabling research to contribute to more equitable policy and practice, the main lesson we drew was that it is possible to infuse a critical dimension into a collaborative action-research project so that issues of social justice (in this case, a focus on inclusion) are considered as practitioners shape their action. We also concluded that the critical friendship of *outsiders* (in this case, ourselves as researchers) is a way of keeping these issues on the agenda.

Lessons from the project

The research process used within this project varied from site to site in response to local priorities and possibilities. In most cases, the school established a small project team, often including the headteacher, and identified a focus for its work. This took the form of an aspect of practice and provision that it wished to review and develop. Evidence was gathered by the schools and university researchers, with meetings between the two teams to exchange information and explore its implications. These processes of dialogue were extended by meetings of schools within each local authority and by four national conferences for schools, local authority officers and university teams from across the Network. Some vignettes illustrate the complex ways in which schools responded to participation in the Network.

VIGNETTE 3.1   Enhancing participation in learning

In an urban high school, university researchers participated with a group of teachers interested in developing their approaches to teaching and learning. The initial discussions of this group gave an insight into the culture of teaching and learning in the school and into some of the barriers to learning experienced by students. The group agreed to evaluate video recordings of their lessons in order to challenge assumptions about certain groups of students and conducted interviews with students about their experience in school. The videos encouraged reflection on thinking and practice and the sharing of ideas about how colleagues could help one another to make their lessons more participative. For example, the recording of a modern language lesson focused the group's attention on issues of pace and support for participation, whilst discussion of the strengths of a science lesson indicated the value of students generating their own questions to deepen their understanding of the subject content. In each case, it was evident that the discussions contained moments of uncertainty for other teachers who were confronted with examples of practice that challenged their own assumptions. This was potentially threatening, particularly because the staff were also involved in carrying out the requirements set by a recent inspection.

VIGNETTE 3.2   Shifting assumptions

In a primary school, students identified as having *moderate learning difficulties* were taught separately from their peers for substantial parts of the school day in a *resource base*. Teachers expressed the view that this was the only way to educate this group. In a series of meetings with teachers, the university team raised questions about the implications of such practice for the way students were valued within the school. This provoked a debate about the inevitability of current practice, which coincided with some work by an advisory teacher on developing group work and problem-solving approaches in classrooms. At the same time as teachers began to integrate these approaches into their teaching, they also began to accept students categorised as *having learning difficulties* into their classrooms and found, to their surprise, that the children could achieve far more than the teachers had supposed. By the end of the project, these students were spending the majority of their time in mainstream classes.

VIGNETTE 3.3   Broadening horizons

Visits between schools were part of the developmental process built into the work of the Network. Schools from two of the local authorities, where the approach to inclusion was low-key and pragmatic, were much influenced by visits hosted by a third local authority with an explicit commitment to developing inclusive cultures, policies and practices. One of the most cautious of the visiting headteachers initially saw the host schools' commitment to inclusion as containing more rhetoric than substance and had been sceptical of the value of Network. Nonetheless, he found his own fundamental assumptions called into question. He felt that the narrow focus of the project in his own school might have been given a greater sense of direction by being viewed within the framework of a broad set of principles. He commented, *I wonder now whether we started at the 'wrong end'? I feel we focused very much on improving learning [practice]. Maybe we should have taken a broader view like [schools in the host authority].*

VIGNETTE 3.4   Trusting in experience

One of the primary schools felt the need to respond to the emphasis on literacy in national policy and, in particular, to the concern about standards of writing. It took the consciously bold step (especially in the context of external school inspections, a prescriptive National Literacy Strategy and the public accountability of schools for *results*) of significantly reducing the amount of time devoted to the explicit teaching of literacy skills and replacing it with group-based language-development activities arising out of shared experiences. As the head explained: *We're going down the route of looking at our teaching strategies, and how children learn, and the skills they need to learn, as learners – not the curriculum bit, but the actual learning techniques and strategies they have. Because that tends to be very limited with our children. And we actually want to broaden their range of learning strategies, their thinking skills. We want to create more opportunities of first-hand experience, the discussion, practising these thinking skills.*

VIGNETTE 3.5   Failing to construct a dialogue

In another of the secondary schools, one with a relatively advantaged intake, teachers expressed concern about a small minority of students who
did not attend regularly or whose behaviour was seen as disruptive. Their
response was to establish a Learning Support Unit, which they thought
would tackle the problems presented by these students, so that teaching
elsewhere could continue undisturbed. When university researchers interviewed some of these students, it became clear that they felt themselves
to be alienated by the culture of the school, as evidenced by teaching
approaches, relations between staff and students and what they saw as fa-
vouritism shown to students from more advantaged backgrounds. When
these findings were shared with the school team, however, the headteacher
made it clear that he did not wish these issues to be pursued and that the
only form of evaluation he was interested in was a quantitative analysis of
reductions in absence and disciplinary exclusions from the school, both
subject to government concern. He did not wish to consider the possibility that there might be limitations in dealing with disruption by seeing it
as only contained within a few problematic students.

Making sense of developments

These vignettes illustrate the extent to which development in each school had
its unique features. However, they also point to some common patterns which
underpinned these differences.

In broad terms, what we saw in schools that participated in the 'Understanding and developing inclusive practices in schools' project was neither the
crushing of inclusion by the Government's standards agenda nor the rejection
of the standards agenda in favour of a radical, inclusive alternative. Certainly,
many teachers were concerned about the impacts on their work on standards,
and some were committed to a view of inclusion which they saw as standing
in contradiction to it. However, in most schools the two agendas remained
intertwined.

So, on the one hand, we sometimes saw ways in which the standards agenda
narrowed and subverted the schools' commitment to inclusion. Invited to
develop inclusive practices, for instance, some schools (as in Vignettes 3.1, 3.2
and 3.5) focused immediately on questions of attainment, seeing such a focus
as the way to be concerned about the achievement of students. Similarly, the
school in Vignette 3.4 saw its learning support unit as the way of maintaining problematic students in the school. Potentially more inclusive approaches
were, in these contexts, passed over.

On the other hand, the focus on attainment in these schools evidently
prompted teachers to examine issues in relation to the achievements and participation of hitherto marginalised groups that they had previously overlooked.

Likewise, the concern with inclusion tended to shape the way schools responded to the imperative to raise standards. This was particularly evident when, towards the end of the Network's life, we asked teachers from schools in the three local areas to consider what outcomes their work had generated for students. Although they saw themselves as producing the *observables* of raised attainment, improved attendance and so on, they did not find that this was possible simply through officially sanctioned practice, such as the national Numeracy and Literacy Strategies that were highly influential during that period. Many of the children they taught did not, they argued, learn effectively from such practices.

Through their involvement in the Network, and its associated development and research processes, the teachers involved attempted to make sense of why this was and to explore different kinds of practice that might be more successful. Some told us that they had to develop the responsiveness of their schools to the characteristics of these students in ways which promoted students' engagement with learning and their sense of themselves as learners. While these actions would eventually be reflected in the measures for which they were held accountable by the government, such holistic developments were, they suggested, valuable *for [their] own sake*, not simply as a means to an end.

There was, therefore, a mutual colonisation of the standards and inclusion agendas in schools' work. If the former in many ways constrained and subverted the latter, there were also ways in which it was itself shaped by inclusive values and offered a focus for the realisation of those values in practice.

An equity research network

The two projects I have described so far clearly have much in common, not least in the way they sought to: stimulate a process of change in practice; formulate action with reference to overarching principles; had a research strand that invited practitioners to inquire into their own practice; and assumed that such inquiry would impact the values on which practitioners act. At the same time, the projects positioned university researchers as critical friends and technical supporters of practitioners.

Between 2006 and 2011, with my colleagues at the University of Manchester, I had a further chance to explore these ideas in more detail through our involvement with yet another group of schools (see Ainscow et al. 2012a, 2012b for detailed accounts of this project). The initiative was located in what we called *Stockborough*, an area characterised by socio-economic disadvantage and social and ethnic segregation. Its secondary school system comprised a hierarchy of 16 schools, some selective on the basis of attainment or religious faith, with others being non-selective and described as *comprehensive schools*.

The Stockborough Equity Research Network (SERN) grew out of an existing partnership of four secondary schools, with ten other schools joining in at various stages over the five-year period. Whilst the four headteachers initially involved had developed very good working relationships, and this had led to some collaborative activities, they felt that the impact had been limited. Consequently, they decided that there was a need to develop ways of working that would challenge the practices, assumptions and beliefs of staff and which would help to create a stimulus for further sustainable improvement. With this in mind, they approached us at the Centre for Equity in Education to support and facilitate the use of research to strengthen their network. The schools agreed to fund our involvement.

Through discussions involving the initial group of headteachers, it was agreed that equity was a central issue facing each of the partner schools. It soon became evident, however, that what this meant was different in each context, not least in respect to the groups of learners who seemed to be missing out within existing arrangements. As a result, it was agreed that the work of the network should take account of these differences by adopting a broad set of research questions to focus its activities, within which each school would determine its own more specific focus. These questions were:

- Which of our learners are most vulnerable to underachievement, marginalisation or exclusion?
- What changes in policy and practice need to be made in order to reach out to these students?
- How can these changes be introduced effectively and evaluated in respect to student outcomes?

In taking the strategic decision to focus attention on groups of learners thought to be missing out within existing arrangements, my colleagues and I were anxious that this might lead to narrowly focused efforts to *fix* students seen as being in some sense inadequate. However, collecting evidence about these groups usually led to a re-focusing of attention around contextual factors that were acting as barriers to their participation and learning. In this way, most of the projects carried out gradually became mainstream school improvement efforts that had the potential to benefit many students.

As with our earlier projects, staff inquiry groups were set up in each school, usually consisting of five or six members representing different perspectives within their school communities. These groups took part in introductory workshops at which we discussed with them an initial analysis we had made of the local area, based on a consideration of various documents, statistics and interviews with a selection of stakeholders, including headteachers, local authority staff, community group representatives and politicians.

Following this process of contextual analysis, we took the staff teams through a process of planning the investigations they intended to carry out. In so doing, we helped them to develop a clearer focus and plan the procedures they would follow. Subsequently, each school team set out to gather evidence about students identified as losing out in some way, the aim being to develop better insights regarding their experiences in the schools. The groups also shared their findings with their colleagues in the partner schools. In these ways, the intention was to deepen understandings of practices, beliefs, assumptions and organisational processes, both within and across the schools in the network.

Taking place as it did over a period of five years of intense government activity to improve educational outcomes, or at least raise the annually reported attainment levels, this was a time of multiple policy initiatives and interventions to *drive up standards*. Consequently, it was not easy to disentangle particular effects and attribute them to the work of the project teams, rather than the pressures imposed generally on schools over this period. Nonetheless, the evidence we collected showed that teachers in the schools themselves felt able to identify changes and trace these to their involvement in the project. It can also be asserted that this contributed fully to the overall increase in examination results recorded in the particular local authority during this period. In fact, the percentage of students gaining five or more A* to C grades in the GCSE (General Certificate of Secondary Education) examinations taken by most students at the age of 16 went up from 54.6% in 2005 to 76.5% in 2010, a rise of 22% (during the same period the national average went from 56.3 to 75.3% or a rise of 19%). Looking at a more inclusive measure of student performance, during the same period the percentage of students gaining five or more A* to G grades went up at almost twice the national average, from 90 to 96.1% (compared to 89 to 92.7% nationally).

Key factors

Our consideration of what this particular network achieved points to a series of factors that seem to be particularly important for the development of more inclusive schools. At their most fundamental, the factors we are concerned with are located in classrooms, where, first and foremost, inclusion is about attitudes. That is to say, teachers and their students can either promote or inhibit a fair, welcoming and inclusive working climate.

In a school that is committed to fairness, all students should expect to be welcome in their classrooms not only in explicit ways, which embrace cultural, social and intellectual differences but also in implicit ways, so they will not feel marginalised because of feedback (or lack of it) on their behaviour and performance. Because all students are welcome, they can expect positive interactions as a normal part of their classroom experience. As a result, they will feel included, valued and acknowledged.

Then there is the issue of practice. If teachers favour one style it will tend to suit those students who are comfortable with that way of working. In effect, strong teaching orthodoxies can disenfranchise students who are less confident with or less engaged by that approach. Equity, therefore, requires practitioners who understand the importance of teaching the same thing in different ways to different students and of teaching different things in different ways to the same students.

The SERN schools could point to examples of good practice in all of these areas before they joined the project. But the issue they were addressing through their involvement was whether they were sure that all students could feel they were embraced within these ways of working. In most of the schools there was evidence, too, of changes in classrooms so that specific groups who felt to be missing out were now more actively engaged in learning, and that this had been achieved through deliberate attention to the attitudes displayed, the language used and interactions engineered in lessons, all of which were reflected in the range of teaching approaches used.

Of course, these are the less difficult aspects of equity to deliver. That is not to deny their value, but simply to accept that while adjustments in classroom practices can have a significant impact on the experiences of particular students, they may not do much to alter the factors that led to these students *missing out* in the first place. Often such factors are more intransigent and therefore more difficult to influence as a single school. A selection of accounts of practice helps to throw light on the complexities involved.

Experiencing surprises

Some of the school inquiries led to significant development in thinking and practice, usually as a result of surprising findings. The experiences described in Account 3.1 were an example of this happening.

> **Account 3.1. Invisible students**. During the first year of SERN, a team of six staff at Valley High School were selected by an assistant head teacher to work with her. They set out to investigate students' allegiances and affinity with the school, as there was a sense that the majority left the school having had a *slightly disappointing* time. The team had a hunch that some young people did not feel that they belonged to the school; instead, they either had strong allegiances to disparate teenage groups, or felt excluded from these groups. It seemed, too, that there might be a connection between this and a more general lack of interest in school amongst students. With this in mind, the team of staff decided to identify learners in Year 9 who appeared to demonstrate this sense of disinterest in the recorded punishments and merits they received via a new behaviour system.
>
> Looking at what had happened during the first weeks of term, the inquiry team was surprised to find that about 25% of the students – with equal numbers of boys and girls – seemed to be *invisible*. Even more surprising was that – contrary to expectations – these students were from across what they described as *the ability range*.
>
> All of this led the staff team to change tack. Clearly, these young people were not being noticed in the classroom, either through their learning or their behaviour. Consequently, the team decided to investigate the experiences of the students more closely to see what this could tell them about practices within the school. With this in mind, they observed the students in class to see what their experiences of learning

and interactions were. The aim was to observe the lessons *through the students' eyes.*

A decision was made to concentrate on 12 students, six of each gender. With the help of one of our university researchers an observation schedule was developed. This focused on four main areas: the interactions and relationships between the student and teacher; the interactions of the student with tasks set; the interactions of the student with peers; and the general dispositions of the students. The team then wrote reflective summaries about what they had found out.

The team then met together to discuss what they had written and experienced. Ground rules were set from the start: in particular, it was decided that names of teachers would not be used, in order to avoid conversations around performance. Despite this, on some occasions staff names were mentioned during the conversations but the team still tried to respect the ethical position they had agreed.

Whilst there were minor differences in what was observed, the staff were struck by how similar the experiences of the students were. In particular, they noticed that their targeted students were rarely named or approached in class. Rather, they were seen to either work through their tasks quietly, often finishing before other students but not then demanding attention, or they were quietly off task, sometimes distracting other students. During whole class question and answer sessions they were generally unassertive in their body language, many of them hardly ever raising their hands or not responding at all.

As a consequence of these further surprises, the team decided to carry out focus group discussions with the students to find out what they had to say about their classroom experiences and the school more generally. The hunches of the staff were that these students did not want to be noticed – that they were happy to not be the focus of attention in lessons. However, once again their assumptions were challenged by what the students said.

It was decided to mix the 12 students with 12 others, picked randomly from Year 9. This was so that these potentially more *visible* students might help to develop a more dynamic and relaxed discussion, as well as providing insights into their experiences of learning. Two researchers from the university conducted the focus groups in order that the students might feel more able to express themselves. They were also mindful of who the target learners were so that they could make sure everyone's voice was heard.

During the focus groups the students were asked to identify and write down a recent learning experience where they had felt involved and engaged in learning, and conversely, activities where they have not felt involved or engaged. They were then asked to expand on these, and to discuss issues around fairness and being listened to within the school. They were told that names of teachers or subjects would be removed, and that anything they said would be treated confidentially.

The students were well able to articulate what they felt worked and did not work for them. They were also acutely and sometimes painfully aware that some students got more attention than they did. Among other things, they articulated their dislike for copying out texts, and their enjoyment of activities where they could think for themselves, as long as tasks were explained clearly and that they *felt part* of the activity.

Some students spoke passionately about their feelings of being ignored during lessons and the sense that this was unfair. For example, one girl explained how she would sometimes put her hand up to ask for advice. Seeing the teacher walking towards her, she would then be disappointed to see that an incident elsewhere in the classroom would distract the teacher's attention. Other students argued that, despite the fact that they attended each day, working hard and always completing their homework on time, they rarely received commendations. Meanwhile they noticed that potentially disruptive students were often rewarded for what seemed like short periods of passive behaviour.

The observation notes and transcripts were then analysed and sections of dialogue on similar themes were grouped together. The team members identified any sections that jumped out at them – that made them stop and think, that taught them something new about their students and the practices and beliefs within the school. This process was repeated several times until, finally, the extracts were organised around the following themes: learning activities, copying, group work, getting help and having tasks explained, treatment of loud and quiet students, teacher talking, and praise for *good* and *bad* students.

Because the experience of gathering evidence had been powerful for the team they decided to consult the headteacher about next steps. As a result, it was agreed that the findings should be presented at a meeting of the senior leadership team. At the meeting – which we attended – some senior colleagues were evidently surprised and taken aback by the evidence. As a result, a whole school meeting was arranged to discuss the implications of the evidence that had been collected.

The meeting was held, after school, with over 90 members of staff in attendance. Some scepticism was voiced about the validity of the data, based on the argument that it was only from a *handful of students*. The response to this from one member of the staff inquiry team was that the power of individual dialogue lies in how it clearly resonates with so many staff. This also led to a suggestion from some staff that the process should be extended to other groups of students, and that it should also be repeated once some changes had been made to see if and how they had impacted on the children. On leaving at the end of the session, some teachers said they would go into their classrooms the following day and make an attempt to name and involve everyone. Whether this happened is not clear.

What is clear in this account is the inquiry team's deepened understanding of the students' experiences and the role of the school processes in shaping their responses. There was also a real sense of them becoming agents of change within their school. Equally powerful was their sense of the crucial different roles and skills that the different team members contributed. One of the team members commented that, before this project, she felt that her status was below that of other colleagues. However, she now realised that she had an equally important role to play in exploring the student experience and bringing this to the attention of the whole staff.

New arrivals

Some of the SERN schools addressed issues that challenge many schools in England, particularly those in urban contexts. One of these is that of how to respond to new arrivals – both students transferring from other local schools and those arriving from elsewhere. As described in Account 3.2, this became a burning issue at Highlands, a school for 11- to 16-year-olds.

> **Account 3.2. Coming and going**. When we became involved in Highlands, the school had a student population of just over 400 students and served some of the most disadvantaged communities in the country. The students were mainly British White, with a small number of Asian and African-Caribbean heritage students, and an increasing group of Eastern Europe students for whom English was an additional language. At that time the school was undersubscribed. Consequently, it had a large number of feeder primary schools: 24 in all, with only 20% of students living locally in a community that was also socio-economically disadvantaged. As a result, many students had long and sometimes difficult journeys to and from school.
>
> The inquiry team members were: a deputy headteacher with responsibility for inclusion, a head of one of the three *houses*, the special needs co-ordinator, a teaching assistant with responsibility for behaviour, and the inclusion administrator. The sixth team member was a specialist teacher in drama and the performing arts. The head was keen to have a teacher with an arts specialism on the team since he was interested in how creativity might change people's lives *by enabling people to be otherwise*.
>
> From the start, the team was keen to investigate issues around mobility in terms of the significantly high number of students who were arriving after the start of Year 7, some of whom moved to Highlands to avoid permanent exclusion from previous schools. The team was also concerned about the number of students for whom Highlands was their second choice. Apparently, the pattern was that some of these chose to leave when places eventually came up in their first choice school.
>
> The team felt that many parents had relatively negative images of the school, largely based on its past reputation. They were also aware that

there was no robust induction process in the school for new arrivals and that it was often difficult to get data about students from their previous schools. They suspected, too, that some of these new students felt isolated, both with respect to their classmates and the teachers. An added challenge to all of this came as a result of a sudden intake of students with little English that, we were told, had *caught the school on the hop*. Some indications of racism had surfaced as a consequence of this intake and, as a result, staff had attempted to develop processes to support the full participation of these students in school life.

A group of eight students who had arrived at the school in Year 10 and 11 were selected for closer attention. The staff team decided to compare the experiences of these students with those of another group who had been in the school since the start of Year 7. This group comprised five girls and one boy, all said to be of relatively high ability. One of the team devised a questionnaire comprising mainly open questions about subject choices, awareness of expected exam grades, confidence in achieving grades, preferred subjects, career choices and aspirations, making friends, and belonging to Highlands. The questionnaires were then used as the basis of focus group discussions and the students also completed them individually. The *mobile students* were divided into two groups of four, as it was felt this would give them more space to speak. This was also to avoid potential disruptive behaviour from two of the students if put together. The students who had been in the school longer discussed the issues as one group.

A researcher from the university facilitated the focus groups so that the students would feel more able to express themselves. The head of house and the teaching assistant were also present. They commented later that their presence did not appear to impact on the established group but sensed it might have done with the mobile groups, since the students had not built up a sense of trust with the staff of how honest they could be.

The staff team then scrutinized the transcripts in order to identify sections of dialogue that stood out, and collated the responses to the questionnaire. They were clearly taken aback by the findings. Significant to them was the difference between the general sense of well-being of the established group and the discomfort that many of the mobile students were experiencing. They had also expected social issues to be the mobile students' main concern but this did not turn out to be the case.

The established students generally felt supported by the school – there was a sense that they had been given a lot of help and advice by staff. They had all been able to take their first choices in their subjects; they were mainly clear what their expected grades were; they felt they could approach members of staff; they felt they were known and knew everyone; and that they belonged to the school. In contrast, the mobile group felt a lot less confident about their subjects. Surprisingly for the staff, this seemed more important to them than the social side of their settling in process. They were not clear what their expected grades were; most of them had not been able to take their first choices in subjects; they were not fully aware of the range of choices they had; and some of them felt they had been placed in classes on an ad hoc fashion.

As regards course work, many of these students felt frustrated that work for exam subjects from their previous schools was not acknowledged. In some cases, too, they felt they were viewed negatively for not having done the appropriate course work and, consequently, not given any support to catch up. The group also talked about not feeling as if they belonged and the difficulty of building up a sense of being known, as well as knowing what to expect from staff and students. Some talked poignantly about the benefits of going to school with the children who you grow up with *on your street*. In addition, some of them commented on how friendly and willing to help they had found many of the staff, and some speculated this was probably because of the school's relatively small size.

The inquiry team decided to observe newly arrived students in class to see what their experiences of learning and interactions appeared to be. Ideally, they would have liked to observe the same Year 11 students they had talked to in the previous discussions. However, it was felt this might be too distracting at an important time of year for these students. Also, the students might be aware of the purpose and react to the presence of the inquiry team member. Instead, five Year 9 students who had arrived in the previous month were identified.

The evidence generated showed that the newly arrived students interacted in similar ways. Most of them seemed to be awkward and self-conscious, and in some cases lacking in confidence. In general, they seemed to be relatively eager to please both the teacher and their peers. On-going negotiation of friendships was evident, sometimes resulting in their being drawn quietly into off-task activities.

The students responded well to attention from the teachers, although on one occasion they were completely ignored. When given attention, they evidently grew in confidence as the lessons proceeded. Attention involved directing easily answerable questions at the new students, providing extra attention on a one-to-one basis, working through examples with them, and naming them more than other students.

Looked at alongside the views of students, the evidence gathered by observation provided a stimulus for discussing the experiences of these young people and, as a consequence, ways of responding. At another level, this began the process of creating a shared language, where the team was able to communicate the subtleties of school processes in relation to student differences.

This account of what occurred at Highfield illustrates how collaborative inquiry can lead directly to changes in practice. In this instance, the school's admissions process was reviewed and new students were met in person by their head of house in order to complete their options process. In addition, the subject option process was refined. It was also agreed that new arrivals would start on a Friday, to meet their tutor and be assigned a *buddy*, before beginning school formally on the following Monday. In addition, staff development activities regarding how to integrate students with English as their second language into lessons were introduced.

Rethinking the agenda

In some instances, an engagement with evidence sometimes led staff within the SERN schools to rethink the way they had formulated their initial agendas. An example of this is described in Account 3.3, which took place in Westbury, a school that had approximately 40% Asian heritage and 60% White British students. There was also an increasing number of refugees and asylum seekers from a wide variety of countries. The Asian British students mainly came from a district that experienced multiple deprivations.

> **Account 3.3. Addressing disaffection.** The community surrounding Westbury comprises almost 100% White British who are traditionally working class. However, some families chose not to send their children to Westbury because of its ethnic mix. Within the school, the students from different ethnic backgrounds were generally harmonious and worked well together. Within classrooms, strict seating plans were used to mix students by ethnicity and gender.
>
> In joining SERN, the headteacher and her senior colleagues decided that they wanted to investigate disaffection in the school. Seven boys had been permanently excluded during the previous year and it had been noted that a disproportionate number of these students, five in all, had been of Asian heritage. The senior staff assumed these difficulties were related to the boys being part of a youth subculture within the Asian community, and a problematic generation gap between the boys and their parents. Their initial focus was to try and reduce the amount of permanent exclusions amongst some of their disaffected Asian British males.
>
> When asked if the staff had felt this might be related to ethnicity or culture, a senior member of staff talked about his belief that these young people's parents were probably relatively unaware of their children's lifestyles outside of the family home. Based on glimpses of a sub-culture, which some members of staff had gleaned from hearing informal conversations between students, they also suspected that these students came into contact with drug related activities, organised fights and a gang culture.
>
> The staff inquiry team, led by a deputy head, identified 26 students whose behaviour had given most concern. These included both Asian and White British students, 24 of who turned out to be boys and most

were from Years 8 to 10. A behaviour database was used to carry out this analysis, although later members of the team realised they could have gone on hunches.

The staff conducted focus student group discussions, facilitated by researchers from the university, all of which were prompted by similar questions, and observed by a member of the pastoral support team. In addition, some staff were interviewed about their views about exclusions and students' behaviour.

In general, the students recognised that they displayed challenging behaviour in school. They felt that, whilst they often were punished because of this, the school's actions were generally fair. They did not pick out any particular teachers or subjects where they felt they were treated less fairly than other students, or where they behaved more badly. They tended to share similar views about lessons, learning, being punished and reasons for feeling disaffected regardless of their ethnicity, and none of their reasons for challenging behaviour and disaffection appeared to be related to race issues. All the students realised that exclusion was serious and that it significantly impacted on their future career opportunities. They also commented that their parents would be upset and disappointed in them if they were excluded.

The focus of attention changed, however, when, on closer analysis it became evident that a common feature of all of these students – White and Asian heritage – was that they all had reading levels significantly lower than their chronological ages, in some cases by more than three years. In contrast, only one out of them recognised that they had a reading problem, and that was a Year 7 student. Clearly this could be because the students did not want to see themselves as having a weakness, or because they saw *getting by* as being enough.

The deputy headteacher explained that they had found that about 40% of all their students between Years 7 to 11 had reading levels below their chronological reading ages, with some of the gaps being *absolutely shocking*. He added that staff were not fully aware of this figure and, similarly, they were probably not fully aware of those young people in their lessons who had weak reading and writing skills, nor the extent of their struggle. Despite some of them knowing about the low levels of literacy across the school, it was still, he explained, confronting to see the correlation between low reading ages and disaffection for the focus groups. Although a relatively small number of the students might have been excluded due to serious disaffection, these might have indicated a much larger number of students who were not as engaged as they could be because of literacy.

Examples were mentioned by the deputy head of when a teacher, not realising a student very well, asked them to read in front of a class. Rather than admit to their inability to read, the student might respond with challenging behaviour or, less evidently, simply switch off. It was noted, too, that learning outcomes tended to dip towards the end of Year 7 and during Year 8, not just because of impending adolescence and peer pressure, but because students found reading and writing a lot harder, *and there is suddenly a lot more of it at a higher level*. As a result of this rethinking, in the following school year attention was focused on ways of fostering literacy across the curriculum, particularly in years 7 and 8.

Some reflections

These accounts of practice from schools involved in the SERN initiative over five years illustrate how a common process of inquiry-based development was interpreted differently in each school. At a general level, the accounts suggest a similar pattern of development in each context as the staff teams moved from their initial focus on particular groups of students – presumed to be vulnerable to various forms of marginalisation – towards a focus on contextual factors that created barriers for these groups. In so doing, this moved attention to processes of overall school improvement in ways that had the potential to improve conditions for larger numbers of learners within a school.

In all these schools, marked shifts became evident at both the individual and inquiry team levels, as evidence contradicted and elaborated prior understandings. It was significant, too, that the extent to which a relatively narrow initial focus widened as a result of the process was shaped significantly by the willingness of school leaders to allow these issues to be explored and by the wider culture of the school. Each team found ways of developing its practice in response to the process. However, external policy constraints opened some channels of development whilst closing many others.

As we saw, in some of the schools the inquiry teams went on to share their evidence with their colleagues at departmental or whole school meetings. These, to varying degrees, challenged and stimulated some staff's thinking and in some instances caused a degree of discomfort. The teams sometimes encountered opposition from colleagues who refused to accept the meaning of the evidence they had generated. In such contexts, evidence generated from student voice proved to be particularly powerful in challenging established meanings.

Some of the investigations led to changes and developments in practices in the schools. These ranged from embedding mutual observations amongst groups of staff to making procedural changes to admissions of new students starting outside the normal starting time, to more subtle individual changes relating to how the staff interacted with students in class.

The accounts are, in many senses, encouraging. They demonstrate the potential of groups of schools to work together, using various kinds of evidence to challenge inequities within their organisational contexts. At the same time, local historical factors continued to limit the impact of their efforts. In particular, trends within the market place of the local education system made some of the partner schools extremely vulnerable. This is a key issue that I return to in later chapters. Meanwhile, I move on to yet another project in order to think about the implications for leadership practices.

Ethical leadership

Building on lessons from our earlier studies in England, a further opportunity was provided to explore the use of collaborative inquiry as a way of developing inclusive schools in a very different context, that of the state of Queensland in Australia, where equity is a long-standing and seemingly intractable challenge. The study involved a research network comprising six schools, spread across what is a large state, and a team of eight researchers from the Queensland University of Technology who, together, explored how ethical leadership could promote ways of interpreting and using various forms of evidence to promote learning and equity. It was funded by the Australian Research Council (see Harris et al. 2017, 2020; Spina et al. 2019, for fuller accounts of the study).

Media reports of the performance of Queensland schools in the high-stakes national testing regime, and comparisons with other state and territory systems in Australia, tended to draw attention to the performance of the state's schools as a source of concern. As in England, schools there faced a broad range of challenges in a context of performativity that is characterised by discourses of choice and competition, high-stakes accountability and moves to increase school autonomy.

In response to these challenges, some schools created data teams, usually made up of school leaders (including deputy principals of department and/or literacy and numeracy coaches) to oversee the work of managing, analysing and reporting on data for the school. These teams, however, did not appear to alleviate the pressure on others in the school to respond to external accountabilities. Rather, they established new structures within schools that would filter state-mandated requirements and develop their own targets for teachers via the use of locally created policies such as school assessment and tracking calendars.

The six schools involved in the network were all involved in broadly the same process of inquiry over a period of three years. They usually started this by exploring how the interpretation of publicly available performance data – developed for the purpose of accountability – might prompt discussions about possible new ways of reaching out to all of their students. Given the emphasis this places on contextual analysis and decision-making within each organisation, it was inevitable that the approaches and forms of interventions that were adopted varied from school to school. What was striking, however, was the influence of local circumstances on the ways that these schools engaged with the study.

The design of the study made use of the idea of an ecology of equity. As explained above, this focuses attention on: within-school factors that arise from existing policies and practices; between-school factors that reflect the characteristics of local school systems; and beyond-school factors, including the wider policy context, family processes and resources, and the demographics, economics, cultures and histories of local areas.

The study was also built around the varied interests and expertise of my colleagues at Queensland University of Technology. Together, they provided extensive expertise in educational leadership, data analysis, collaborative action research, school change, assessment and inclusion.

The research design

A version of the strategic model developed in the earlier projects, with its parallel strands of activity, was adopted in the Queensland study. The first of these strands was built on the ongoing development of knowledge within each school, drawing on various forms of evidence and using processes of collaborative inquiry – planning, acting, observing and reflecting – led by groups of staff and supported by the university research team. Based on our earlier work, the assumption was that the interpretation of data and engagement in collaborative inquiry would lead to changes in practice that would support more equitable schooling.

The second strand of inquiry was central to the concerns of the university research team. It focused on four research questions that were developed beforehand:

- How can an evidence-based inquiry approach be used to support efforts to achieve equity within schools?
- What forms of leadership are needed to support such developments?
- How can networking allow educators to examine expectations and achievement, and take action to improve student learning?
- How can all of this be achieved in the context of high-stakes accountability policies?

These four research questions formed the foundation of the *understanding* strand of the research design. This involved a more traditional research stance, which involved the collection of evidence through a range of methods, including observation, interviews, data analysis and preparation of accounts of practice. Here, an intended outcome was to make contributions to knowledge about social justice and ethical leadership in a policy context dominated by accountability and managerialism.

Taking lessons from the earlier studies, a key feature was the ways in which the two strands interconnect. As noted earlier, we viewed these multiple interactions as a process of knowledge generation, occurring when researchers' and practitioners' knowledges meet in particular sites. In this way, our aim, once again, was to produce new knowledge about ways in which broad values might be better realised in future practice. Ethical leadership practices were a major focus of this project. This focused specifically on the efforts of school principals and other senior staff to improve educational outcomes for all students.

Project activities

Initially, we worked mainly with school leadership teams, usually consisting of principals, deputy principals and heads of departments, to engage in intensive reviews of publicly available student outcome data, plus the collection and analysis of statistical data from within their schools. In working with school leaders and the school-based research teams, we tried to stimulate critical reflection on current practices, starting particularly with discussions about data and equity. Our expectation was that the situational analyses using publicly available data, alongside insider knowledge, would point to potential *levers for change* (Ainscow 2005). Within these contexts, the task of the team from the university was to help school staff to interpret and reflect upon school data and plan strategies to improve the learning of all of their students.

The schools then established one or more staff research teams to design and carry out plans for investigating and managing change as part of their engagement in the collaborative inquiry process. The range of inquiries was diverse and included the collection and analysis of multiple forms of evidence, involving school leaders, teachers, students and members of the broader community. These initiatives focused on issues such as: assessment practices and the use of data to support equitable school-based systems and procedures; challenging deficit views about students; the development of a coaching model for implementing school change; developing new approaches to feedback for senior school students; strategies to engage students as active agents in writing; and interventions for enhancing student engagement. At least two university researchers worked with each of the schools, acting as critical friends throughout the three years, supporting and collecting evidence in order to report the inquiry processes.

Meanwhile, in order to address the research questions in the *understanding* strand of the strategic model, school leaders were occasionally interviewed regarding their understandings of ethical leadership in the context of high-stakes accountability (Ehrich et al. 2015). In addition, during research network meetings, discussions were facilitated by university researchers to gauge their collective thoughts regarding ethical leadership as experienced by the leaders and to learn more about ethical dilemmas that they experienced and worked to resolve in their schools.

Drawing lessons

We were particularly interested in the impact of accountability data on all of this, not least the pressures this placed on school leaders in relation to the performance of their schools. Whilst not dismissing the dangers associated with such policies, it did seem that they could be turned to advantage when practitioners are driven by a commitment to inclusion and fairness. Such a conclusion echoes the conclusions of the earlier studies in England. As I explained, these had all taken place in the context of government efforts to improve standards in public education, as measured by test and examination scores. This involved the creation of an educational *market-place*, coupled with an emphasis on policies fostering greater diversity between types of schools.

Within the Queensland study, we found that the research network meetings, as well as workshops organised for the participating schools by the university researchers, helped to strengthen the partnerships between all those involved. In particular, they provided contexts in which expertise was shared with the aim of helping schools to develop locally relevant strategies for improving outcomes for all their students. In these ways, knowledge was generated both within schools and in the emergent understanding of how the research network schools were all working towards quality and equity, whilst at the same time addressing their own contextual challenges.

Leaders from the schools were also involved in occasional meetings with the university research team, where the focus was to examine the challenges involved in leading their school teams in cycles of inquiry to support equity. Gradually these shared experiences helped to cultivate a context of openness and trust, where school leaders could challenge ideas and share their experiences.

Using data

A vignette provides a flavour of the developments in the Queensland schools.

VIGNETTE 3.6   Starting with test scores

In another secondary school, the initial catalyst for the inquiry was the repeated poor performance of their Year 9 student cohorts on the national writing test. These results were used as both a measure of the school's improvement agenda and as an indicator of areas to target in terms of teaching and learning. In other words, the initial premise of the collaborative inquiry was to *resolve educational problems and improve educational practice* (Carr and Kemmis 2003, p. 109), as determined and measured by the writing test.

The concerns about student performance on the tests were complemented by discussions of observations carried out by teachers of their students' approaches to writing in their classrooms. Their conversation with university colleagues led the teachers to consider the extent to which student performance on the tests reflected a lack of confidence as writers, which was impeding their learning in English and subsequently limiting their achievement in assessments. In this way, the test results were used as both a measure of the school's improvement agenda and as an indicator of areas to target in terms of teaching and learning.

The principal actively encouraged a team of five teacher-researchers to engage in collaborative inquiry to enhance students' writing. In order to achieve these goals, they were given a generous amount of time to work with members of the university team.

In this school, the role of the principal in supporting the staff inquiry teams proved to be significant, a theme that I return to in Chapter 6.

Engaging with voices

In analysing the school-led collaborative inquiries within the Queensland study, we saw the process as involving an engagement with a series of *voices*:

- *The voice of authority*, as indicated in policy documents and accountability systems
- *The voice of practitioners* who find themselves dealing with competing expectations
- *The voice of students* who experience the way policies are interpreted and enacted within classrooms
- *The voice of those beyond the school gate*, including colleagues in other schools and community partners
- *The voice of school leaders* as they seek to move their schools forward within existing policy pressures

In addition, there were the voices of researchers, each bringing their different interests and expertise to the inquiry process. And, importantly in our study, the coming together of these different interests and areas of expertise proved to be a splendid source of innovative thinking.

In these contexts, the role of the university team as critical friends was a complex one. While offering advice and challenging current approaches and thinking, there were opportunities, too, where the engagement in this project facilitated more open communication and understanding around the new structures the schools had implemented. We also grew to appreciate the role of collaborative inquiry in helping teachers and leaders to develop a discerning eye regarding current (in)equitable practices and to take appropriate action following further exploration and analysis. Detailed explanations are provided of the processes involved, including the relationships within the network, between schools and the team of researchers and the strategies used to collect data in order to draw lessons from the study, in Harris et al. (2017, 2019).

The experiences of the schools in the Queensland study illustrated how collaborative inquiry does not always involve a smooth, rapid or assured path to more equitable school development. In fact, in some instances, we saw how collaboration can be the means by which progress is blocked, leading stake-holders to collude with one another in resisting change. Efforts to develop opportunities for collaboration can also be hampered by a range of barriers of the sorts described earlier in this chapter, including varied levels of support from school leaders, different understandings of the purpose of the research, as well as time pressures in schools. We also saw evidence of what Hargreaves (2000) refers to as *contrived collegiality*, i.e. artificial arrangements that may lead to ineffective collaborative relationships.

In addressing these challenges, the fact that the university team involved members with very different expertise, stances, methodological preferences and, indeed nationalities, proved to be a particular strength. At the same time, our varied ideas occasionally led to moments of dispute and tension, with different viewpoints having to be resolved in order to determine the next steps. During these periods of uncertainly, each of us was further challenged in our thinking. Fortunately, our partnership helped us to cope with these disturbances, such that they often became critical incidents that led to the development of new ideas. In these ways, we explored the outer limits of collaboration in ways that proved to be both productive and enriching.

Drawing lessons

Reflecting on the work of the various collaborative research networks described in this chapter points to some lessons that may be helpful to others wishing to promote inclusion and equity. These are likely to be of particular relevance to those working in policy contexts characterised by competition and increasing accountability of the sort experienced in Australia and England. As we have seen, such contexts place new pressures on schools to improve student performance within high-stakes testing regimes. Our experiences have thrown light on the way that this generates dilemmas for schools as they face strategic decisions.

Thinking about such contexts, the experiences underline the importance of **school leaders having a moral responsibility to promote equity**, broadly defined as being about inclusion and fairness. These experiences also offer guidance that can help in making this happen. This guidance is based on an assumption that the potential exists within school communities for addressing this agenda. As we have seen, strengthening collaboration within and between schools is a means by which this potential can be mobilised.

The approach I have outlined is not about the introduction of particular techniques or organisational arrangements. Rather it places emphasis on processes of social learning within particular contexts. **The use of evidence as a means of stimulating reflection and experimentation** is seen as the key strategy for moving such processes in a more inclusive direction.

The studies also confirm how the use of evidence to study teaching within a school can help in **generating a language of practice**. As I explained in Chapter 2, without such a language, teachers find it difficult to experiment with new possibilities. However, it is vital in fostering the development of practices that are more effective in reaching hard-to-reach learners. Specifically, it can create space for rethinking by interrupting existing discourses. As we have seen, the starting point for such processes is often with a consideration of statistical evidence regarding student progress, particularly school performance data collected by schools as part of accountability requirements. However, the need to dig deeper into factors that influence progress usually requires an engagement with more targeted and often qualitative forms of evidence.

All of this has major implications for leadership practice at different levels within schools. In particular, it calls for efforts to encourage **coordinated and sustained efforts by whole staff groups** around the idea that changing outcomes for all students is unlikely to be achieved unless there are changes in the behaviours of adults. Consequently, the starting point must be with staff members: in effect, enlarging their capacity to imagine what might be achieved and increasing their sense of accountability for bringing this about. This may also involve tackling taken-for-granted assumptions, most often relating to expectations about certain groups of students, their capabilities and behaviours.

However, our experiences also indicate that collaboration can sometimes be the means by which progress is blocked, leading stakeholders to collude with one another in resisting change. This form of collusion is encouraged where there is a collective view that some students are in some way deficient, such that it is taken for granted that they are unlikely to make progress. We have seen, however, that there is an alternative way of thinking, one that sees **learner differences as having the potential to stimulate experimentation**. This can lead to practices that are likely to benefit all students within a school.

As I have shown, **engaging with the varied voices of different players**, within and outside a school, can provide a powerful means of making this happen. More specifically, this can help in finding space to think differently. Collecting and engaging with different forms of evidence is a way of hearing these voices, some of which may normally be silent. However, this is likely to challenge existing thinking and practice within a school. At the same time, it can prompt moments of reflection which lead to the questioning and challenging of systemic rigidity and restrictions.

Conclusion

The work of the research networks described in this chapter further confirms how partnerships within and between schools can help mobilise the resources available to promote inclusive developments. However, they have also revealed another set of barriers, ones that make such forms of collaboration difficult within education systems that emphasise market forces. As I have shown, these barriers create particular dilemmas for school leaders, particularly those working in schools serving more disadvantaged communities, as they struggle to stay with their principles within policy contexts which create competing demands.

One of the most significant lessons that can be drawn from the work of these research networks relates to how these challenges can be addressed. Specifically, I have described how those taking on leadership roles supported and challenged one another regarding the dilemmas they face in trying to maintain their ethical stances. In a way that I had not anticipated, involvement in the networks created a ground-up movement that both worked within and challenged some of the restrictions of the current context of data-driven high-stakes accountability. Joking about all of this with our school colleagues in Queensland, we concluded that we were a group of resistance workers operating in an occupied country.

Finally, all of this has significant implications for national policy makers. In order to make use of the power of collaboration as a means of achieving equity in schools, they need to foster greater flexibility at the local level in order that practitioners have the time and space to analyse their particular circumstances and determine priorities accordingly (Hargreaves and Ainscow 2015). This means that policy makers must recognise that the details of policy implementation are not amenable to central regulation. Rather, these have to be dealt with by those who are close to and, therefore, in a better position to understand local contexts.

Furthermore, policy makers need to provide practitioners with the time to carefully and strategically consider how their responses to policy directives will impact all of their students. With time and flexibility, schools can engage with systemic directives in ways that can better support the learning of all students and challenge existing inequities, as we see in the examples provided in the next chapter.

4 Promoting inclusive practices

With colleagues, I contributed to a project in Mpika, an isolated rural area in the north of Zambia, which showed how engagement with evidence generated within schools can help promote inclusive thinking and practices. The process involved collaborative inquiry amongst teachers, parents and children.

Each class was divided into groups. Three of these groups were given digital cameras, and the children were asked to work cooperatively in their groups to take photographs in the school environment of *welcoming/unwelcoming places.* Once the photos had been printed, the children used them to make posters telling stories of what makes the school welcoming or unwelcoming.

Some of the groups were asked to look around the school environment to identify places they liked and disliked, whilst others created role plays depicting something that happens which makes them happy or unhappy to come to school.

Set within a context that has limited resources available, these experiences demonstrated further benefits of evidence-based collaborative inquiry. In particular, they pointed to the potential of such approaches for opening doors to more child-focused, interactive classroom practices.

Moving practice forward

As I have explained, over the last 25 years or so, I have been privileged to work with many colleagues in contexts such as Zambia, using collaborative inquiry as a strategy for inclusive school development. I see this approach as a process of knowledge-generation, occurring when researcher and practitioner knowledge meets in particular sites, aimed at producing new knowledge about ways in which broad values might better be realised in future practice.

In this chapter, I draw on more of these experiences to consider how partnerships between practitioners and researchers can facilitate developments in practice. As I will explain, this involves engagement with evidence generated through a range of methods, much of which involves listening to the voices of those involved in the process of education. Such evidence can make the familiar unfamiliar in ways that challenge assumptions, encourage the sharing of ideas and stimulate joint efforts to develop more inclusive practices. It is important to note, however, that none of this provides a simple way forward.

DOI: 10.4324/9781003438014-4

To gain the potential benefits, it is necessary to address the challenges involved in using processes of collaborative inquiry within the busy contexts of schools.

The approach requires particular types of relationship between practitioners and researchers, in the way that is outlined helpfully by Hiebert, Gallimore and Stigler (2002). They suggest that fruitful forms of collaboration require a reorientation of values and goals amongst both groups. So, they argue, teachers need to move away from the dominant view that teaching is a *personal and private activity*. Rather, they have to adopt the *more risky view* that it is an activity that can be continuously improved, provided it is made public and examined openly. At the same time, Hiebert and his colleagues argue that researchers must stop undervaluing the knowledge teachers acquire in their own classrooms. In this way, researchers will be able to recognise the potential of *personal knowledge as it becomes transformed into professional knowledge*.

Professional development

Central to the developments presented in this chapter is the need to create the conditions within which teachers are involved in processes of evidence-based professional learning within their schools. With this focus in mind, I begin by drawing on findings from our review of international research that are relevant to this agenda (see Messiou and Ainscow 2016)

According to Opfer and Pedder (2010), teacher professional development relies heavily on supportive interactions amongst staff members at all levels of a school in order for the development process to be effective. They also indicate that the term *development* signposts that this is intended to lead to changes in practice and, therefore, increased effectiveness: the implication being that successful teacher development is largely dependent on what practitioners perceive effectiveness to be. This means that much of teacher development must occur within schools and, in particular, within classrooms. In this way, there is a direct focus on the concerns of individual teachers and their workplace contexts.

All of this demands organisational flexibility and the active support of senior staff who must be prepared to encourage and support processes of experimentation (Leithwood and Riehl 2003). Where this is focused on issues related to learner diversity, it is also likely to involve challenges to the thinking of those within a particular organisation (West, Ainscow and Nottman 2003).

Locating professional development within schools and classrooms is a way of making better use of the expertise that already exists (Ainscow et al. 2012a). It also relates to what is known about how practices develop within the workplace. Significant here is the influential thinking of Etienne Wenger (1998), who explains how practice develops through processes of social learning. In so doing, he provides a framework that can be used to analyse learning in social contexts, such as schools. At the centre of this framework is the concept of a *community of practice*, a social group engaged in the sustained pursuit of a shared enterprise within a particular context.

As a result of a review of publications about teacher professional development over ten years, Avalos (2011) highlights the importance of collaboration as a facilitator for learning amongst teachers, in particular for altering or reinforcing teaching practices. There is also an assumption that practitioners have to take greater responsibility for their own professional learning. So, for example, Hayes (2000) suggests that effective teacher development can be promoted if and when used in line with collaborative and context-specific involvement of teachers, who have ownership over their personal development.

The importance of collaboration in professional development is also highlighted by a series of research syntheses from the Centre for Evidence-Informed Policy and Practice in Education. In particular, one of its reviews concludes that collaboration among teachers, coupled with active experimentation, may be more effective in changing practice than reflection and discussion about practice alone (Cordingley et al. 2005). In addition, Hill, Beisiegel and Jacob (2013) argue that: *Through studies conducted over the past two decades, scholars have identified programme design elements thought to maximize teacher learning, including a strong content focus, inquiry oriented learning approaches, collaborative participation, and coherence with school curricula and policies* (p. 476).

Collaborative participation is, therefore, an essential factor in maximising teacher learning. This explains the recent emphasis on the use of forms of collaborative inquiry to facilitate teacher development in research carried out in a variety of contexts, such as Canada, Europe and the USA (e.g. Bleicher 2014; Butler and Schnellert 2012; Cain and Milovic 2010; Horn and Little 2010; Jaipal and Figg 2011; Vaino, Holbrook and Rannikmae 2013). It also points to the possibility of joint practice development, which Fielding et al. (2005) define as learning new ways of working through mutual engagement that opens up and shares practices with others. Joint practice development, they suggest, involves: interaction and mutual development related to practice; recognises that each partner in the interaction has something to offer; and is research-informed, often involving collaborative inquiry. Through such activities, teachers develop ways of talking that enable them to articulate details about their practices. In this way, they are able to share ideas about their ways of working with colleagues. This also assists individuals to reflect on their own ways of working, as well as the thinking behind their actions.

It is important to bear in mind, however, that such sharing of ideas is far from easy in the context of schools, partly because of the intensity of the day but also because of the nature of teacher knowledge. Commenting on this, David Hargreaves (2003) draws attention to how much of teachers' knowledge is tacit and therefore difficult to articulate. He argues that this is the main reason why it has proved so difficult to transfer good practice from one teacher to another. This leads him to conclude that what he describes as *social capital* is needed within teaching communities. Social capital here represents shared values and assumptions that, because they are commonly *owned* by community members, are available for all members of the community to draw on when transferring knowledge and understandings. For Hargreaves, building social capital involves the development of networks based on mutual trust, within which good practice can spread in natural ways.

Using similar thinking, Talbert and McLaughlin (2002) argue that strong collaborative teacher communities engender *artisanship* in teaching by sustaining teachers' commitment to improving practice. They suggest that this occurs through dialogue and collaboration about ways in which students can be helped to engage, and by sharing and inventing effective classroom practices.

Developing practices

In thinking about the practical implications of these ideas, it is also important to note research which suggests that developments in practice are unlikely to occur without some exposure to what teaching actually looks like when it is being done differently (Elmore, Peterson and McCarthy 1996). Furthermore, this has to be addressed at the individual level before it can be solved at the organisational level. Indeed, there is evidence that collaboration without some more specific attention to changes at the individual level can simply result in teachers coming together to reinforce existing practices, rather than confronting the difficulties they face in different ways (Lipman 1997).

Florian and Black-Hawkins' (2011) study of how practitioners make sense of a policy of inclusion led them to argue that it is not *what* but *how* support is provided that is important. This finding preceded the development of their *inclusive pedagogical approach* (Black-Hawkins and Florian 2012), which argues that assistance can be used to provide rich learning opportunities in ways that are ordinarily available in the community of the class rather than as additional provision for some, different to that which is available to others.

Inclusive pedagogy is an approach to teaching and learning whereby learners' differences are presented as a challenge for teachers to respond to in ways which encourage an open-ended view of students' potential (Florian and Black-Hawkins 2011). Difficulties that students may face are understood as factors to be given consideration in learning and teaching. Extending forms of activity in order to widen opportunities for everyone to learn can meet individual needs by encouraging participation and allowing students to monitor their own progress at their own pace within the learning community of the class. The belief underpinning this approach is that every student has potential and will make progress in a different way and at a different pace.

This thinking echoes the ground-breaking *Learning without Limits* initiative, which examined ways of teaching that are free from predetermined assumptions about the abilities of pupils within a class (Hart 2003; Hart et al. 2004). This involved researchers in working closely with a group of teachers who had rejected ideas of fixed ability, in order to study their practice. They started from the belief that constraints are placed on children's learning by ability-focused practices that lead young children to define themselves in comparison to their peers.

Susan Hart and her colleagues argued that the notion of ability as inborn intelligence has come to be seen as *a natural way of talking about children* that summarises their perceived differences. However, the teachers involved in their study based their practices on a different perspective, one that adopted a belief that things can change and be changed for the better, recognising that whatever a child's present attainments and characteristics, given the right conditions, everybody's capacity for learning can be enhanced. Approaching their work with this mind-set, the teachers involved in the study were seen to analyse gaps between their aspirations for children and what was actually happening.

At the heart of the processes in schools where changes in practice do occur is the development of a common language with which colleagues can talk to one another and, indeed, to themselves about detailed aspects of their practice (Huberman 1993). Without such a language, teachers find it very difficult to experiment with new possibilities. As I have suggested, much of what teachers do during the intensive encounters that occur within classrooms is carried out at an automatic, intuitive level, as they respond to unpredictable events. Furthermore, this goes on in contexts where there is little time to stop and think. This is why having the opportunity to see colleagues at work is so crucial to the success of attempts to develop practice. It is through shared experiences that colleagues can help one another articulate what they currently do and define what they might like to do (Hiebert, Gallimore and Stigler 2002). It is also the means whereby space is created within which taken-for-granted assumptions about particular groups of learners can be subjected to mutual critique, something that is crucial in relation to responding to student diversity.

The role of evidence

At this stage in my argument, it is important to stress that collaboration by itself does not necessarily lead to the sorts of experimentation with new practices needed in order to respond to learner diversity within schools. Indeed, it can lead to forms of collusion that resist such developments.

Relevant to this, our research has revealed more about how social learning processes within schools influence people's action and, indeed, the thinking that informs their actions (Ainscow et al. 2003). Often, this is stimulated by an engagement with various forms of evidence that create periods of turbulence in relation to existing ways of thinking and working. Particularly powerful techniques in this respect involve the use of mutual observation, sometimes through video recordings, and evidence collected from students about teaching and learning arrangements within a school (Ainscow et al. 2012a). Under certain conditions, such approaches provide interruptions that stimulate self-questioning, creativity and action. In so doing, they sometimes lead to a reframing of perceived problems through processes of reflection that, in turn, draw attention to overlooked possibilities for addressing barriers to participation and learning (Lamote and Engels 2010; Lewis, Perry and Murata 2006; Yost, Sentner and Forlenza-Bailey 2000).

However, none of this provides a straightforward mechanism for the development of more inclusive practices. We have found that any space for reflection that is created as a result of engaging with evidence may sometimes be filled by conflicting agendas. Indeed, we have documented detailed examples of how deeply held beliefs within schools can prevent the experimentation that is necessary in order to foster the development of more inclusive ways of working (Ainscow and Kaplan 2005).

An inquiring school

Our research has led me to argue that *schools know more than they* use (Ainscow 2020). This means that the starting point for strengthening the work of a school is with the sharing of existing practices through collaboration amongst staff, leading to experimentation with new ways of working that will reach out to all students. Vignette 4.1 illustrates what this might involve.

VIGNETTE 4.1   All different all equal

The school, which caters for about 500 students in the age range 3–11, serves a multicultural community. Today, there are 23 different nationalities, with 19 different languages spoken amongst the families.

An assistant headteacher worked with a group of her colleagues to co-ordinate efforts to strengthen the commitment to inclusion in the school. She began by holding a staff meeting to brief her colleagues. Specifically, she asked them to work in small groups to identify children they considered to be at risk of marginalisation or exclusion.

Both the head and the assistant head agreed that all of this *was a bit scary.* For example, the discussions that took place brought to the surface potentially uncomfortable issues, such as, attitudes towards immigration, *children who smell* and feelings about a child who was considered to be odd.

Further information was gathered from parents using a questionnaire, which had to be translated for some families. Another staff meeting was devoted to discussion as to how the views of children could be gathered. This started with a consideration of existing practices in the school for listening to the voices of students, which led to a list of such activities.

The assistant head and her colleagues analysed the responses for each class and then for the whole school. Though this was time-consuming, they believed that it was helpful in drawing attention to issues in the school that needed addressing. They felt that it was particularly important to capture the views of new arrivals.

At a further meeting, the staff had a chance to look at the evidence that had been collected. As a result, it was decided to allocate a two-week period for the use of various student voice activities in every class. The assistant head organised a schedule for this.

As each teacher carried out the activities in their classes, a colleague would observe the process, looking specifically at the way individual children responded. In this way, they were able to integrate student voice activities into their day-to-day teaching and learning, something that subsequently became a part of usual practice across the school.

By the end of the school year, there was strong evidence that the strategies used had led to significant changes in thinking and practice. As part of this process, safety in the school became a major area of discussion, something that had not been anticipated.

At the heart of processes in schools like this, where professional learning takes place, is the development of a common language with which colleagues can talk to one another and, indeed to themselves, about detailed aspects of their practice. As noted above, without such a language, teachers find it difficult to experiment with new possibilities.

Much of what teachers do during the intensive encounters that occur every day in classrooms is carried out at an automatic, intuitive level. Furthermore, there is little time to stop and think. This is why having the opportunity to see colleagues at work is so crucial to the success of attempts to develop practice, as is evident from the research reported earlier in this book. It is through shared experiences that colleagues can help one another articulate what they currently do and define what they might like to do. It is also the means whereby space is created within which taken-for-granted assumptions about particular groups of learners can be subjected to mutual critique.

An engagement with evidence of various kinds to study teaching within a school can help in generating a language of practice within a school. This, in turn, can foster the development of practices that are more effective in engaging learners who are seen as hard to reach. Specifically, it can create space for rethinking by interrupting existing discourses and questioning usual ways of working.

The starting point for such processes is often a consideration of statistical evidence regarding student progress. However, the need to dig deeper into factors that influence learner progress usually requires engagement with qualitative forms of evidence. Particularly powerful techniques in this respect involve the use of mutual lesson observation, sometimes through video recordings, and evidence collected from students about teaching and learning arrangements within a school (Ainscow and Messiou 2017).

Under certain conditions, such approaches help to make the familiar unfamiliar in ways that stimulate self-questioning, creativity and action. In so doing, they can sometimes lead to a reframing of perceived problems that, in turn, draws the teacher's attention to overlooked possibilities for addressing barriers to participation and learning. In this way, differences amongst students, staff and schools become a catalyst for improvement.

Here, the concern with the principles of inclusion and equity means that there also has to be a focus on the thinking that lies behind actions and the impacts of such thinking on practices (Sadker et al. 2009). In particular, there must be a concern with the attitudes and assumptions that influence what teachers do, some of which may be unconscious, and how these can be modified through dialogues with others, especially with learners themselves (Messiou and Ainscow 2020).

Schools learning together

The approach I have outlined so far is based on the idea of those within schools collecting and engaging with various forms of evidence in order to stimulate moves to create more inclusive practices. The research summarised in the previous chapter provides encouraging evidence of the potential of this approach. However, it has also thrown light on the difficulties in putting such thinking into practice, particularly within policy contexts that put pressure on schools to compete. This points to some of the limitations of within-school strategies, suggesting that these should be complemented with efforts to encourage greater cooperation between schools, as seen in Vignette 4.2.

VIGNETTE 4.2   Learning from differences

A network of primary schools worked in partnership with university researchers, following a model of collaborative inquiry that draws on teachers' professional expertise and wider research knowledge, to explore new ways of supporting learners from economically disadvantaged backgrounds. Overall, the aim was to improve the learning opportunities, experiences and outcomes of all children by identifying and addressing overcoming barriers to their learning.

Each school determined its own focus for research, starting by identifying issues that were causing concern or were puzzling in some way. They then followed a structured research programme in which the teachers and university researchers collected and shared evidence about the school's practices so that they could develop a rich, deep understanding of what is happening to learners in school, and from wider research. This evidence was then used to stimulate new thinking and professional learning about current practices, and to identify strategies for responding to the research findings.

The schools used exchange visits to generate evidence regarding their shared focus on developing more inclusive practices. The aim of these visits was to look specifically at relative strengths and weaknesses within schools in the network, using differences to stimulate new thinking.

The most successful visits were usually characterised by a sense of mutual learning amongst hosts and visitors. It was noticeable, too, that the focus for these visits often took some time to identify and clarify. Indeed, the preliminary negotiations that took place were in themselves a key aspect of the process.

During one such visit, the visiting teachers were each invited to observe two children. A simple observation framework, designed by the staff research group in the host school, focused on children's interactions with peers and teachers.

The children to be observed were chosen by the class teacher, who was the deputy head of the school. They were nominated on the basis that they were the children he knew least about in his class. In addition to observations, the visiting teachers were asked to interview these children. Again, a loose structure was devised, but the main emphasis was on the visiting teachers following up on things that they had seen during observations.

Afterwards, one of the visiting teachers said that the day had been *absolutely fascinating* .... She added, *There is no way in your own school you could do th*is. This seemed to be borne out by some of the imagery used by students about their teacher during the interviews that day. For example, one commented, *He's like a piranha looking round the class. He knows when I'm not listening.* And another student remarked, *He could be a really good teacher if he could explain but he gets too frustrated.* The joking response by the class teacher to such statements was *I want to go home! I've had enough now!*.

The personal nature of these observations and the teacher's willingness to listen to this feedback with colleagues from his own and another school present illustrate the extent of the challenge that was sometimes involved in this sort of collaboration.

We have generated considerable evidence suggesting that forms of school-to-school collaboration of this kind can strengthen improvement processes by adding to the range of expertise made available (e.g. Ainscow 2015; Ainscow and Howes 2007; Muijs et al. 2011). These studies indicate that collaboration among schools has enormous potential for fostering the capacity of education systems to respond to learner diversity. More specifically, they show how such partnerships can sometimes help to reduce the polarisation of schools, to the particular benefit of those students who seem marginalised at the edges of the system, and whose progress and attitudes cause concern.

There is also evidence that when schools seek to develop more collaborative ways of working, this can have an impact on how teachers perceive themselves and their work. Specifically, comparisons of practices in different schools can lead teachers to view underachieving students in a new light. In this way, learners who cannot easily be educated within a school's established routines come to be seen less as having problems but as encouraging teachers to re-examine their practices in order to make them more responsive and flexible.

Beyond the school gate

Ensuring that all children receive support from their families and communities is essential to the promotion of equity. This in turn means ensuring that schools can build on the resources offered by families and support the extension of those resources, as illustrated in Vignette 4.3.

VIGNETTE 4.3   Crossing boundaries

The word *boundaries* frequently comes up during a visit to this primary school, which serves a diverse, multicultural community. First of all, the visitor notes the metal fence with pointed spikes that stakes out the physical boundaries of the school, whilst at the same time discouraging would be intruders. Then, there is much talk of the cultural boundaries children cross each day as they move between contexts that are influenced by different traditions, religions and languages. There is also a sense of boundaries created by the well-articulated rules and procedures that dictate the ways in which staff and children go about their business.

This example is particularly interesting in that not so long ago, the behaviour of students in the school was a major problem. Nowadays, things are much improved.

The school takes particular steps to support children and families as they move between different cultures. On first arrival in the nursery, many of the children have limited language and this has to be a priority, leading to what is often rapid progress. Staff are also sensitive to the fact that some of the children attend additional lessons at the local mosque in the late afternoon.

Considerable efforts have been made to ensure parental support for the school's efforts to foster a more cooperative working atmosphere. The head explains that she has tried to convince parents that it was necessary to *break the cycle of violence*.

There was a period when some parents, particularly some of the fathers, would come into school to be abusive to the head teacher and other members of staff. Sometimes the head used what she referred to as *veiled threats*, for example: *I've told them that I would exclude their child if things don't improve.*

In fact, the head is opposed to the exclusion of students, although at times she has been forced to use this approach, not least in order to attract support from outside the school. Gradually, however, the views of parents have become much more positive, as reflected by their involvement in morning assemblies and support for other school events. Here, the family literacy programme that the school introduced has proved to be particularly successful.

At the same time, tensions between home and school do still exist. For example, one teacher comments that some of the children are related and sometimes they bring family disputes with them into school. Differences in expectations also surface on some occasions. The head explains:

For example, some mothers will dress the boys and leave the girls to dress themselves.

One teacher, talking about her class of 11-year olds, notes:

Every single boy here smokes. They steal cigarettes from home.

Nevertheless, the visitor is struck by the quiet atmosphere, and the sense of calm and order around the school. Senior staff explain how they have worked with the parents to foster this atmosphere. One explained, *We tell them, you have to model the behaviour you want from the children.*

So, what is it that has led to these striking improvements? In particular, what forms of leadership practice have been used? It seems that there have been two overlapping phases of development, each emphasising rather different approaches.

During the first of these two phases, much of the leadership seemed to have been centred around the head teacher herself. More recently, a different approach has emerged, one that is characterised by an emphasis on collaborative inquiry approaches that involve staff, students, family members and, in some situations, community representatives.

In explaining all of this, the headteacher seemed to be particularly sensitive to the challenges faced by her colleagues. She noted, *there is too much pressure on everybody.* Having said that, she appears to have been successful in developing a sense of common purpose and a commitment to mutual support that stretches beyond the school building. Here, too, there is little evidence of any distinction between the roles of teaching and non-teaching staff. One support assistant commented, *We're all involved in everything.*

My colleagues and I have seen many examples like this of what can happen when what schools do is aligned in a coherent strategy with the efforts of other local players: families, employers, community groups, colleges, universities and public services (Ainscow 2016b; Drever, McLean and Lowden 2021). This does not necessarily mean schools doing more, but it does imply partnerships beyond the school gate, where partners multiply the impacts of each other's efforts. Our experience suggests that the success of such partnerships is dependent upon a common understanding of what those involved are trying to achieve and, once again, an engagement with various forms of evidence to stimulate collective effort.

Such area-based initiatives are intended to involve a wide range of partners working together in a coordinated manner. Schools are often the key to these partnerships and may be their principal drivers. However, this is not simply about enlisting other agencies and organisations in support of a school-centred agenda. Rather, they are aimed at improving a wide range of outcomes for children and young people, including but not restricted to educational outcomes – much less, narrowly conceived attainment outcomes. Health and well-being, personal and social development, thriving in the early years and positive employment outcomes are all as important as how well children do in school.

None of this arises from a down-grading of the importance of attainment but from a recognition that all outcomes for children and young people are inter-related. Furthermore, the factors which promote or inhibit one outcome are very likely to be the factors which promote or inhibit outcomes as a whole.

As a result, the focus of such initiatives is the population of an area, rather than the population of schools per se, and they may be led by non-educational organisations, such as housing associations or regeneration partnerships. Moreover, they are envisaged as being long-term and are committed to acting strategically, basing their actions of a deep analysis of the local area's underlying problems and possibilities (Kerr, Dyson and Gallannaugh 2016).

Such approaches draw on the principles underpinning the highly acclaimed Harlem Children's Zone in the USA (Whitehurst and Croft 2010). This project involves efforts to improve outcomes for children and young people in areas of disadvantage through an approach that they characterise as being *doubly holistic*. That is to say, they seek to develop coordinated efforts to tackle the factors that disadvantage children and enhance the factors which support them, across all aspects of their lives, and across their life spans, from conception through to adulthood. The Harlem project has been described by researchers as *arguably the most ambitious social experiment to alleviate poverty of our time* (Dobbie and Fryer 2009, p. 1).

Developments such as these have implications for the various key stakeholders within education systems. In particular, teachers, especially those in senior positions, have to see themselves as having a wider responsibility for all children and young people in their local area, not just those that attend their own schools. They also have to develop patterns of working that enable them to have the flexibility to cooperate with other schools and their wider communities.

Making sense of the process

Underlying the use of collaborative inquiry to promote inclusive practices within schools is a common pattern. Most importantly, it involves an engagement with evidence collected by practitioners with support from university researchers. Usually, this begins with a consideration of an established set of practices that are largely taken for granted. An interruption occurs that problematises these practices and provokes consideration of why current practice is the way it is and how it might be improved. This may then lead to actual changes in practice, but not always.

Given my focus on the possibilities of developing more inclusive ways of working, this begs two important questions:

- What is it that provokes the problematisation of established practice?
- And why does this necessarily lead to more inclusive ways of working?

In addressing these questions, we have found it helpful to draw on a range of theoretical resources. One that has proved particularly powerful is the idea of *communities of practice*, as developed by Etienne Wenger (1998), focusing specifically on the way he sees learning as *a characteristic of practice*.

Wenger explains practice in terms of those things that individuals within a community do, drawing on available resources, to further a set of shared goals. This goes beyond how practitioners complete their tasks, to include, for example, how they make it through the day, commiserating about the pressures and constraints within which they have to operate. Practices are thus ways of negotiating meaning through social action, which underlines the importance of the conversations embedded in teachers' day-to-day work, as referred to earlier in this chapter.

In explaining this process, Wenger argues that communities *reify* their practices by producing concrete representations of them, such as tools, symbols, rules and documents (and even concepts and theories). However, these reifications have to be given meaning through a process of participation, which consists of the shared experiences and negotiations that result from social interaction within a purposive community. The implication of this is that ideas and materials generated within one context cannot simply be lifted and transferred elsewhere.

Wenger offers some helpful guidelines for judging whether a particular social collective can be considered a community of practice. Since such a community involves mutual engagement, a negotiated enterprise and a repertoire of resources and practices, its members should be expected to:

- Interact more intensively with and know more about others in the group than those outside the group;
- Hold their actions accountable (and be willing for others in the community to hold them accountable) more to the group's joint enterprise than to some other enterprise;
- Be more able to evaluate the actions of other members of the group than the actions of those outside the group; and
- Draw on locally produced resources and artefacts to negotiate meaning, more so than those that are imported from outside the group.

By these criteria, the staff teams in the studies reported in this book can, to varying degrees, be seen as communities of practice. Much of the evidence for this assertion rests on what was witnessed of the ongoing and informal interactions between groups of teachers. So, for example, amongst staff inquiry groups, hours of meetings, shared experiences and informal discussions over hurriedly taken lunches were observed. These sometimes involved the development of particular meanings of frequently used phrases, such as *raising standards*, *equity* and *inclusion*. These shared meanings help to define a teacher's experience of being a teacher. In the same way, it can be assumed that groups of colleagues doing similar work in another school have their own shared histories that give meaning to being a teacher in that particular context.

There is no reason to suppose that teachers are conscious of such processes for the most part, though occasionally they may be able to articulate their importance for developments in their schools. What was significant in some of our project schools, however, was not simply the high level of collaboration that was claimed by the teachers (such claims can, of course, be challenged), but the implication that *good practice* is defined through such collaborative processes. In these contexts, good practice is defined not by what researchers or policy makers say, or others do elsewhere, but by what *we* think *works here*.

Once again, the notion of communities of practice is important here in that it views practice as being intimately bound up with the norms, values, beliefs and assumptions of a group of teachers, in a particular school context. The implication is that practices cannot be understood – or, more to the point, changed – without also understanding and changing those local patterns. What is needed is something that disturbs existing assumptions and provokes some sort of reformulation, both of practice and of the thinking on which it is based.

Changing practices

This relationship between practice and local meaning-making suggests that external agendas cannot simply be *imposed* on communities of practice. Specifically, external proposals for change, however powerfully enforced, have to be endowed with meaning within local contexts before they can inform practice. This implies that schools (or, at least, the communities of practice within schools) may well negotiate local meanings for those agendas that are different from those of the formulators themselves or, indeed, of other schools.

The significance of communities of practice is usefully summed up by Wenger when he argues:

> *Communities of practice are not intrinsically beneficial or harmful.... Yet they are a force to be reckoned with, for better or for worse. As a locus of engagement in action, interpersonal relationships, shared knowledge, and negotiation of enterprises, such communities hold the key to real transformation – the kind that has real effect on people's lives... The influence of other forces (e.g. the control of an institution or the authority of an individual) are no less important, but they are mediated by the communities in which their meanings are negotiated in practice.*
>
> *(Wenger 1998, p. 85)*

There is an important caveat here. Communities of practice *are not intrinsically beneficial or harmful* precisely because the values and assumptions to which they will subscribe are determined locally. In terms of the development of practices, there is nothing inherent in even the most dynamic community of practice which predisposes it towards generating more equitable outcomes. Indeed, a dynamic community that defends the status quo or moves rapidly in a non-inclusive direction is entirely conceivable. So, for example, Yurkofsky et al. (2020) argue:

> *Educators who believe in supporting equitable schools can still carry implicit biases that affect their practices, and teachers who aspire to improve their pedagogy may in practice have trouble giving up the belief that external factors (e.g., parental and neighbourhood influence) – as opposed to their own actions as teachers – are the primary determinants of students' achievement.*
>
> *(p. 415)*

What, then, makes the difference between instances where collaborative meaning-making creates a potential for the development of inclusive practices and those where such practices actually arise? For this, two sets of concepts from the literature on organisational development are helpful: Argyris and Schön's (1996) idea of *single and double-loop learning*; and Skrtic's (1991) distinction between bureaucracies and adhocracies, together with his notion of the recognition of *anomalies* as the catalyst for the transition from one to the other.

Taking the ideas of Argyris and Schön first, they argue that organisations are capable of learning, but to different extents and, indeed, at different levels. What they refer to as single-loop learning takes the form of what in an educational context might be called the improvement of existing practices, but without any fundamental reconsideration of the assumptions upon which those practices are based. On the other hand, double-loop learning asks questions about the underlying aims of practice and about the implicit theories which underpin it. In the examples I have presented we see how an engagement with evidence generated within schools can sometimes encourage reflections that lead to such changes in focus.

Similarly, Skrtic also presupposes a fundamental distinction in the way organisations solve problems. He argues that bureaucratic organisations deal with such problems by creating different sub-units and specialisms to contain them, leaving practice elsewhere in the organisation undisturbed. So, for example, a school may decide to establish a separate unit to deal with the problems of disruptive behaviour, such that it avoids the need to examine ways in which its own practices may have helped to generate these problems. On the other hand, what Skrtic calls adhocratic organisations see such problems as an opportunity to rethink their existing practices in fundamental ways. Moreover, he argues that bureaucratic organisations can become adhocratic if enough of their members recognise *anomalies* in existing practice.

It seems, then, that faced with some form of disturbance – what I referred to earlier as an interruption – some schools will close the problem down and make largely technical responses. Others may open the problem up and use it as the basis for a critical interrogation and reformulation of practice, and the assumptions on which practice is based. However, as Skrtic argues, someone has to recognise a problem as an anomaly and convince others of its significance.

Conclusion

In this chapter, I have explained how I have worked alongside teachers, supporting their efforts to facilitate the presence, participation and achievement of all the children in their classes. What has most stayed with me as a result of all these experiences are the efforts of many teachers to find ways of achieving this goal, including some who work in challenging contexts with limited material resources to support their efforts.

As I have explained, the overall approach I am describing involves what I refer to as *an inclusive turn*. This involves moves away from explanations of educational failure that concentrate on the characteristics of individual children and their families, towards an analysis of contextual barriers to participation and learning experienced by students within schools. In this way, students who do not respond to existing arrangements come to be regarded as *hidden voices* who, under certain conditions, can encourage the improvement of schools.

This thinking calls for coordinated and sustained efforts within schools, recognising that changing outcomes for vulnerable students is unlikely to be achieved unless there are changes in the attitudes, beliefs and actions of adults. The starting point must therefore be with practitioners: enlarging their capacity to imagine what might be achieved, and increasing their sense of accountability for bringing this about. This may also involve tackling negative assumptions, most often relating to expectations about certain groups of students, their capabilities and behaviours. The next chapter offers practical advice regarding ways of putting this thinking into action.

5 Using collaborative inquiry

Currently I am working with a partnership of schools in a city in the north of England, using the thinking presented in this book to foster inclusion and equity. The schools mainly serve areas of economic disadvantage. There are also many children from families who have arrived in the country in recent years.

As part of their improvement strategy, the schools work in what they call *learning threes* to support their professional development activities. Recently I spent a morning with school leaders from one of these groups as they spent time gathering information about practices in a partner school. Their efforts were focused around the indicators and questions provided in *Reaching Out to All Learners*, the resource pack of professional development materials I developed for the International Bureau of Education-UNESCO.

Many good ideas emerged from the visit that I will pass on to other schools. For example, taking photographs and using these to create powerpoint presentations is a brilliant way of using the peer inquiry process to stimulate further discussions within partner schools. I also thought the emphasis placed on listening to the views of children was particularly valuable, as was the idea of book scrutiny. I know that such approaches are used elsewhere but what was important here was the engagement of groups of senior staff from partner schools in the discussions that took place.

What most stood out for me, however, was the way that differences that were noted during the visit were used to encourage colleagues to reflect on their own schools. For example, during the review discussion at the end of a morning visit, one colleague said, *I've written this question down to ask back at school*

Much of the discussion focused on matters of detail. For example, there was discussion of the roles of lighting and background music as ways of creating an engaging classroom. However, one interaction that stood out for me led to discussion of the importance of oracy in relation to students from economically disadvantaged backgrounds. Having noted what she had witnessed in the early years' classrooms, one colleague commented, *We noticed that unless there is an adult present, the children don't talk*. She went on the reflect on this experience in relation to her own school: *I don't think that this has hit me so much as seeing it in another school!!*.

DOI: 10.4324/9781003438014-5

My colleagues and I have previously written about such incidents as creating *interruptions* (Ainscow et al. 2006). Under certain conditions, such experiences can help to make the familiar unfamiliar in ways that stimulate self-questioning, creativity and action. In so doing, they can sometimes lead to a reframing of perceived problems that, in turn, draws the attention of practitioners to overlooked possibilities for addressing barriers to participation and learning. In this way, differences amongst students, staff and schools can become a catalyst for improvement. In referring to the use of such approaches, leadership expert Viviane Robinson and her colleagues (2008) note that taking part in collaborative inquiries into improving teaching and learning is the most impactful action a school leader can take to improve educational outcomes for students.

Starting points

As I have explained, the approach to inclusion that I am suggesting involves *a process of increasing the participation of students in, and reducing their exclusion from, school curricula, cultures and communities.* In this way the notions of inclusion and exclusion are linked together because the process of increasing participation of students entails the reduction of pressures to exclude. This link also encourages us to look at the various constellations of pressures acting on different groups of students and acting on the same students from different sources.

For these reasons, therefore, I am suggesting that a starting point for the development of practice within a school has to be with a close scrutiny of how existing practices may be acting as barriers to participation and learning. This means that attention has to be given to helping practitioners to develop a reflective attitude to their work such that they are continually encouraged to explore ways of overcoming such barriers. With this in mind, the approaches discussed in this book place considerable emphasis on the need to observe the process of schooling and to listen carefully to the views of those involved, particularly those of children and young people.

Drawing on the experiences of carrying out the studies reported so far, this chapter offers practical guidance on the use of collaborative inquiry to promote inclusive developments in schools. It is important to stress that this guidance, which has been used in a variety of forms in a range of settings, should not be seen as a blueprint to be followed rigidly. Rather, it is intended to be adapted by those leading developments to suit particularly contexts.

Collaborative inquiry

I refer to the overall approach I am recommending as collaborative inquiry. As summarised by Deppeler and Ainscow (2016), what distinguishes this approach from more traditional research is that it involves a commitment to forms of inquiry that involve the following:

- An engagement with the views of different stakeholders, in the belief that the bringing together of the expertise of practitioners (and, sometimes, students) and academic researchers can challenge taken-for-granted assumptions, not least in respect to vulnerable groups of learners, stimulate new thinking and encourage experimentation with new ways of working (Ainscow, Dyson, Goldrick and West 2012a; Deppeler 2013; Messiou and Ainscow 2015).

- The improvement of practice within schools through the sharing of expertise and forms of collaborative action that stimulate efforts to find more effective ways of engaging students who are seen to be *hard-to-reach* (Hiebert, Gallimore and Stigler 2002; Lo, Yan and Pakey 2005; Messiou 2019).
- Collaboration and networking within and across classrooms, schools and systems in order to move expertise around within education systems (Ainscow 2015; Muijs, West and Ainscow 2010; Fullan, Rincon-Gallardo and Hargreaves 2015).
- The development of local capacity for sustaining change through the linking of the efforts of schools to wider resources. This requires the use of more holistic strategies that seek to connect schools, communities, and external political and economic institutions (e.g. Kerr, Dyson and Raffo 2014; Lipman 2004).

Developing a strategy

In using collaborative inquiry, we encourage schools to create a group made up of members of staff chosen on the basis of their capacity to provide leadership and work with colleagues to drive improvements in their schools. Ideally, this inquiry group should provide a variety of perspectives and have a willingness to see difference as an opportunity for critical reflection and change. It is important that one member of the group is a senior member of staff, which signals that what happening is core business, as opposed to just another short-term project.

The tasks of the staff inquiry group are as follows: to facilitate and engage their school in collaborative action research; support and challenge one another in relation to these activities; and present and discuss their experiences at various school and cross-school events. Participation in such groups can also open up opportunities for individual career development.

We have found it helpful for staff inquiry groups to use the framework that follows to plan collaborative inquiry activities, although this should be used flexibly, taking account of factors and circumstances within individual schools. The framework consists of six interlinked elements, each with its own set of issues for consideration. Although presented in sequence, some of the elements will probably develop simultaneously.

The **elements of the framework** are as follows:

1 **Analysing our context.** In order to develop effective strategies for reaching learners who are vulnerable to underachievement, marginalisation or exclusion, there is a need to analyse the contexts within the school and its community. In this way, initial *hunches* can be developed as to the sorts of

barriers experienced by these learners and what actions might need to be taken to overcome them. This is why it is helpful for members of the inquiry group to have different perspectives on the life of the school.

Issues to consider:

- Which students are missing out within our school?
- What do we know about these learners?
- Which group(s) should we focus attention on?
- What are our hunches about the factors that lead to their marginalisation?

2 **Collecting evidence.** Building on initial hunches, arrangements need to be made to collect additional evidence of various forms to deepen the inquiry group's analysis. Here evidence can take many forms. It is likely to start with a consideration of statistical material that is readily available within the school, such as attendance and performance data. This may point to individuals and groups for whom there is concern. In a sense, this gives a general picture of what is happening in the school in relation to these students. The next step involves a much more specific analysis of the situation using qualitative data, including evidence provided by the students themselves. Our research has found that such evidence can provide a powerful means of moving schools forward, not least because it may challenge the assumptions of staff as to why some students are vulnerable to marginalisation, exclusion and underachievement. It may also draw attention to students who are being overlooked.

Issues to consider:

- What further information do we need about these students?
- How can we collect, record and analyse this information?
- Who needs to be involved?
- What forms of support do we need?

3 **Making sense of the evidence.** Having collected and considered various kinds of evidence, the inquiry group will need to plan ways of orchestrating a widespread discussion within their school community as to the issues that need to be considered. This is likely to involve placing the matter on the agendas of the senior management team, appropriate staff meetings, the student council and parent groups. Some schools have found it useful to involve local authority support staff and representatives from their partner schools in these discussions, not least because *outsiders* can helpfully ask questions and note patterns that *insiders* are overlooking. In a sense, this is a way of *making the familiar unfamiliar* in order to encourage deeper processes of reflection within the school community. Where this is well led, it is a means of drawing people together around a common sense of purpose. Our research suggests that such involvement is the most effective means of encouraging school development. Another important role of the inquiry group is to coordinate and stimulate this process. At the same time, it is essential that members of the senior management team are seen to be actively involved.

Issues to consider:

- What does the evidence suggest about the experience of this group of students?
- What factors appear to be associated with their lack of progress?
- Who needs to be involved in making sense of this evidence?
- What might we do to address these factors?
- What aspects of our school need to be considered?

4 **Moving forward.** Having established areas for development, it will be necessary for the inquiry group to formulate strategies for involving the school community in moving forward. Here, the overall approach is based on the assumption that schools know more than they use and that the logical starting point for development is with a detailed analysis of existing ways of working. This allows good practices to be identified and shared, whilst, at the same time, drawing attention to ways of working that may be creating barriers to the presence, participation and learning of some students. At this point it is helpful to remember the old adage, *school improvement is technically simple but socially complex.* In other words, planning the actions that are needed is likely to be relatively straightforward; the challenge for the inquiry group is to find ways of getting everybody involved. Inevitably, the actual strategies adopted will depend upon the nature of the areas being addressed.

Issues to consider:

- What action are we proposing to improve the experience of this group of students?
- What aspects of our school do we need to change?
- Who needs to be involved in moving forward?
- What actions should we take to involve them?

5 **Involving partners.** The contributions of external partners, especially family members, will be important as the school moves forward in relation to its plans. This also has the potential to make an important contribution to multi-agency working. Here, too, there is considerable evidence that school-to-school collaboration can add value to the efforts of individual schools to develop more equitable ways of working. This shows how collaboration between schools can help to reduce the polarisation of schools, to benefit in particular those students who are marginalised at the edges of the system and whose performance and attitudes cause concern. There is evidence, too, that when schools seek to develop more collaborative ways of working, this can have an impact on how teachers perceive themselves and their work. Specifically, sharing and comparing practices can lead school staff to view underachieving students in a new light. Rather than simply presenting problems that are assumed to be insurmountable, such students may be perceived as providing feedback on existing classroom and school arrangements. In this way they may be seen as sources of understanding as to how these arrangements might be developed in ways that could be of benefit to all school members.

Issues to consider:

- Who do we need to involve from outside the school?
- How can we get them involved?
- In what ways can they add value to our efforts?

6 **Monitoring progress.** As the school moves forward with its plans, it is necessary for the process of implementation to be carefully monitored. Evidence gathering will also be needed in order to determine the impact in terms of the presence, participation and achievements of students. The inquiry group has a key role in coordinating this work. Senior and middle managers must also be involved in gathering, generating and interpreting information in order to create an inquiring stance throughout the school. It is anticipated that as these activities develop they will have a wider impact. In this way, the initial focus on groups of learners seen as being *at risk* is likely to challenge existing practices within the schools. This locates the work of the inquiry group firmly at the centre of the schools' overall development plans. It should be noted, too, that, in practice, *monitoring progress* merges with *analysing our context* and so the elements of the framework interlink.

Issues to consider:

- What are the outcomes we are seeking?
- What do we expect to see happening in the process of achieving these outcomes – in the short, intermediate and longer term?
- How do we monitor these actions and their impact on student presence, participation and progress?

Forms of evidence

As illustrated by the examples presented in this book, evidence can take many forms and it is usually necessary to combine more than one approach. In what follows, possibilities for generating evidence are explained.

Statistics. Large quantities of statistical information are usually available in schools regarding, for example, attendance, behaviour and student progress. These are often an excellent starting point for a school-based investigation.

In recent years the extent and sophistication of such data have improved, so much so that the progress of groups and individuals can now be tracked in considerable detail, giving a much greater sense of the value that a school is adding to its students. If necessary, further relevant statistical material can be collected through questionnaire surveys of the views of students, staff members and, where relevant, parents and carers.

Recently, I have been introduced to another useful way of generating relevant statistical data, *social network analysis*, by my colleague at the University of Glasgow, Thomas Cowhitt. This is an approach that helps researchers and practitioners think about and characterise social systems by *focusing our attention on the relationships among the entities that make up the system* (Borgatti et al., 2018, p. 2).

Social network analysis can provide an *over-head* view of the social system within a school or group of schools. It can then track changes in actor relationships over time. For example, in our current project in the city of Dundee[1] use is being made of social network analysis to map the relationships that connect the city's schools to each other and to wider stakeholder organisations, identifying key individuals, groups and organisations within the network and the associations between them. By repeating this mapping exercise at intervals, we are charting how relationships in the city are changing in volume and nature.

It is important to stress that statistical information on its own tells us very little. What brings such data to life is when *insiders* start to scrutinise and ask questions together as to their significance, bringing detailed experiences and knowledge to bear on the process of interpretation. Even then, there are still limitations that need to be kept in mind. Statistics provide patterns of what exists: they tell us what things are like but give little understanding as to why they are as they are, or how they came to be like that. This is why research methods experts tend to promote the idea of using mixed research methods. It is also why evidence collected through qualitative approaches is needed to supplement statistical data. More specifically, qualitative research methods can help us to address *how* and *why* questions, in order to determine what actions need to be taken to initiate change within a school.

Qualitative methods. These can take many forms, some of which involve informal ways of generating intelligence about the situation within a school through forms of conversation. When used effectively, these approaches can help develop a deeper understanding of the way participants within schools and classrooms construct meaning about their experiences. Possible methods for generating such evidence include the following:

- **Interviews** are usually a key element of data collection. There are many possible approaches to conducting interviews as part of school-based action research. They may be guided by a set of pre-arranged questions that require almost predictable responses; on the other hand, they may take the form of a focused discussion around a set of prompting themes. Interviews may take place with individuals or in groups. Focus groups are an attractive method, especially when conducting research with students in schools, not least because it is possible to include a larger group of participants. However, there is a danger, particularly with young people, that the views of particularly confident individuals may shape the contributions of others.
- **Taking a learning walk.** These are organised visits around a school's learning areas by groups of colleagues. In some instances, students may also be involved. The walks may be pre-focused on an agreed agenda or kept open in order that those involved pick out *thing they notice*. During and following the walk, colleagues are encouraged to reflect on what they have seen in a way that is intended to encourage sharing of ideas and mutual challenge. Another version of this approach involves groups of staff from

partner schools in scrutinising examples of children's work in a way that encourages those involved to reconsider their working definitions of quality.

- **Observation.** This is an essential element of attempts to improve practices within a school, since research suggests that such developments are unlikely to occur without some exposure to what teaching actually looks like when it is being done differently. Observations can take different forms, depending on the nature of the improvement agenda. So, for example, they may be guided by a relatively focused set of indicators, or, at the other extreme, by a series of open questions or themes. In addition, unexpected events can reveal something of significance to the inquiry. Learning how to observe within classrooms and in a school environment is a challenge – there is always a great deal going on, and it is easy to become distracted. Sometimes it helps to make video recordings, although, again, there are advantages and limitations to this method of data recording. It is useful to be able to replay the recording in order to look at sections in more detail, and it is for groups of colleagues to discuss a video recording. On the other hand, the video camera can only record what is within the frame and important events may be missed.

Seeing things differently. Beyond conventional observation and interview procedures, there is room for the use of more creative approaches in order to capture the views of others, particularly those of children. For example, shadowing groups of youngsters through a school day can provide adults with new and sometimes disturbing insights into what it is like to be a learner in their school. In one secondary school, for example, it was surprising for staff to discover how some students go through the whole day without hearing an adult use their name. Such experiences remind us of the subtle ways in which some young people can come to feel marginalised.

Visual methods, too, can be a particularly powerful way of engaging children. So, for example, drawings can be useful as a stimulus for individual or focus group interviews. In a similar way, asking students to take photographs of different aspects of their school experience has proved to be particularly successful in enabling adults, and other children, to see school life through the eyes of the learner who has taken the photograph.

Lesson study. We have found it helpful to combine methods for generating and making use of evidence. Here, a powerful approach is that of lesson study, a systematic procedure for the development of teaching that is well established in Japan and some other Asian countries (Lewis, Perry and Murata 2006).

The goal of lesson study is to improve the effectiveness of the experiences that teachers provide for all of their students. The core activity involves collaborative research on a shared area of focus that is generated through discussion. The content of this focus is the planned lesson, which is then used as the basis of gathering data on the quality of experience that students receive. Called *research lessons*, they are used to examine the responsiveness of the students to the planned activities.

Members of the group work together to design the lesson plan, which is then implemented by each teacher in turn. Observations and post-lesson conferences are arranged to facilitate the improvement of the research lesson between each trial. It should be noted here that the main focus is on the lesson and the responses of class members, not the teacher.

The collection of evidence is a key factor in lesson study. This may involve the use of video recordings. Emphasis is also placed on listening to the views of students in a way that tends to introduce a challenging edge to the discussions that take place.

In introducing the approach, we have found it useful to hold an initial workshop for the staff involved to introduce guidelines for setting up lesson study groups, led by researchers from the university who have previous experience of using this approach. Then, over a period of a few weeks, the staff involved follow a version of the following step-by-step procedure:

1 Staff form trios, usually made up of colleagues with varied experience. They work together to trial and evaluate the idea of lesson study as a means of strengthening teaching and learning in relation to themes that are seen to be relevant, e.g. learner engagement; responding to diversity; encouraging independent learning.
2 Each trio chooses and plans a lesson that they will each teach. The aim of this research lesson will be to put together best available expertise.
3 As each member of staff teaches the lesson, their two colleagues observe the process, focusing specifically on the way students respond. If possible, the lesson should also be recorded on video, and a sample of students interviewed to determine their reactions and the extent of their learning.
4 After each research lesson the trio reflect on what has happened, using their notes, the views of students and the video recording to analyse processes and outcomes. They then make adjustments to the lesson plan before it is taught by the next member of the trio.
5 Once the lesson has been taught by each member of the trio, a short report is prepared, summarising the findings of the process and recommendations for future practice.

At the end of the lesson study period, a further staff meeting may be held at which each trio presents the findings of their research and the conclusions they have reached. The whole group then go on to consider implications for policy and practice within their school.

The learning goals provide the reason for teaching and for observing the lesson. Teams usually begin by selecting a subject, concept, theme or topic in the course they want to study. Many are drawn to topics that are particularly difficult for students to learn, or for teachers to teach. Others select a topic that comes later in the term, so they have enough time to plan and design the lesson. Still others focus on topics that are new to the curriculum, or that are especially important in building students' understanding.

As far as possible, learning goals should be stated in terms of what students will understand and what they will be able to do as a result of the lesson. Goals specify desired forms of student learning, thinking, engagement and behaviour. Whatever the teachers decide to do in the class will be considered in the light of these goals.

During the planning stage, team members usually begin by sharing how they have taught or would teach the lesson, discussing and debating the merits of different types of class activities, assignments, exercises and so forth. To keep the focus on student learning, though, teachers also pool their knowledge of how students in the past have learned or struggled to learn the topic at hand. Once past experiences and personal approaches are on the table, the team can begin to design a research lesson that will help students achieve the chosen learning goal.

Throughout the process, teachers are encouraged to look at the subject matter from the student's point of view. In particular, when planning the lesson, teachers predict how students will perceive, interpret and construe the subject matter and the lesson activities. In these ways, lesson plans are designed in a way that anticipates student responses in terms of learning, thinking and engagement.

In preparation for teaching the lesson, teams should think about how to collect evidence that will help them determine the extent to which the learning goals are achieved. Participant may also develop an observation protocol based on their predictions of student responses and decide what types of evidence will be collected from students.

Before the actual class period, it may be helpful to inform students about the research lesson and the observers that will be in the classroom. Prior to the lesson, the observers are introduced to the class, explaining that the overall aim is to find ways to improve their learning.

Traditional classroom observations tend to focus on what the teacher does during the class period. However, observations of research lessons focus on students and what they do in response to teaching.

The analysis phase addresses three questions:

- In what ways did students accomplish the lesson goals?
- How could the lesson be improved?
- What did we learn from this experience?

After the lesson is taught, while it is still fresh in everybody's minds, the group – and any invited observers – should meet to discuss and analyse what happened. Participants offer their observations, interpretations and comments on the lesson. The purpose is to analyse and evaluate the lesson thoroughly in terms of student learning, thinking and engagement.

To prepare for this post-lesson session, it helps to identify someone to take careful notes and to collect the additional data from lesson observers. Japanese teachers refer to these post-lesson sessions as a *colloquium*, during which the lesson study teacher, group members and, where appropriate, outside observers discuss the research lesson. The person who taught the lesson is given the opportunity to speak first, followed by lesson study group members and other observers. The discussion should focus on the lesson (not the teacher) and on analysing what, how and why students learned, or did not learn, from the experience.

Lesson study involves further research cycles during which the group revise and test the lesson once again. Analysis of the evidence leads the group to consider ways to improve the lesson. Groups may modify the learning goal(s), lesson design, and also change their strategies for collecting evidence. After deciding on revisions, the group re-teaches the lesson.

Coaching. Similar to the idea of lesson study, I have worked with some schools that have found it helpful to introduce coaching into their teacher partnerships. This is based on the idea that developments in practice require exposure to someone who can help teachers understand the difference between what they are doing and what they aspire to do.

The approach incorporates all the elements that research suggests create powerful forms of professional development. Specifically, it is located mainly in classrooms; builds on the expertise available within the school; involves teacher collaboration; helps to develop a language of practice; and uses evidence as a stimulus for reflection and experimentation. The process usually involves four steps: (i) two teachers assist one another in preparing a lesson they will each teach; (ii) prior to each of the two lessons, the teachers meet with a senior colleague who has been trained as a coach to discuss their lesson plan; (iii) as the two each teach the lesson their colleagues observe, focusing in particular on students who are thought likely to experience difficulties in achieving the goals; and (iv) following each of the lessons, the coach orchestrates a process of review on what has taken place.

Inclusive inquiry. This is an approach to collaborative inquiry that emphasises the involvement of students. It was developed through two linked studies led by Professor Kiki Messiou at the University of Southampton. I acted as the methodological consultant for both of these initiatives.

The first study involved eight secondary schools in cities in England, Portugal and Spain (Messiou et al. 2016). Building on the findings of this research, the second study involved a two-stage collaborative action research study, carried out in primary schools in five countries (i.e. Austria, Denmark, England, Spain and Portugal). These schools were invited to take part because they were known to have diverse student populations (Messiou and Ainscow 2020).

During the first phase of the study, trios of teachers in one primary school in each country involved students in efforts to develop inclusive classroom approaches. Then, in the second phase, these schools became hubs to promote the approach within a network of primary schools in their local area. This meant that a total of 30 schools took part. In each country a team of university researchers supported, recorded and analysed the action research as it occurred in each of the schools, using observations, interviews and surveys.

The approach used in the study involved a series of interconnected processes, as shown in Figure 5.1. Central to these are discussions amongst teachers and their students about how to make lessons more inclusive. This involves students becoming researchers who learn how to use research techniques to gather the views of their classmates, as well as observing lessons.

The dialogues that this encourages are focused on learning and teaching. More specifically, differences amongst students and teachers are used to challenge existing thinking and practices in ways that are intended to encourage experimentation in order to foster more inclusive ways of working. This, in turn, sets out to break down barriers that are limiting the engagement of some learners, not least by challenging taken-for-granted assumptions about the capabilities of particular students.

In practical terms the inclusive inquiry approach involves trios of teachers cooperating to find ways of including all children in their lessons, particularly those who are seen as *hard to reach*. These might be, for example, migrants, refugees or students with disabilities, as well as others, who do not belong to a particular group that is receiving special attention. They might also include learners who teachers feel are being overlooked, perhaps because they are quiet or shy.

There are three phases to the Inclusive Inquiry approach – planning, teaching and analysing – all of which involve dialogue amongst children and teachers. In practical terms these phases require teachers to use a set of steps. We found that the implementation of these steps can be challenging, not least because of the difficulties of finding the time that is required. There is also a

Figure 5.1 Interconnected processes of inclusive inquiry.

related worry that the approach will be watered down in ways that will reduce the impact and, as a result, lead the approach to be discredited.

In response to these concerns, we developed a way of monitoring implementation based on an approach that we had used in previous projects (e.g. Ainscow, Gallannaugh and Kerr 2012). Influenced by work carried out in Texas many years ago (Hall et al. 1975), it involves a *levels of use* instrument, which attempts to *assess what the individual innovation user actually does in using an innovation* (p. 52). This enables trios of teachers to determine how far they have used the approach. In this way, members of a trio can identify areas that need further development. We also found it helpful for university researchers to join this process in a way that further encourages critical reflection, collaborative learning and mutual critique, as recommended by Wasser and Bresler (1996).

Peer inquiry. This approach involves the creation of groups of colleagues within a partnership of schools that work on solving real problems through cycles of inquiry and reflection. In this way, the peer inquiry process encourages the sharing of expertise, whilst also offering challenges to existing thinking and practices.

The starting point for peer inquiry is the existing experience and knowledge of its members. Colleagues in the group are seen as sources of challenge and support, bringing their experiences and perspectives to the discussions that take place.

The suggested steps are as follows:

1 The headteachers and leads from each school's inquiry group spend a morning together in each of their establishments, in order that the visitors can gather evidence about how inquiry-based improvement plans are being implemented. This might include discussions with a sample of staff and students, possibly through a series of learning walks. It is suggested that the host school determines the exact focus for inquiry.
2 Towards the end of the morning, the visitors meet to agree a list of thoughts regarding what has emerged. It is important to stress that these commentaries are **not intended to be evaluative**. Rather, they are a summary of interesting ideas that emerged during the visit.
3 The commentaries are intended to be used as the basis for discussion about the implementation of evidence-based improvement strategies within the host school. Later, they can also be used to stimulate discussion with other colleagues within the partner schools.

One of the most significant features of the visits carried out using peer inquiry is the way in which colleagues from different schools support one another in reviewing aspects of practice. It has been found that these linking activities can shed new light on familiar situations, both for visitors and visited.

This adds support to research which suggests that an engagement with evidence can, under certain conditions, help staff in schools to strengthen their practices. As I have explained, this involves the creation of *interruptions* to the usual ways of thinking that exist within a school in order to create space and encouragement for reflection and mutual challenge. However, we have found that this is not in itself a straightforward mechanism for change. To have a chance to move practice forward, interruptions must be welcomed and they must follow an invitation to engage in dialogue.

With this in mind, links between schools are made on the basis that the visitors are primarily there to assist the development of practices in the host school by generating evidence and reflecting together on the possible implications. In this way, visitors go both as colleagues and co-researchers, invited to find out more about the impact of existing practices. In Chapter 6, I provide accounts of the use of peer inquiry related to the development of leadership practices.

Moving practice forward

In supporting collaborative inquiry projects of the sort proposed in this chapter, it is helpful to engage those involved in professional development activities in relation to the themes being addressed. In such contexts, the following accounts of practice have sometimes been used to stimulate discussion within workshops. These examples illustrate the flexible ways in which schools have used some of the approaches described so far to identify and address barriers experienced by students in their schools.

> **Account 5.1. Challenging expectations**. In this primary school, the staff inquiry group noticed that assessment evidence showed that a significant proportion of children were struggling with writing, as compared to their scores in mathematics. The original emphasis had been informed by national debates on boys' underachievement, and certainly it was a group of boys who struggled most with their writing. Nevertheless, a focus on boys alone was clearly unjustified, given that boys were also some of the highest performers and that many girls were barely outperforming the lowest performing boys.
>
> Further evidence was generated by interviewing a small number of children while they were writing, some of which pointed to their feelings of fear of failure. Members of the staff inquiry group were fascinated by these responses and wondered about how widespread were these feelings about writing. With this in mind, they decided to devise a questionnaire, which was completed by all children in years five and six, with teaching assistants scribing for some children. Once again, the staff were surprised and intrigued by the factors that children identified as barriers to good writing and began to consider how their own practices might be changed to alleviate some of these issues.
>
> It was decided that this was a moment to engage other staff in the school. So, the group decided to use the data from interviews and the questionnaires, alongside examples of children's writing, to inform

the planning of a teacher development day. The emphasis throughout was on interpreting the data from *their* children and how they might respond in terms of their own practice. The meeting generated a lot of debate, with many teachers giving examples of how they intended to try new ideas in relation to the insights gained.

Teaching assistants were involved in these discussions, providing valuable and specific insights from their one-to-one work with students. elements of *fun* during the day – for instance, trying out a drama activity linked to writing a story – also helped to remind staff of the continuing good relationships within the school and encouraged discussion about their priorities in the face of many challenges. Even so, follow-up interviews with some teachers revealed how they struggled to see ways of changing their practice within the constraints of the school's policy. Indeed, only later, after inspectors had judged the quality of teaching in the school to be *outstanding*, did teachers start to trust their own judgement again in determining how they might develop their practice.

Significantly, two years later a number of staff were still using data from the questionnaire to inform continuing developments. *Trials* of different approaches to encouraging writing also continued to take place, with a continuing emphasis on checking things out with the children concerned.

Account 5.2. Teachers moving out of their comfort zones. Three teachers in a secondary school adopted the idea of lesson study, an inquiry-based approach to professional development. In planning a joint lesson, they identified students within each of their classes who they saw as being particularly vulnerable. They felt that by thinking about the lesson with these individuals in mind they might create new and different ways of facilitating the learning of all of their students. So, for example, one teacher talked about a student who had an understanding of language but would not speak, even when invited. Another teacher focused on one of his students who had severe dyslexia.

This led the teachers to discuss how they might plan their lessons differently; for example, they talked about getting the students to write on the whiteboard, and getting students to rehearse verbally what they wanted to say, rather than writing arguments down.

In addition, the trio decided that they needed to work with some of their students before teaching the lessons to get an idea of how they preferred to learn. They also wanted to consider how best to plan the lesson to support the many differences amongst the students. With this in mind, they selected seven students, each from a different ethnic background, six of whom were born outside the country.

The teachers got these students together at lunchtime and asked them to rank their preferences regarding different classroom activities that can be used when studying poetry. As a result of these discussions, they decided that they as teachers would have minimal input into the activity.

The overall aim of the lesson that was planned was to develop confidence in and awareness of a variety of dramatic techniques. Each teacher taught the lesson with their colleagues watching, making changes in the light of the regular discussions that took place as they proceeded. It was noticeable that these became increasingly focused on matters of detail and, as a result, led to a greater emphasis on mutual challenge and personal reflection. For example, after one of the lessons, a conversation took place during which two teachers were heard thinking aloud about their own ways of working as a result of watching their colleague:

Teacher 1: *I thought it was noisy. I knew it was OK, but I felt a bit uncomfortable with it, as I can't imagine having the same level of noise in my class and being in control. I'm not sure I could let them go like that.*

Teacher 2: *You can tell you've (Teacher 3) done a lot of group work with your class. You've built up that relationship of letting them work more autonomously over time so it's not just a one off.*

Teacher 1: *I would structure my lesson more. You gave them both tasks together. You did not really go through them before the lesson started but circulated among them when they were doing their first task, drama features, to check they were OK for the second task. I'd divide it into two tasks, the first being carrying out the dramatic feature, and then the second one being the one where they reflect on what the important aspects are of each feature of drama. I would do one task, then stop them all and bring them back to me, and then I'd tell them what to do for the second task. I might be doing them a disservice but I don't think they could cope. Or maybe I just want to feel in control.*

Teacher 2: *It really surprised me how they just got on and read their packs of information in their groups. I'm envious. What surprised me was the way you were able to give them instructions and rely on them to read through them. You have obviously been teaching them to be autonomous.*

All of this led on to a consideration of the different teaching styles used by the members of the trio:

Teacher 1: *I think (teacher 3) has got a very calm style. It rubs off on the kids. I watched how she circulated round the class. That calm style wouldn't work with my group, or is that the way we've moulded them? They're a lot lower ability and it takes a lot of energy to get them to put pen to paper. There are a lot of behavioural issues. I feel shattered at the end. If I was calmer perhaps they would mellow? I would be nervous about my students being able to be so independent. You didn't quite tell them everything they needed to do. My students couldn't do* *that, or maybe it's about my expectations of my student? It's partly to do with who the students are but it's also to do with expectations.*

The conversation went on to consider ways of mobilising hidden strengths amongst the students:

Teacher 2: *I also liked the way you chose leaders for each of the groups. You chose people who you knew would be confident to lead the groups.*

Teacher 1: *We don't draw on their strengths enough. Take for example Student Y, he is low in everything but he runs for the city. Student X is very involved in the cadets, perhaps he would be good at leading this activity. Just because he is not very good in English doesn't mean we can't draw from their strengths in other areas.*

Teacher 2: *I don't really know what makes them tick, what groups or clubs they belong to, what gets them going. We've got to show that they are good at something and draw on their strengths.*

By the end of the process the three teachers all commented that they had been challenged to rethink their lesson planning and facilitation. Through this, they realised that the new approaches had given them opportunities to learn outside of what they referred to as their *comfort zones* and, in so doing, move beyond their expectations about the capabilities of their students.

Conclusion

This chapter has provided practical guidance on the use of collaborative inquiry to promote inclusive developments in schools, plus further illustrative examples of what this looks like in action. This guidance should not be seen as a blueprint to be followed rigidly. Rather, it is intended to be adapted by those leading developments to suit particular contexts.

In order to support such development activities, I worked with colleagues from a range of countries to design *Reaching Out to All Learners*, a resource pack of materials, for the International Bureau of Education-UNESCO. The pack is available free, in a variety of languages at: https://www.ibe.unesco.org/en/node/103?hub=41

These materials address the practicalities of addressing the challenges facing schools and other education centres, such as early years and further education provision, as they seek to include all of their students.

The focus of the resource pack is on three strategic questions:

- How can schools be developed in order to respond positively to student diversity?
- How can classroom practices be developed that will ensure that lessons are inclusive?

- How can practitioners engage families, partner schools and the wider community in their efforts to become inclusive and equitable?

Whilst the materials can be read by individuals, they are designed to encourage collaborative forms of professional learning in the following settings:

- Within individual or groups of schools to promote the development of policies and practices;
- In-service courses or workshops for teachers;
- Collaborative action research projects involving schools working with the support of university staff; and
- Pre-service teacher education courses (although some of the activities may need to be revised in light of the limited experiences of participants).

There is an introductory video that explains the content of the resource pack and how it is intended to be used. Suggestions for further reading and additional relevant resources are also provided.

Other resources that I have found to be helpful in planning professional development workshops are as follows:

- *Inclusion and Education: All Means All.* This short animation video is particularly useful as an introduction to the importance of inclusion and equity in education: https://youtu.be/kEyjlqixq9c
- *Promoting Equity in Education.* These materials provide a stimulus for professional development sessions, which can be used live or online – within schools or elsewhere: https://futureschooling.co.uk/inclusive-schooling/promoting-equity-in-education/
- *Every school is inclusive: to some degree.* During this interview, I explain international developments over the last 30 years in relation to inclusion and equity in education: https://youtu.be/oKz09ngdNcA
- *Promoting inclusion and equity in education: Lessons from international* **research.** I gave this short talk at the Atlantic Rim Collaboratory Summit, Oslo, May 2023: https://youtu.be/9E9fawfkHWk
- *Empowerment, equity and excellence.* In this presentation I address the theme of changing education systems in relation to inclusion and equity: https://www.youtube.com/watch?v=ir058B2_Z1A
- *The Universal Design for Learning.* A framework that is widely used internationally to make learning inclusive and transformative for everyone: https://www.cast.org/impact/universal-design-for-learning-udl
- *Reaching the Hard to Reach.* These professional development materials focus on teacher/student dialogue as a strategy for promoting inclusive classrooms (available in five languages): https://reachingthehardtoreach.eu/
- *The UNESCO Open File on Inclusive Education.* An introduction for policy makers and managers who have an important role to play in bringing about the changes needed to make inclusive education a reality: https://www.eenet.org.uk/resources/docs/132164e.pdf

- *Developing children's zones for England: What's the evidence?* This report argues that children's zones, based on the principles underpinning the Harlem Children's Zone, offer a way of improving outcomes for children from economically poorer backgrounds: https://www.savethechildren.org.uk/content/dam/global/reports/advocacy/developing-childrens-zones.pdf
- *Children's Neighbourhoods Scotland.* Reports a project that took a place-based approach to improving outcomes for children, young people and their communities: Children's Neighbourhoods Scotland
- *Time for an inclusive turn.* In this blog I consider developments in Portugal, one of the most inclusive education systems: https://internationalednews.com/2022/03/30/time-for-an-inclusive-turn-mel-ainscow-on-inclusion-as-a-guiding-principle-for-educational-reform-in-portugal/

Before using any of these resources, it is important to ensure that the content is appropriate from a cultural perspective.

Having focused on the practicalities of using collaborative inquiry to promote inclusive developments in schools, in the following chapter I consider the implications of these suggestions for leadership practices.

Note

1 https://www.gla.ac.uk/schools/education/news/headline_896988_en.html

6 Leading inclusive school development

Having observed a lesson in a school serving an economically poor community in the city of New Delhi, India in which the children engaged in a role-play activity about families, I asked the teachers how this had been planned. They explained how during the previous year a newly appointed headteacher had instigated occasional Saturday morning workshops to discuss their work.

Around the walls of the school were colourful posters developed during these professional development gatherings. It was these discussions, the teachers explained, that had stimulated them to try out different approaches to teaching. However, they explained that it was not just the meetings that had encouraged their innovations. They had also developed the idea of what they called *partnership teaching*, whereby they occasionally have opportunities to work together in one another's classrooms. It was this, more than anything, they argued, that had stimulated their experimentation.

I asked about how they found time for this, given the large number of children in each class. They explained that sometimes the headteacher takes a class to release a teacher to work with a colleague. Other times they might put two classes together, but this usually meant that they would have to work outside, since the classrooms were too crowded.

School cultures

Experiences such as this one have convinced me of the importance of creating a climate within which more inclusive relationships and practices can be developed. The nature of such positive contexts can take many forms, and, therefore, attempts at generalisations are difficult. Nevertheless, my monitoring of developments in schools over time suggests a series of organisational conditions that facilitate the risk-taking that seems to be associated with movements towards more inclusive practices. More specifically they indicate that such movement is not about making marginal adjustments to existing arrangements, but rather about asking fundamental questions about the way the organisation is currently structured, focusing on aspects such as patterns of leadership, processes of planning and policies for staff development. In this way the development of inclusive schooling comes to be seen as a process of school improvement.

DOI: 10.4324/9781003438014-6

There is considerable evidence that norms of teaching are socially negotiated within the everyday context of schooling (e.g. Rosenholtz 1989). It
seems that the culture of the workplace impacts on how teachers see their
work and, indeed, their students. However, the concept of culture is difficult
to define.

Schein (1985) suggests that culture is about the deeper levels of basic assumptions and beliefs that are shared by members of an organisation, operating unconsciously to define an organisation's view of itself and its environment.
It manifests itself in norms that suggest to people what they should do and
how. In a similar way Hargreaves (1995) argues that school cultures can be
seen as having a reality-defining function, enabling those within an institution
to make sense of themselves, their actions and their environment. A current
reality-defining function of culture, he suggests, is often a problem-solving
function inherited from the past. In this way today's cultural form created
to solve an emergent problem often becomes tomorrow's taken-for-granted
recipe for dealing with matters shorn of their novelty. Hargreaves concludes
that by examining the reality-defining aspects of a culture it should be possible
to gain an understanding of the routines the organisation has developed in
response to the tasks it faces.

My impression is that when schools are successful in moving their practice
forward, as in the example from New Delhi, this tends to have a more general
impact on how teachers perceive themselves and their work. In this way the
school takes on some of the features of what Senge (1989) calls a learning organisation, i.e. *an organisation that is continually expanding its capacity to create its future* (p. 14). Or, to borrow a useful phrase from Rosenholtz (1989), it
becomes *a moving school*, one that is continually seeking to develop and refine
its responses to the challenges it meets. The New Delhi experience points to
the important roles of senior staff in making this possible.

As schools move in such directions, the cultural changes that occur can also
impact on the ways in which teachers perceive students in their classes whose
progress is a matter of concern. What may happen is that as the overall climate
in a school improves, such children are gradually seen in a more positive light
(Rosenholtz 1989). Rather than simply presenting problems that have to be
overcome or, possibly, referred elsewhere for separate attention, such students
may be perceived as providing feedback on existing classroom arrangements
and school policies. Indeed, they may be seen as sources of understanding as
to how these arrangements might be improved in ways that would be of benefit to all students.

It is important to recognise, of course, that the cultural changes necessary
to achieve schools that are able to hear and respond to the *hidden voices* are in
many cases highly significant. Traditional school cultures, supported by rigid
organisational arrangements, teacher isolation and high levels of specialisms
amongst staff who are geared to predetermined tasks, are often in trouble
when faced with unexpected circumstances. On the other hand, the presence
of children who are not suited to the existing *menu* of the school provides

some encouragement to explore a more collegiate culture within which teachers are supported in experimenting with new teaching responses. In this way problem-solving activities may gradually become the reality-defining, taken-for-granted functions that are the culture of a school that is moving in an inclusive direction.

A common sense of purpose

The approaches to collaborative inquiry explained in the previous chapter are intended to support schools in making such moves. They require coordinated efforts to bring stakeholders together around a common sense of purpose (Ainscow and Sandill 2010). With this in mind, they place an emphasis on processes of social learning within particular contexts. The uses of evidence as a means of stimulating experimentation, and collaboration within and between schools, and between schools and the communities they serve, are all seen as key strategies. None of this will happen by chance, however. Rather, it requires forms of leadership that will make it happen.

All of this further underlines the importance of the deeper levels of basic assumptions and beliefs that are shared by members of an organisation, operating unconsciously to define how they view themselves and their working contexts. The extent to which these values include the acceptance and celebration of difference, and a commitment to offering educational opportunities to all students, coupled with the extent to which they are shared across a school staff, relates to the extent to which students are enabled to participate (Kugelmass 2001).

Changing the norms that exist within a school is difficult to achieve, particularly within a context that is faced with so many competing pressures and where practitioners tend to work alone in addressing the problems they face (Fullan 2007). On the other hand, the presence of learners who are not suited to the existing menu of the school can provide some encouragement to explore a more collaborative culture within which teachers support one another in experimenting with new teaching responses. In this way, problem-solving activities gradually become the reality-defining, taken-for-granted functions that are the culture of a school that is more geared to fostering inclusive ways of working.

The implication of all of this is that becoming more inclusive is a matter of thinking and talking, reviewing and refining practice, and making attempts to develop a more inclusive culture. Such a conceptualisation means that inclusion cannot be divorced from the contexts within which it is developing, nor the social relations that might sustain or limit that development (Dyson 2006i). This suggests that it is in the complex interplay between individuals, and between groups and individuals, that shared beliefs and values and change exist, and that it is impossible to separate those beliefs from the relationships in which they are embodied. Nias (1989) describes a culture of collaboration developing as both the product and the cause of shared social and moral beliefs.

Similarly, Hopkins et al. (1994) contend that in organisations striving to-wards change, school culture is constantly evolving. This evolution takes place through interaction of members of a school with each other and through their reflections on life and the world around them (Coleman and Earley 2005).

Other researchers argue that in order to bring about the cultural change that inclusion demands, it is essential to consider the values underlying the intended changes (Corbett 2001; Kugelmass 2001). Thus, cultural change is directed towards a *transformative view of inclusion, in which diversity is seen as making a positive contribution to the creation of responsive educational settings* (Ainscow et al., 2006). This involves developing the capacity of those within schools to reveal and challenge deeply entrenched deficit views of *difference*, which define certain types of students as *lacking something* (Trent, Artiles and Englert 1998). Writers who are involved in facilitating and evaluating such processes in schools repeatedly identify the role of leadership as critical for sus-taining such changes, both in developed and developing contexts (e.g. Kugel-mass and Ainscow 2003; Leo and Barton 2006; Lipsky and Gartner 1998; Zollers, Ramanathan and Yu 1999).

Levers for change

Research on school development indicates that teachers' beliefs, attitudes and actions are what create the contexts in which children and young people are encouraged to participate in learning activities (Seashore-Louis 2020). This being the case, the task must be to develop education systems within which teachers feel supported as well as challenged in relation to their re-sponsibility to keep exploring more effective ways of facilitating the learning of all students. This raises the question of what actions are needed to move thinking and practice forward; in other words, what are the *levers for change*? (Ainscow 2005)

Senge (1989) sees *levers* as actions that can be taken in order to change the behaviour of an organisation and those individuals within it. He goes on to argue that those who wish to encourage change within an organisation must be smart in determining where the high leverage lies. Too often, he sug-gests, approaches used to bring about large-scale changes in organisations are *low leverage*. That is to say, they tend to change the way things look but not the way they work. Possible examples of low leverage activity in the educa-tion field include the following: policy documents, conferences and in-service courses. Whilst such initiatives may make a contribution, they tend not to lead to changes in thinking and practice. Our aim, therefore, must be to identify what may turn out to be more subtle, less obvious and yet higher leverage efforts to bring about change in schools.

It seems, then, that the UNESCO principle that *every learner matters and matters equally* is likely to require challenges to the thinking of those within a particular organisation and, inevitably, this again raises questions regard-ing forms of leadership. Our review of literature concluded that the issue of inclusion is increasingly seen as a key challenge (West, Ainscow and Nottman 2003). In relation to this, Leithwood, Jantzi and Steinbach (1999) suggest that with continuing diversity, schools need to thrive on uncertainty, have a greater capacity for collective problem-solving and be able to respond to a wider range of learners. Sergiovanni (1992) also points to the challenge of student diversity and argues that current approaches to school leadership may well be getting in the way of improvement efforts. A particular concern is also to understand how leadership and student behaviour are linked. This means that forms of leadership that can facilitate improvements in student behaviour are particularly important (Ainscow and Fox 2000).

Certain forms of leadership are known to be effective in promoting inclusion in education (Riehl 2000). These approaches focus attention on teaching and learning; they create strong supportive communities of students, teachers and parents; they nurture the understanding of a culture of education among families; and they involve multi-agency support.

Lambert (2005) argues for constructivist leadership as a strategy for responding to learner diversity. This involves reciprocal processes that enable participants in an educational community to construct meanings that lead towards a common purpose about schooling. They use this perspective to argue that leadership involves an interactive process entered into by both students and teachers. Consequently, there is a need for shared leadership, with the principal seen as a leader of leaders. Hierarchical structures have to be replaced by shared responsibility in a community that becomes characterised by agreed values and hopes, such that many of the control functions associated with school leadership become less important or even counterproductive. As highlighted, this requires a cultural shift across levels and most importantly at the level of school leadership. At the same time, it is important to note that factors that influence such transitions may lie outside the school setting, for example at the district or local authority levels. This is particularly so in more centralised education systems.

Relationships

Much of the literature on the role of leadership in relation to school improvement places emphasis on the importance of social relationships. Johnson and Johnson (1989), two key figures in the field of social psychology, argue that leaders may structure staff working relationships in one of three ways: competitively, individualistically or cooperatively. Within a competitive structure, teachers work against each other to achieve a goal that only a few can attain; an individualistic structure exists when teachers work alone to accomplish goals that are unrelated to the goals of their colleagues, whereas a cooperative structure exists when teachers coordinate their efforts to achieve joint goals. They go on to argue that to maximise the productivity of a school, principals have to challenge the status quo of traditional competitive and individualistic approaches to teaching, inspire a clear mutual vision of what the school should and could be, empower staff through cooperative team work, lead by example, using cooperative procedures and taking risks and encourage staff members to persist and keep striving to improve their expertise. Within this overall formulation, Johnson and Johnson place a strong emphasis on the need to build cooperative teams.

Leithwood and Riehl (2003) refer to two approaches to school leadership, one with an orientation to student achievement and the other with a focus on meeting the needs of individuals. They further contend that leaders serving diverse schools need to use both approaches in order to perform their role effectively (see, e.g. Shah 2006; West, Ainscow and Stanford 2005). Gross, Shaw and Shapiro (2003) echo this by arguing that school leaders need to strike a continual balance between concern for people and accountability. Johnston and Hayes (2007), among others, contend that student learning is linked to professional learning and that students are likely to be more successful at school if their teachers are actively engaged in learning how to teach within the local context of the school. As a result of their research in schools in challenging circumstances, these authors assert that professional learning requires a pedagogy that disrupts the *default modes of schooling*. Consequently, as they indicate, practitioners in schools need to *learn new things* not only to *do new things*, conceptualising professional learning as the pedagogical practice of educational leaders.

The most helpful theoretical and empirical leads regarding leadership and inclusion, however, are provided by Riehl (2000), who, following an extensive review of literature, develops *a comprehensive approach to school administration and diversity*. She concludes that school leaders need to attend to three broad types of tasks: fostering new meanings about diversity, promoting inclusive practices within schools and building connections between schools and communities. She goes on to consider how these tasks can be accomplished, exploring how the concept of practice, especially discursive practice, can contribute to a fuller understanding of the work of school principals. This analysis leads Riehl to offer a positive view of the potential for school principals to engage in inclusive, transformative developments. She concludes: *When wedded to a relentless commitment to equity, voice, and social justice, administrators' efforts in the tasks of sensemaking, promoting inclusive cultures and practices in schools, and building positive relationships outside of the school may indeed foster a new form of practice* (p. 71).

Coordination

All of this has major implications for leadership practice at different levels within schools and education systems. In particular, it calls for efforts to encourage coordinated and sustained efforts around the idea that changing outcomes for all students is unlikely to be achieved unless there are changes in the behaviours of adults. Consequently, the starting point must be with staff members: in effect, enlarging their capacity to imagine what might be achieved and increasing their sense of accountability for bringing this about. This may also involve tackling taken-for-granted assumptions, most often relating to expectations about certain groups of students, their capabilities and behaviours.

My argument is, then, based on the assumption that schools and their communities know more than they use and that the logical starting point for inclusive development is a detailed analysis of existing arrangements. As we have seen, this allows good practices to be identified and shared, whilst, at the same time, drawing attention to ways of working that may be creating barriers to the participation and learning of some students. However, as I have stressed, the focus must not only be on practice. It must also address and sometimes challenge the thinking behind existing ways of working.

As a result, it is possible for schools to develop the characteristics of a *learning organisation*. That is to say, they can become contexts that *prioritise learning, growth and innovation in every facet of its culture* by:

- Developing and sharing a vision centred on the learning of all students;
- Creating and supporting continuous learning opportunities for all staff;
- Promoting team learning and collaboration among staff;
- Establishing a culture of inquiry, innovation and exploration;
- Establishing embedded systems for collecting and exchanging knowledge and learning;
- Learning with and from the external environment and larger learning system; and
- Modelling and growing learning leadership.

(Kools and Stoll 2016)

In moving forward this list of features provides another useful guide for planning.

Developing leadership practices

Within our various projects, my colleagues and I have explored ways in which leadership practices can be strengthened in order to create contexts where the sorts of approaches described in earlier chapters can be introduced. This was a particular area of focus in a network we set up in England in 2011 (see Ainscow et al. 2016, for a more detailed account).

We called the network the *University of Manchester Coalition of Research Schools*. In setting it up our intention was to work with a small number of carefully chosen schools that had the capacity to take forward a pioneering agenda within their organisations and with their partner schools. During the subsequent period, 11 schools were involved (primary, special and secondary), all of which were recognised as being outstanding as a result of inspections. Eight of them had become formally designated as *teaching schools* as part of a national policy initiative which involved schools seen as being successful in taking a lead in providing support to other local schools.

Our hope was that involvement in the Coalition would increase creativity within these schools through the use of the sorts of collaborative inquiry I have described in earlier chapters. In this way, our aim was to challenge them to aspire to excellence by placing inquiry at the heart of everything that goes on. This meant they would become schools that are on the move, always seeking new ways to reach out to all of their students, particularly those who miss out within existing ways of working. In other words, they would be concerned with finding effective ways of improving the achievement of all of their students, particularly those from disadvantaged backgrounds.

Involvement in the Coalition required schools to each nominate a staff team to act as research coordinators, empowered to lead developments in their own school. Members of our university group supported these teams in identifying areas where inequities persist, collecting and analysing contextual evidence, developing and implementing an improvement plan and evaluating its impact. As these developments occurred, the schools were occasionally assisted in making use of recommendations from research carried out elsewhere.

These activities were reinforced by a series of workshops that were intended to stimulate whole-school development and research. Links across the network of schools were also developed, such that they could learn from one another's research. At the same time, this enabled the university team to develop evaluative accounts of practice and impact and facilitate cross-school analyses of the collective findings.

Impact

As we worked with the schools, we saw further evidence of the impact of the collaborative inquiry approach developed through our earlier work. For me, this was an indication of the development within the schools of an inquiring stance. Our sense was that this was helped along by the relatively strong leadership practices that existed within the schools. In particular, there seemed to be a confidence within the organisations regarding how to get things done efficiently and a belief that these actions were likely to lead to positive outcomes.

Despite the presence of these positive features, however, the schools did occasionally experience forms of turbulence of the sort we had seen in our earlier projects. In particular, staff and senior leaders described how their involvement in collaborative inquiry often led them to feel confused and uncertain as to how they should proceed. In some instances, this included a sense of doubt regarding the roles of our university team, who, they assumed, were going to take a lead in deciding how best to proceed. At times, too, this led to tensions within the staff inquiry groups, as they tried to determine an appropriate way forward. In one case this led a school to withdraw from the project.

Evocative images were used by various senior colleagues to explain what this felt like, e.g. *wood for trees*, *lost in the fog*, *muddy waters* and *herding sheep*.

One headteacher explained this in a way that was typical of what happened in most of the schools:

> *I think we struggled at first because we'd not done anything like this before, and I think it was allowing ourselves to not know. I think what we've got to do is to think it's ok to not know the answer to something: that's the very reason that we're doing this. So, what is it that's bothering us? What is that we want to find out more about? And let's just open our minds to it, and find out the answer and see what it picks up along the way....*

She went to argue:

> *So, we've learned something, definitely, and I think that it's given us that vehicle to go and find out. This has helped us to think let's go and talk to the children, let's go and talk to the staff, let's shadow students, let's do all those things that are involved in research and see what we can find out.*

It seemed to us that all of this opened up potentially important spaces for new professional thinking regarding leadership practices, as colleagues learnt how to learn from one another in new ways. The challenges this creates, however, have obvious implications for the way such initiatives are led, as another head explained:

> *What we had to do was actually remind everybody that this was not going to be straightforward. It wasn't following a formula, because you've got different personalities that like different things.*

The involvement of our university team as *outsiders* – seeing things in different ways, asking questions and bringing ideas from elsewhere, including from formal research – added a further set of challenges into this process. As a result, the area of focus for the inquiries frequently changed, as new evidence led to the rejection of what seemed like promising ways forwards, whilst also pointing to new possibilities that had to be considered. In these ways, well established ways of working were sometimes reconsidered. For example, another headteacher commented:

> *Well, I think if you've got a philosophy you've got to be able to back it up with the fact that it's been effective; and I think you have to question how effective it's being and look at alternatives, because otherwise you can become quite stagnant and not really look at what you're doing.*

We related comments such as this to the idea of *double-loop learning* (Argyris andSchon 1996), mentioned in Chapter 4. This is based on the view that practice within an organisation is guided by some more-or-less deep-seated sets of assumptions and values. For the most part, routine problems can be overcome within the framework provided by these assumptions and values. As a result, emphasis is placed on making existing techniques more efficient in a way that is referred to as single-loop learning. However, from time to time something, or someone, throws the underlying assumptions into doubt leading to double-loop learning. What follows is not simply the improvement of existing practices, but new ways of thinking about practice – new sets of assumptions and newly configured sets of values – leading to greater creativity in respect to ways of moving forward.

Action learning

The overall aim of the Coalition of Research Schools project was to support the participating schools in developing their capacity to use collaborative in-quiry to improve outcomes for all of their students, particularly those from disadvantaged backgrounds. Given the status of some as teaching schools, we intended that this way of thinking would inform their wider roles.

By its nature this was a significant change that was likely to challenge think-ing and practice within the schools, as evidence confronts those involved with ideas that may not fit with their existing assumptions. From our earlier studies we knew that, under the right organisational conditions, this had the potential to stimulate the sharing of expertise and, indeed, experimentation with new ways of reaching those learners whose progress is a cause for concern.

Crucial to all of this were forms of leadership that would encourage an inquiring stance amongst school staff and a climate that supports a degree of risk-taking. With this in mind, heads involved in the Coalition participated in a further strand of activity focused on the strengthening of leadership practices. The approach we explored was that of *action learning* (Revans 1972). This involves the creation of action learning *sets*, i.e. groups of colleagues that work on solving real problems through repeated cycles of action and reflection. In this way, the action learning process encourages the sharing of expertise, whilst also offering challenges to existing leadership practices.

The starting point for the work of such an action learning group is the existing experience and knowledge of its members. Colleagues in the group are seen as sources of challenge and support, bringing their experiences and perspectives to the discussions that take place. Within such contexts, written accounts of practice are used to stimulate further reflection and creativity.

We suggested that the process should focus directly on the implications for leadership practice in schools using the Coalition's collaborative inquiry strat-egy. At the same time, it is likely to lead to discussion of wider issues regarding school management and leadership.

The action learning process we adopted involved the following steps:

1 Action learning sets are made up of three headteachers and one university researcher.
2 Members of the set spend a morning together in each of their schools in order that the three visitors can gather evidence about leadership practices.

This might include discussions with a sample of staff and students, possibly through a series of learning walks.

3 Towards the end of the morning, the visitors meet to agree on a commentary on what they have learnt. This is then shared with the headteacher (and possibly other senior staff). Together, the group agree a summary of what has emerged.

4 Following the visit, the university researcher writes a draft account of practice based on the summary. This draft is then agreed with the other members of the action learning set.

These suggestions drew on the experience of an earlier project on the role of leadership in respect to student behaviour that we carried out on behalf of the National College for School Leadership (Fox and Ainscow 2006). One of the most significant features of the visits carried out during that initiative had been the way in which colleagues from different schools supporting one another in reviewing aspects of leadership practice. It was found that these linking activities had the potential to shed new light on familiar situations, both for visitors and visited.

This adds support to our earlier research suggesting that an engagement with evidence can, under certain conditions, help staff in schools to rethink their practices. As I have explained, this involves the creation of *interruptions* to the usual ways of thinking that exist within a school in order to create space and encouragement for reflection and mutual challenge. However, we have found that this is not in itself a straightforward mechanism for change. To have a chance to move practice forward, interruptions must be welcomed and they must follow an invitation to engage in dialogue.

With this in mind, links between the Coalition schools were made on the basis that the visitors would primarily be going to assist the development of leadership practice in the host school by generating evidence and reflecting together on the possible implications. In this way, visitors went both as colleagues and co-researchers, invited to find out more about the impact of existing practices. Subsequently, we named this approach *peer inquiry* (Hadfield and Ainscow 2020).

Addressing the challenges

The action learning approach we explored proved difficult to introduce and sustain, not least because it tends to challenge existing assumptions and well-established ways of working. We found that there is a need to foster both support and challenge within such action learning groups. Our experience suggests that the following factors are important in this respect:

• **Commitment** – Progress requires a commitment from participants to the group, as well as to the process. There is also a need to recognise that the processes involved require a commitment over time in order that they can be effective. In other words, it has to be understood that this is not a *quick fix*.

- **Willingness** – Alongside this sense of commitment there is a need for those involved to be prepared to have an open mind and to be prepared to follow the model of adult learning involved.
- **Relationships** – It follows that much of this is about relationships. In particular, the forms of self-questioning that are involved require a degree of openness and trust amongst group members.
- **Agreed purposes** – Motivation seems to arise from a sense that the processes involved will have a pay-off for individuals. This is why it is essential that areas of focus are negotiated and agreed within the group.
- **Power** – Such negotiations will sometimes lead to tensions, as different group members argue their corners in respect to their own priorities and interests. This is why, in our experience, it is better to have groups within which there are members who have a similar status.

It was agreed that the accounts of practice would be shared with all the heads in the Coalition prior to a seminar at which the wider implications would be discussed. The two examples that follow provide a flavour of the accounts that were developed. They were each developed as a result of a half-day visit I made with the headteachers of two partner schools. These visits began with a briefing from the host headteacher. This was followed by a *learning walk*, usually led by students, and included informal classroom observations. Then there were focus group discussions with students and members of staff.

The visits concluded with the sharing of impressions with the head and, sometimes, other senior members of staff. Notes were kept during this discussion in order to prepare for the subsequent writing up of the account of practice. The examples that follow are adapted from two of these accounts. In reading them, it is important to note that school leaders in England have considerable influence over policies, including budgets. At the same time, they are subject to significant processes of accountability regarding the progress of students in their schools.

A school on the move

Sunshine primary school has 640 or so students and serves an urban area. All but a handful of the children are from minority ethnic backgrounds, the largest group having Pakistani and Bangladeshi heritages. There are said to be 26 different languages spoken in the homes of the children, and, on arrival into the early years provision, most have little or no spoken English. Nevertheless, there is massive support for the school from parents. The importance of this to the school's success is recognised, and considerable efforts are made to keep families involved, as can be sensed from the account of practice that emerged from the visit.

> **Account 6.1. Learning from differences.** The new principal at Sunshine, who took up post almost two years ago, immediately had the tasks

of strengthening the profile of the staff and developing an improvement strategy. He was fortunate to be joined at the same moment by a new vice principal who has particular strengths in leading professional development, particularly around the teaching of maths.

On his arrival, the new principal's instinct was that the school was fortunate not to be in special measures. Following the retirement of his predecessor there had been two temporary heads. Perhaps unsurprisingly, there were few systems in place, teaching was at best *patchy*, and there were many staff on temporary contacts. The principal commented, *The data simply did not make sense*. The good news, however, was that the school's budget was healthy, which gave the new management team an opportunity to make immediate changes: *I never had to ask can we afford it*. There were also good practices to build on: *Three or four classes with strong teaching*.

The view of the vice principal is that it was important that the new management team started work before the summer beak. Their urgent priority was to get in place a full quota of teachers for the start of the school year. Echoing the words of the management guru, Jim Collins, the principal explained, *We had to get the right people on the bus*. At the same time, a few members of staff had to be moved on. The overall staff now consists of approximately 130 people.

Priorities. The reshaping of the staff team gives strong indications of the priorities of the new leaders. Inevitably, there was an urgent need to achieve rapid improvements in attainment in order to respond to external policy pressures. Talking about this, the principal explained, *We had a narrow curriculum in year 6 last year. In fact, progress measures from year 3 to 6 were remarkable*. He added, *Short term we needed to drive up standards, but longer term the aim is to create a beyond outstanding school*.

Within these longer-term goals, the importance of responding to the particular circumstances, and needs of the students and their families, created other priorities. It was explained, for example, that many of the children have limited experiences of what is available within the city. Concerns such as this have led to a massive commitment to providing a broad and enriching curriculum experience. With all of this in mind, the school has developed a programme of field visits. It was also decided to appoint a number of specialist teachers, to cover PE, music and Spanish.

Responding to diversity. At the same time, the new management team saw the need to address the challenge of diversity within its population. It was therefore decided to invest in a greater number of support personnel, not least to ensure strong support for students arriving from other parts of the world. Care was taken about the titles given to these colleagues, stressing that *they are not there to help teachers*. Rather, titles such as *learning assistant* and *learning mentor* are intended to signal the concern with supporting children's progress.

In talking about what has happened, the principal said that in the first few months many things needed strengthening. He commented, for example, that sport was weak. Now the school takes part in many different external sports event. The big thing now, he added, is *to win something*.

Leadership and coordination of much of the school's activities is through key stage teams. This seems to make sense in such a large organization. There are, however, dangers in this, as noted by the principal: *You can get into a silo mentality in phases. We need to keep a whole school perspective.*

Engagement. Walking around the school the visitor is struck by the sense of engagement amongst students and staff. Much use is made of corridors and small breakout rooms to provide additional support for learning. The walls are full of visual symbols regarding the commitment to enrich the children's learning experiences, such as *wonder walls* and *pride displays*. Attention is also given to signalling the importance of reading, with posters on classroom doors stating the book that the class is reading currently and, at the same time, the one that the teacher is reading. Reflecting on this, the principal recalled his surprise that so few of the children had been able to tell him what was their favourite book.

The good use of space is also seen in the playgrounds, where careful attention is given to avoid overcrowding. There are also lots of play options for children to choose. Meanwhile, groups of older students act as guardians of safety.

Drawing lessons. We were interested to hear the views of staff and students on what had enabled the school to move forward so quickly. Senior staff we talked to emphasised, once again, the importance of staff appointments. One commented: *Appointing the right people is the key.*

Long serving staff talked of the revolution that occurred 18 months ago. In explaining what this had involved, reference was made to the feeling that there is now a *common sense of purpose*. Another talked of the importance of *consistency*, explaining, *we used the word a lot in the past but it never came to life*. Reference was also made to good *communication: Having the same message – it's a huge school*. Underpinning all of this is the emphasis placed on collaboration. Indeed, the deputy principal commented that this is *the key word*. Another significant comment came from a well-established teacher who, commenting on the leadership team, said: *They are here to stay!*

A newly appointed senior teacher explained that what struck him when he arrived was the emphasis on reflection amongst the staff. It seems likely that this is the result of the massive investment in staff development though what is referred to as *reflective inquiry*. This incorporates all the elements that research suggests create powerful forms of professional development. Specifically, it involves four steps: (i) two teachers assist one another in preparing a lesson they will each teach; (ii) prior to each of the two lessons, the teachers meet with a senior colleague who has been trained as a coach to discuss their lesson plan; (iii) as the two each teach the lesson their colleagues observe, focusing in particular on students who are thought likely to experience difficulties in achieving the goals; and (iv) following each of the lessons, the coach orchestrates a process of review on what has taken place.

Using this approach on a regular basis requires an enormous commitment of human resources. On the other hand, it seems to have paid off, both in terms of improvements in the quality of teaching and in the strengthening of staff collaboration. Staff members talked enthusiastically about what it meant to them, noting its importance in enabling *teachers to learn from each other* and the value of having *another pair of eyes*. Stressing the importance of seeing this as being totally separate from performance management, the vice principal explained that *the notes are for the teachers only*.

Alongside this emphasis on professional learning, the school does have strong systems for ensuring quality, including regular lesson observations by senior staff. The principal explained that little of this had gone on previously. Inevitably, therefore, the introduction of such strategies led initially to some moments of turbulence. That said, it seems that longstanding staff quickly warmed to the style of the new regime. One commented, *It could have led to turmoil*. Another added, *As older staff we had had so much turmoil we wanted someone to tell us*. It was perhaps significant that she added that her and her colleagues had helped the new management team get an understanding of the local community and what it expected of the school.

The sense of pride about what has been achieved came though strongly as these ideas were discussed. One teacher commented, *Very often you get thanked for what you do*. Similarly, another said: *Confidence is growing in our school*. A senior teacher, recently arrived, commented: *If I was starting my career I would have loved to be here*. Frequent mention was also made of *fairness*, a concept that was stressed by the principal. One teacher summed what this meant for her: *All classes should have good teaching*.

Within this highly collaborative context there is an obvious question as to what happens if a member of staff is not performing. Commenting on this, the vice principal noted: *If somebody is not good enough we would support them*. She added, *There is a line however*.

It was interesting, too, to hear the views of some of the older students, all of who were entirely positive about their schools. One girl summed this up: *The school's perfect*.

Running through this account of the visit to Sunshine primary school is a story of cultural change. What we saw was the use of various strategies that are intended to coordinate the actions of teachers and others behind agreed policies. However, these have to work in ways that do not reduce the discretion of individual teachers to practise according to what they see as the needs of their students. Consequently, teachers must have sufficient autonomy to make instant decisions that take account of the individuality of their students and the uniqueness of every encounter that occurs.

What is needed, therefore, seems to be a well-coordinated, cooperative style of working that gives individual teachers the confidence to improvise in a search for the most appropriate responses to the students in their classes. This becomes particularly important in a school that has such a highly diverse population.

From what happened at Sunshine, it seems that relationships are the key to establishing greater coordination. As explained earlier in this chapter, school relationships may be structured in one of three ways: individualistically, competitively or cooperatively. In schools with an individualistic form of organisation, teachers tend to work alone to achieve goals unrelated to the goals of their colleagues. Consequently, there is little sense of common purpose, no sharing of expertise and limited support for individuals. Furthermore, such schools often move towards a more competitive form of organisation.

In a competitive system, teachers strive to do better than their colleagues, recognising that their fates are negatively linked. Here the career of one teacher is likely to be enhanced by the failure of others within the school. In this win-lose struggle to succeed, it is almost inevitable that individuals will celebrate difficulties experienced by their colleagues, since they are likely to increase their own chances of success.

Clearly, the organisational approach which is most likely to create a positive working atmosphere is one that emphasises cooperation. In such a school, individuals are more likely to strive for mutual benefit, recognising that they all share a common purpose and, indeed, a common fate. Furthermore, individuals know that their performance can be influenced positively by the performance of others. This being the case, individuals feel proud when a colleague succeeds and is recognised for professional competence. Furthermore, a school such as Sunshine, which is based upon a cooperative structure, is likely to make effective use of the expertise of all its personnel, provide sources of stimulation and enrichment that foster their professional development and encourage positive attitudes to the introduction of new ways of working.

A school on the move

Keeping these ideas in mind, I move on to another account of practice that emerged from a similar peer inquiry process. This involved two headteachers and myself visiting a secondary school.

During the visit we tried to make sense of what had happened in recent years, focusing in particular on attempts to make sure that all students get a fair deal. We were particularly interested in what this meant for leadership practice.

Account 6.2. Getting a fair deal. Lakeside is an 11-16 high school serving a diverse range of communities from a series of townships. It is reported that 40% of the students live in areas of high deprivation as defined by national indicators. Despite this, Lakeside is said to have high standards of behaviour, achieves examination results which consistently exceed national averages, has very few former students designated as being out of employment or education, and is recognized as being outstanding by inspectors. Not surprisingly, it is the most consistently oversubscribed school in the local area.

The current principal was appointed four years ago, having previously been deputy head in the school. He and other members of staff explained that the previous principal had been successful in creating a well-disciplined environment, brought about by a leadership approach that was characterised as being autocratic. Explaining the features of this approach, the current principal explained that *the focus was on behaviour*, the aim being that *kids do as they are told*. His sense that whilst this had undoubtedly created *a strong achievement culture*, that had led to improvements in results, it had not encouraged a *strong learning culture*. However, he also felt that that this style of management was *self-limiting*, in the sense that it left limited space for independent thinking amongst staff, or amongst students. He recalled, for example, how one member of staff had asked the principal's permission to go home at 3.30.

Strategy. In moving the school forward, the principal made use of a chart on which he has described the stages that a school might go through to move from *satisfactory to good*, from *good to outstanding*, and from *outstanding to world class*. The staff we met were well aware of this formulation, suggesting that it has become a means of creating a common understanding of the strategic direction that the school is attempting to take.

The principal explained that through an on-going debate across the school, the aim is to define what a world class school would look like. This formulation has informed much of the work of senior staff in fostering improvement efforts at different levels of the organisation. So, for example, he recalls saying to a head of department: *If this was the best science department in the world, what would it look like?* Similarly, a recent discussion has focused on ensuring that catering arrangements are world standard, which led to the appointment of a highly qualified chef to lead this aspect of the school.

Culture and leadership. School culture is sometimes defined as *the way we do things round here*. Certainly, our impression was that recent years have seen significant changes in the way that decisions are made at Lakeside, all of which have been influenced by the aim of giving staff more space to act independently. Commenting on this, the principal explained: *There is a clear vision of what we want to achieve, but license to get there in different ways.*

Our discussions with senior and middle leaders tended to confirm all of this, with them recognising a significant move away from a top down management style towards one in which most developments are formulated and led within departments. For example, one middle leader noted: *The senior leadership team trust the departments to deliver.* All of this is set in the context of what the principal describes as *high levels of accountability*. These include: rigorous performance management procedures; regular line management meetings; consistent use of student data; and thorough processes for departmental improvement.

An example of how this works relates to how lesson observations are organized. A deputy head commented: *Five years ago heads of department did no lesson observations.* Now, he explained, they are mainly managed by middle leaders, albeit with support from senior staff. There seem to be three forms used: formal observations for the purpose of performance management; occasional informal observations to prepare inexperienced staff for the formal ones; and cooperative arrangements within staff groups that are intended to foster the sharing of practices and experimentation with new ways of working. These latter activities are referred to as *teaching and learning communities*. In addition, senior leaders do two-day reviews of the work of each department once a year.

A younger teacher felt that all of this represented an *interesting mix of formal observation and sharing of expertise*. Taking about younger staff, a head of department explained, *People aren't left to flounder here*. Remarkably, there seems to be little need to take more formal steps with regard to poor performance. Indeed, the head of one of the larger departments explained: *I've not had experience of a capability case in this school*.

Department roles. Each subject department seems to have its own approach to the marking of student work and book scrutiny. This has been developed and customised from a whole school Marking to Improve policy. One teacher explained that *the school standard is that books must be marked once every six lessons, although in our department we might do more sometimes*. A head of department talked about how her colleagues used learning walks to stimulate the sharing of ideas about teaching and learning. Commenting on the emphasis that is placed on mutual observation amongst staff, a deputy head said: *There is amazing practice here. Our challenge is to spread it across the school*. With this in mind, another teacher made reference to there being *an ethos of sharing practice*.

Heads of department explained their own approaches. One said, *We try to separate professional development from performance management*. In terms of student outcomes, another of the middle leaders explained, *We look at trends, not knee-jerk reactions to blips* – an idea that we had already heard stressed more than once by the principal.

Staff perspectives. Importantly, the principal frequently emphasised the importance of teachers as learners. As an example, he told the story of how he had encouraged a member of staff of Asian heritage to lead a workshop for his colleagues on how to cook curry. The principal explained: *This workshop was part of a staff 'wellbeing' activity – no students* *were present but it was good as a member of staff to learn in the same context as our students. It reminded me of having to ask lots of questions, wanting the 'teacher to check' my work (culinary insecurity), and of having my work (OK, my, quite frankly, delicious curry) scrutinized by others.*

Staff members made reference to the challenges that exist in some of the local districts, contrasting this with the atmosphere in the school. One described how a visitor had commented that he thought the school had a middle-class population, before expressing surprise on hearing the profile of their socio-economic backgrounds. Another teacher commented: *As a teacher I am surprised what happens in the community. We don't have that in school.*

Atmosphere. Walking around the school a pervasive positive working atmosphere was clearly evident wherever we went. It was also interesting to note that the school no longer needs to have an *on-call system* or withdrawal arrangements to deal with difficult behavior. Rather, difficulties are dealt with through staff cooperation within departments.

Interestingly, teachers recognise that the ways of working that were established under the previous headteacher continue to have an influence. There are, we were told, consistent expectations and an emphasis on maintaining routines, albeit within an atmosphere that is now far more relaxed. One teacher explained: *We still consolidate behaviour but now the main focus is on teaching and learning.* Another commented about how the ethos amongst the students has changed: *They come to work now.*

The principal is conscious of his own behavior in this respect, and the messages it gives to staff and students. He explained, for example, that he no longer expects the students to stand when he enters a room, explaining that this created an unnecessary interruption to the flow of a lesson. He added that, at first, some colleagues were uncomfortable about this change.

We noted that decisions about approaches to teaching and learning are also largely developed within individual departments, in whatever ways seem to be appropriate. So, for example, talking of how students are grouped for teaching, the principal explained: *We talk about it but the departments decide.* The principal commented that a wide range of approaches are possible but whatever is chosen *must be fully justified.*

What most surprised us most was that the students we met who had been in the school for the last five years or so also recognised the way that the school has developed. They were particularly conscious that the way they are dealt with has changed, not least in the sense that they are expected to take more responsibility for their own behaviour and learning. One student said: *There are many staff who want us to think outside the box. We are stretched academically.* At the same time, some students still feel that there is *too much focus on discipline.* In this respect we were not surprised to hear mention of the emphasis placed on wearing the correct uniform

Responding to diversity. The principal explained that there is now far less within-school variation in respect to quality of practice and student outcomes. Of particular note here is the examination results of those students from economically disadvantaged backgrounds. Having said all of that, Lakeside continues to face an enormous challenge of responding to differences within a richly diverse school community.

It was fascinating to hear the views of older students on this issue. In a way that suggested that this had been discussed with them on other occasions, they were able to see the *dilemmas* that it creates for the staff. In particular, they were able to debate the question of whether *fairness* meant treating everybody the same, or should it involve providing differential support to those with a greater need. By and large they favoured the second position, although this sometimes seems unfair. For example, one student felt that some of his classmates are *given more leeway*. And a high achieving girl commented, *Some of us are left to fend for ourselves sometimes*.

What was also striking was the fact that these young people were conscious of – and, indeed, could articulate – the way the school has changed over recent years. Noting the commitment to be a *world class school*, one student commented, *There is now a lot more drive from the senior leaders, so that they know where the issues lie*.

Navigating dilemmas. Our strong impression was that Lakeside is a school on the move. Whilst it does extremely well for most of its students, those involved are still not satisfied and want to do more.

With this in mind, the move towards greater freedom for staff to decide on how to move forward seem eminently sensible, as does the greater emphasis being placed on student involvement. Indeed, having had the privilege of hearing the views of some of the young people at the school, it struck us that this and many other schools could do much more to use their energy and insights to provide a *further* source of leadership for school improvement.

This account of Lakeside High School relates to the argument of Valli, Stefanski and Jacobson (2018) who suggest that school leaders working to enhance equity *must learn to navigate 'enduring' dilemmas, not simply solve problems* (2018, p. 34). These dilemmas include the need to open school boundaries to parents, the local community and other agencies, while also *protect[ing] the core … of teaching and learning against unnecessary and unproductive* (p. 34). The skills of leaders in managing such tensions, and building consensus and reciprocity around a shared sense of educational purpose, are therefore crucial. Furthermore, the more extensive developments become, and the more widely leadership is shared, the more these skills will be tested.

Conclusion

The accounts of practice presented in this chapter suggest that attempts to develop inclusive schools should pay attention to the building of consensus around shared values within school communities. This implies that school leaders must have a commitment to the ethics of *care* and *justice* and a capacity to lead in a participatory manner (Ehrich et al. 2015).

My experiences in England – as well as in Australia – have thrown light on some of the challenges involved in adopting such a stance within education systems dominated by standardised testing, leading to increased competition and marketisation of education. These challenges present dilemmas for school leaders as they attempt to maintain their own values in a policy context that pulls them in different directions. Meanwhile, these experiences remind us – in case we forget – that sustainable school improvement takes time.

All of this means that, in thinking about the use of the overall approach to the development of leadership practices described in this chapter, it is essential to recognise that it does not offer a simple recipe that can be lifted and transferred from place to place. Nor is it a quick fix. Rather, it defines an approach to improvement that uses processes of contextual analysis in order to determine strategies that fit particular circumstances. This involves an engagement with various forms of evidence, leading to the development of locally determined strategies. In this way, those involved probe beneath the surface of headline performance indicators to understand how local dynamics shape particular outcomes for students. In so doing, this helps to identify barriers to progress as well as resources that can inject pace into efforts to move things forward.

What is most distinctive about the approach is that it is mainly led from within schools. It is predictable, however, that this will lead to periods of organisational *turbulence* (Hopkins, Ainscow and West 1994). The nature of this phenomenon will vary from place to place, but in general it arises as a result of the reactions of individuals within a school to ideas and approaches that disrupt the status quo of their day-to-day lives. It is worth noting, however, that there is research evidence to suggest that without periods of turbulence, successful, long-lasting change is unlikely to occur. In this sense turbulence can be seen as a useful indication that things are on the move. At the same time, it underlines the importance of sensitive, supportive leadership.

7 Changing education systems

Oakwood High School serves a public housing estate in an English city, where the residents are mainly from economically disadvantaged backgrounds. For years the school has had a bad reputation in the area because of poor student attendance, behaviour and performance on national tests and examinations. However, the school year 2009–2010 saw a sudden and dramatic improvement. Student attendance improved significantly, and in the national examinations taken by students at the age of 16, the overall school performance improved by over 20%.

Across the city, about ten miles away, Victoria Grammar School, serves a very different community. There, students are selected for the school as a result of tests taken at the age of 11. In the main they come from relatively better-off families, indeed, some could be described as wealthy. Predictably, the performance of its students on national examinations is outstanding, making it an attractive choice for aspirational parents, many of whom move into the area in the hope that their youngsters will gain a place.

The rapid progress made at Oakwood arose as a result of its partnership with the Grammar School. Through this unusual relationship – involving the crossing of various social boundaries – new energy and expertise were made available to Oakwood. Commenting on what happened, the headteacher of the Grammar School explained:

> *I spend about three days a week over at Oakwood and one of my assistant headteachers works 50% of the time with the senior leadership team there to build capacity.*

She also commented on the benefits gained for her own school, not least with respect to the opportunities it had provided for some of her staff to address new professional challenges. This story is one of many examples of how partnerships of various kinds can help to stimulate improvements in practice and expectations.

DOI: 10.4324/9781003438014-7

Moving knowledge around

In their influential book, *The Spirit Level*, Wilkinson and Pickett (2009) seem to have situations like this in mind when they argue:

> *Although good schools make a difference, the biggest influence on educational attainment, how well a child performs in school and later in higher education, is family background.... Children do better if their parents have higher incomes, and do better if they come from homes where they have a place to study, where there are reference books and newspapers, and where education is valued.*
> *(pp. 103–105)*

My primary concern is with the challenges that are created by this type of inequality. Specifically, my focus is on finding more effective ways of creating schools that can *reach out* to all children and young people, whatever their personal characteristics and family circumstances.

As I have worked on improvement projects over the last 25 years, I have become increasingly aware of the extent to which schools can be supported in addressing this challenge through the creation of partnerships that can help *move knowledge around*, as in the one involving Oakwood and Victoria. Such arrangements are much influenced by contextual factors, not least those associated with national policies as they are implemented at the local area level.

With all of this in mind, in this chapter I draw on my experience of working with policy makers in attempting to move thinking and practice forward in relation to inclusion and equity. These examples all took place in the United Kingdom, where equity is a major concern within the four national education systems (Ainscow 2023). It is important to understand, however, that these initiatives tend to be focused on relatively narrow views of learning outcomes, as defined by the performance of students on tests of attainment.

My involvement in these projects was as a part-time adviser, where possible, using forms of collaborative inquiry to encourage innovations. This gave me privileged access to information about the way decisions are made within an education system, from the levels of government ministers, senior civil servants, school leaders and classroom teachers. It also provided frequent reminders of the cultural, social and political complexities involved when trying to bring about changes in the way that an education system does its business.

Reflecting on these experiences leads me to outline a series of propositions that can help create the conditions for promoting equity within education systems. I also illustrate the sorts of factors that make it difficult to implement these ideas, including the current emphasis on the so-called *what works* approach to educational improvement.

A city-wide strategy

Much of the earlier literature on school improvement underplays the significance of local context. There is, however, research to suggest that what goes on at the district level has a significant role to play with respect to processes of school improvement (e.g. Elmore 2004; Fullan and Gallagher 2020; Hargreaves and Ainscow 2015).

Between 2004 and 2006, my colleague Andy Howes and I carried out a study on behalf of the government of an improvement process known as *Transforming Secondary Education* in a city where the performance of the school system was a cause for considerable concern. The initiative attempted to use collaboration within four networks of secondary schools as the main route to sustainable higher achievement (Ainscow and Howes 2007).

Since collaboration is essentially a social process, we felt that it was important to pay attention to the various perspectives of those involved, including teachers and other members of staff, school leaders, local authority officers and the private company working with them – and to observe and reflect on how they worked together in pursuit of the objectives. Our conclusions were drawn from variations in responses to this process in the various collaborative groupings. These variations suggested that the necessary negotiation of interdependent relationships between schools, local authorities and their wider communities requires increasingly skilful and considered approaches from leaders at all levels in the system. The evidence of the study supports the idea that this is particularly true in the general context of competing educational agendas and uncertainty about forms of governance.

Certainly, some features of the local educational context at the beginning of this process were not conducive to the establishment of systematic and sustainable collaborative working. Schools in the city had long competed for students, and, at the stage of transition to secondary school, student migration was widespread as more aspirational parents sought out places in relatively high-attaining schools. In addition, falling roles required the closure of two secondary schools during the two years of the project.

Our research led us to a positive conclusion about the role that collaboration played in creating pathways for improvement in the city. After a relatively short period, the schools demonstrated how collaborative arrangements can provide an effective means of solving immediate problems, such as staff shortages; how they can have a positive impact during periods of crisis, such as during the closure of a school; and, how, in the longer run, schools working together can contribute to the raising of aspirations and attainment in schools that have had a record of low achievement. Meanwhile, statistical data showed that attainment levels increased between 2002 and 2004 in all four groupings. There was also strong evidence that collaboration helped reduce the polarisation of the education system, to the particular benefit of those students who are on the edges of the system and performing relatively poorly, although the impact was uneven.

However, none of what we found applied across the board – each of the 18 secondary schools, and the people managing and developing them, had their own orientations, ethos and context, and it would be arrogant to assume that their intentions, capabilities and achievements can be summed up in a few pages. Nevertheless, we drew out some lessons that proved to be relevant to the other system change initiatives described later in this chapter.

The project involved the creation of what were referred to as quadrants of schools. Additional government funding (in excess of £1 million) was provided to support the process, and a private company was hired to work alongside the local authority in setting up the project. Whilst whole-hearted involvement in the project could not be mandated, the assumption was that all the city secondary schools would participate. In practice, most schools were enthused by the prospect of collaborating in small groups, although a minority of schools were less willing.

Developing the strategy

A steering group was set up to manage the project. This included the director of education and other senior officers, representative headteachers, experienced staff from another local authority, senior government advisers and staff from the private company. On a day-to-day basis, the core project team consisted of just two people: a member of the private company (himself a highly regarded local ex-headteacher) and a local authority officer working full-time on the initiative. Early on, the private company played an essential role in creating additional capacity for brokering between schools.

Headteachers were consulted extensively over the membership of the quadrants, which were organised not on geographical proximity but in order to bring together schools at different stages of development and with varied levels of success in examinations. Representatives from schools in another local authority with a history of collaborative working were attached to each quadrant. As I explain later in this chapter, these features offered leads for what was to develop later in Greater Manchester and Wales.

The project design featured a *twin-track* approach. The first track involved short-term initiatives aiming at assisting schools in raising standards for all students. In particular, the goal was to meet the then Government's *floor target* requirements within two years, according to which all schools were to have at least 25% of their Year 11 students attaining five or more A* to C GCSE grades. These initiatives included the production of revision guides in some subjects, booster classes for students just under the attainment targets and rapid introduction of alternative courses taught with additional staffing in key areas. Some of these initiatives were put in place through coordination between schools at a subject level. Unusually, teachers were paid additional money for attending project meetings outside of school. These activities were promoted through collaborative structures and encouraged some sharing of ideas and experiences. However, they entailed little collaboration between staff in the schools.

The second track was a longer term strategy based on strengthening collaboration amongst the city's schools. As a relatively small local authority, the city's education department was seen to have insufficient resources to meet all the development needs of schools without input from expertise already located in the schools. Collaboration was intended to facilitate more sharing of resources than had proved possible under earlier schemes. The implication too was that changing relationships between schools would gradually be mirrored by changing relationships with officers of the education department. With this in mind, a school improvement adviser was allocated to work with each school grouping.

Collaboration in action

Significantly, the four school groups developed in quite different ways, reflecting their varied contexts and histories. It is helpful, therefore, to consider accounts that describe these differences, highlighting significant developments in each case.

> **Account 7.1. Quadrant A** consisted of four schools: a strong traditional foundation school, a school that had reopened after failing to improve following inspection, one newly opened school and one marked for closure. They were geographically closer than those in the other groupings, and a particularly close collaboration developed through the sharing of resources. Headteachers decided to manage the group directly, to ensure that activities fitted in with existing school development priorities. They quickly learned that they could rely on each other for support and challenge, as noted by one of the heads: *The project takes pressure off people... Knowing that you can ring someone galvanises you to do things sometimes.*
>
> At that stage, whilst encouraging collaboration as a general principle, the group only involved teachers where it fulfilled a strategic need that they had identified.
>
> A critical stage for this group concerned the closure of one of the four schools and the *takeover* of the buildings by a stronger school – which could have caused great conflict. In practice, the help given by the group resulted in the school's final cohort of students attaining more highly in examinations than their predecessors in previous years. This is significant in that often school closures lead key staff to move on, leaving a feeling of a sinking ship. The school grouping helped to avoid this by creating a sense of continuity, working together on joint projects, sharing resources, and requiring staff newly appointed to the group to work in the school for the first year of their contract.
>
> The head of the closing school explained that *we were able to get at a field of staff which we couldn't get at before.* Significantly, too, the school continued to offer some resources in return. The other headteachers were a ready source of support and advice for him (*I'll go to them much quicker than to the local authority, if I have an issue*) and he was able to offer strong teachers in subjects, such as art, to work part-time in the other schools, to everyone's benefit.

A lot was learnt from this process. The headteacher of the traditional school talked of *bussing by consent*, describing the possibilities for creating a good social mix in all the schools in the group. There was an *important* social dimension to this, which suggested that increased collaboration amongst schools may be an important way of tackling the ethnic divide building up between schools in the city.

Account 7.2. Quadrant B successfully developed a sustainable working pattern as a result of a struggle to be more strategic about collaboration for improvement. The five secondary schools involved, together with another school from the partner local authority, worked in diverse contexts and with varied levels of attainment. The headteachers quickly decided that they were committed to the project and to each other, prioritising their meetings, speaking openly about difficulties, focusing increasingly on teaching and learning, and contributing substantial funds to a communal pot. The decision to appoint and pay for a coordinator at the level of deputy headteacher was critical in creating greater capacity for sustained collaboration after the end of the funded project.

One school was in the special measures category following inspection and benefited from a pot of additional money, as the headteacher explained: *Our thanks to the other schools for the financial support for continuing collaboration – it is extraordinary.*

Interestingly, the school in trouble contributed significantly to the group. In this case, their inspection-driven focus on teaching and learning influenced the other schools to pay more direct attention to classroom processes. All the schools had skilful teachers who actively assisted counterpart departments in other schools in the group. This process began through an orchestrated training day and continued through individual contact, encouraged by school leaders.

The group coordinator was involved in making connections, such as facilitating support for particular teachers at the struggling school and linking up with initiatives that were otherwise seen as *innovation overload*. However, her role was full of uncertainty, which required her to go beyond institutional structures, resulting in periodic dilemmas as to where she should place her effort. She more than anyone grappled with the question, *How do we set something up which is sustainable?* It was this struggle that led to a group application for another government initiative and a consequent reshaping of stated priorities, whilst maintaining the significant relationships that the group had built.

Moving on, Quadrant C comprised five schools, one of which was, at the time, a new-style *city academy*, another of which had already become successful in improving achievement amongst learners from disadvantaged backgrounds, and three schools said to be in challenging circumstances.

Account 7.3. Quadrant C. Collaboration in this group was first and foremost a mechanism for working effectively with externally available resources. A particular focus was the 14–19 curriculum, and the production of joint resources for revision and supported self-study. Progress was impeded, however, by the expectation that all schools would participate. One headteacher in particular chose not to engage with the project, saying that it did not address *real problems*, and that leaders of schools in challenging circumstances did not have time for planning meetings.

Only once the group had agreed to appoint a coordinator was there a significant push forward with activities. As the coordinator said: *I'm making myself the focus for their loyalty. I'm the person who will be banging on the door complaining if they don't do what they said they would. I'm encouraging them to take part.*

The experience of this group supported the argument that collaboration requires the commitment of key stakeholders and that self-interest is, in practice, a predictable and important component of inter-dependency. This suggests that a necessary (but not sufficient) condition for a successful large-scale intervention based on collaboration is an appeal to self-interest and not simply altruism.

Account 7.4. Quadrant D. This group included five secondary schools: four seen to be *facing challenging circumstances* and one that at the outset of the project had been placed in *special measures* by the national inspection agency, Ofsted. The fifth school was a large, highly successful voluntary aided school affiliated to a large church. There was also a special school linked to the group.

Although collaborative activities were slow to materialise across this quadrant, the sense of imposition was a mainly positive factor: *It was imposed on us, otherwise we certainly would not have seen it as a priority. But you can't make the gelling happen.*

New headteachers were appointed to three of the five schools over the period of the project and this slowed down collaboration, although it did not prevent it. Initial activities were well received but unfocused. Gradually, however, initiatives involving the sharing of resources between schools took shape. One example concerned English teaching, where the headteachers together paid for and managed a shared member of staff. One of them explained:

We realised in a group meeting that we were all in dire straights in English. Only one school had a head of English. The headteacher there said I've got an excellent teacher who is looking to move. Our local authority adviser knew the teacher, and she managed and facilitated the appointment. It is a middle leader post, and we four schools each share a quarter of the cost.

This was a strategic development for schools whose relatively patchy reputation was making it impossible for them to appoint suitably qualified teachers. It was later repeated in other subjects, such as music, where three schools were unable to offer the subject because of a lack of qualified staff, while another school in the group had more than ten music teachers. The group tackled the problem through another initiative to share resources, by coordinating a joint link with influential institutions beyond school in a way that individual schools would find impossible.

Drawing lessons

The striking observation from these accounts of the developments in the quadrants is how each of the school groupings quickly became distinctive. Nevertheless, our analysis of examination results, together with an understanding of what processes were taking place in schools through the project, suggested strongly that there was a positive impact on student attainment in all of the quadrants. It is impossible to be sure that this would not have occurred without an emphasis on collaboration, but previous years' results suggested that this was unlikely.

From an early stage there was also evidence in some of the quadrants of a critical edge to discussions about priorities and what they really needed to address. However, as one local officer explained, '... *within school groupings, the primary thing is to preserve the harmony of the group*'.

In some cases, explicit challenges were apparent but this had not been easy to achieve. So, for example, peer review amongst groups of heads proved difficult to engage in initially. However, such review processes, supported by local authority officers, were eventually carried out in all groups and widely seen as a useful and productive process. It seems, therefore, that collaboration involves working not with an abstract or distant model of *good practice*, but through learning directly from partner schools what is possible in the context of the inevitable tensions and compromises with which school leaders and teachers have to deal.

The stories of the four groups show how headteachers with different priorities tended to emphasise different resolutions of these tensions and how these differences can be very productive. The different levels of provision for lower and higher attaining students in schools in Quadrant A, for example, led to a productive exchange of resources and mutual learning and eventually to a systematic widening of the curriculum on offer through course places for students from the other schools. Meanwhile, in Quadrant D, the direct link with the special school led to developmental work on areas that might have otherwise received little attention in the push for targets.

As we saw, in two of the school groupings coordinators played an important role in sustaining improvement efforts in the context of competing pressures. It was noticeable, for example, how they were able to create momentum through particular projects, seeking out opportunities, and building allegiances. On some occasions, they were seen to hold back where they judged attempts to engage in a collaborative effort to be counterproductive. This led us to conclude that collaboration for school improvement requires someone who can take challenges to a headteacher, or group of heads, and, at the same time, maintain a forward-looking dialogue that helps to expand horizons beyond the individual school.

The evidence of this study offered important pointers for what was needed in order to facilitate progress in relation to equity across an education system. In particular, it pointed to certain conditions that are necessary in order to make school-to-school collaboration effective. These are as follows:

- The development of relationships amongst schools serving different districts and, in some instances, from another local authority;
- The presence of incentives that encourage key stakeholders to explore the possibility that collaboration will be in their own interests;
- Headteachers and other senior staff in schools who are willing and skilled enough to drive collaboration forward towards collective responsibility, coping with inevitable uncertainties and turbulence;
- The creation of common improvement agendas that are seen to be relevant to a wide range of stakeholders; and
- Coherent external support from credible consultants/advisers (from the local authority or elsewhere) who have the confidence to learn alongside their school-based partners, exploring and developing new roles and relationships where necessary

This experience also led us to conclude that national policy makers would be naive to overlook the influence of what happens at the local level. This is particularly so in urban contexts, where local history, interconnections between schools and established relationships are always significant.

Just to add, during a visit to the city some ten years after the *Transforming Secondary Education* project, a teacher informed me that Quadrant C was still going strong. Incidents like this remind us that the full impact of time-limited initiatives is likely to take time. Of course, this does not fit with the timelines of policy makers who are likely to have the next election in mind.

Together with evidence about the limits of improvement based on individual schools, this particular study suggested that a national education strategy for improving opportunities for all students, in all schools, requires the systematic and locally organised redistribution of available resources and expertise through a contextually sensitive strategy for collaboration. This thinking was to influence the development of City Challenge, a major initiative to promote equity across urban conurbations in England, which began in London.

London Challenge

As noted earlier, the English education system is a particularly relevant context when thinking about the challenge of equity, as noted in a 2007 OECD study which reported that the impact of socio-economic circumstances on young people's attainments was more marked than in any other of the 52 countries considered. Benn and Millar (2006) argue that one of the biggest problems the country faces is *the gap between rich and poor, and the enormous disparity in children's home backgrounds and the social and cultural capital they bring to the educational table* (page 145).

In seeking to address this concern, various interventions were launched in England during the period of Labour Governments (1997–2010). This led to a series of centralised national strategies to strengthen practices of teaching and leadership. At the same time, competition between schools was seen to be one of the keys to *driving up standards*, whilst further reducing the control of local authorities over provision.[1] All of this was intended to *liberate* schools from the bureaucracy of local government and establish a form of market place. In this way, it was argued, families would have greater choice as to which school their children would attend, informed by school reports from the national inspection agency, Ofsted, and the annual publication of school test and examination results.

During that period, there were also a number of policy efforts to address factors which lie beyond schools. These recognised that children's academic progress cannot be divorced from other aspects of their development and what happens to them outside school – in their families, neighbourhoods and more widely. These initiatives sought to improve and equalise educational outcomes, by aligning schools' core business of teaching and learning with interventions targeting other aspects of children's lives. All of this was part of a Children's Plan which set out a framework for organising child and family services based on the principle that *Every Child Matters*, i.e. that all children should be healthy, stay safe, enjoy and achieve, make a positive contribution and achieve economic well-being.

London Challenge was a further element in this reform programme. This initiative began in 2003, concentrating on the improvement of secondary schools. By 2007, Ofsted was reporting that standards in these schools had improved *dramatically* and that the city recorded its best ever examination results, with its state secondary school students leading the rest of the country for the third year running (Ainscow 2015).

As a result of their research into the implementation of the London Challenge, Kidson and Norris (2014) conclude that it was a distinctive example of public service improvement that was practitioner-focused, highly collaborative and applied across a system. They note, too, that all the people they interviewed felt that the initiative had made a major contribution to the exceptional improvement in the capital's schools. This was attributed to: the way credible professionals supported their peers; the powerful sense of moral purpose and positive framing; and the close working relationships of officials, advisers and ministers, which was focused on a shared, data-led view of where there was strength and weakness in the schools.

There are, however, a range of other views about what made the difference in London. For example, Lowe (2015) points out that other government interventions taking place around the same time may also have had an impact. He mentions Teach First, a graduate recruitment scheme launched in 2002 to coax top young graduates into the classroom, which was widely used in London. He also notes the possible impact of the national inspection agency, Ofsted, and new transparency in relation to school results. In addition, Lowe argues that the role of primary schools cannot be ignored, noting that the national strategies in literacy and numeracy were perhaps taken up far more enthusiastically in London than elsewhere. Burgess (2014) introduces another perspective, suggesting that the basis for London's progress was the ethnic composition of its school population. It is worth noting, too, that there is a view that London schools benefited from preferential financing.

A further worrying factor that should not be overlooked are subsequent reports that London schools had seen increases in both temporary and permanent exclusion rates.[2] This reminds me of a comment made by a key figure involved in the London Challenge who referred to how they had learnt to *pull some tricks* in order to improve results. All of this underlines the complexities involved in system change and the problems that exist when trying to establish the nature of the *local causality* at play within it (Hadfield and Jopling 2018).

In the light of this success, in 2008 the government extended the London programme for a further three years and expanded it to primary schools. At the same time, the creation of a generic City Challenge programme was announced that would include two other regions, the Black Country, in the West Midlands, and Greater Manchester. Meanwhile, the academic debates to determine what were the key features of the *London effect* have continued.

The Greater Manchester Challenge

In 2007 I was appointed as the Chief Adviser for the Greater Manchester Challenge, a three-year initiative involving over 1,100 schools in ten local authorities, with a government investment of around £50 million (see Ainscow 2015, for a detailed account of this initiative). The decision to invest this large amount reflected a concern regarding educational standards in the city region, particularly amongst children and young people from disadvantaged backgrounds. It is important to note that both the London and Greater Manchester Challenge programmes each had the active involvement of a Government Minister. In terms of the impact, the presence of high-status political leadership should not be overlooked.

An analysis of the context led to the conclusion that plenty of good practices existed across Greater Manchester schools. Consequently, it was decided that collaboration and networking between schools of the sort that had occurred in London would be key strategies for strengthening the overall capacity of the system to reach out to vulnerable groups of learners. More specifically this involved a series of interconnected activities for *moving knowledge around* in order to build a self-improving school system (Ainscow 2012, 2015).

In an attempt to engage all schools in the Greater Manchester city region in processes of networking and collaboration, as in London, Families of Schools were set up, using a data system that groups schools on the basis of the prior attainment of their students and their socio-economic home backgrounds. There were 58 primary and 11 secondary Families, each of which had between 12 and 20 schools from different local authorities. The strength of this approach is that it grouped together schools that served similar populations whilst, at the same time, encouraging partnerships amongst schools that were not in direct competition with one another because they did not serve the same neighbourhoods.

Figure 7.1 is a graph taken from the Families of Schools data system. It illustrates how schools within a Family can be compared in terms of the overall attainment levels of their students (i.e. the horizontal axis) and the improvements that have occurred over the previous three years (i.e. the vertical axis). So, for example, in this case – which is for secondary Family 6 – why does school number 1 seem to be doing so poorly compared with schools 15 and 98?

Such varied performance amongst Family members offers possibilities for using differences as a resource to stimulate the sharing of expertise and joint efforts to innovate in order to: improve the performance of every school; increase the numbers of outstanding schools; reduce the gap between high and low performing groups of learners; and improve outcomes for particular vulnerable groups of students.

We found, however, that for this to happen schools had to dig more deeply into the comparative data in order to expose areas of strength that can be

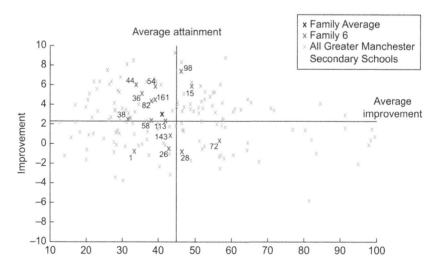

Figure 7.1 Families of schools.

used to influence performance across their Family, whilst also identifying areas for improvement in every school. In so doing, they must be wary of the dangers associated with what Simon (1978) refers to as *satisficing*. This involves attempts to meet criteria for adequacy, leading to an acceptance of a merely satisfactory outcome, rather than aiming for the best possible levels of improvement.

With this in mind, the average performance for each Family – both in terms of overall attainment and recent improvement trends – provided a benchmark against which overall goals for each of the partner schools could be set. At the same time, the analysis of data with regard to sub-groups of students (e.g. boys and girls; those eligible to free school meals; minority groups) and different subject areas also enabled a Family to work on the issue of within-school variations. The collective goal was then to move all of the Family members in a *north-easterly* direction on the performance graph.

In thinking about how to make this happen, we found that it was important to be sensitive to the limitations of statistical information. What brings such data to life is when *insiders* start to scrutinise and ask questions as to their significance, bringing their detailed experiences and knowledge to bear on the process of interpretation. The occasional involvement of colleagues from partner schools can deepen such processes, not least because of the ways in which they may see things, or ask questions, that those within a school may be overlooking.

Even then there remain limitations that need to be kept in mind. Statistics present patterns of what exists: they not only tell us what things are like but also give little understanding as to why things are as they are or how they came to be like that. This is why qualitative evidence is needed to supplement statistical data. For example, our earlier research had demonstrated how mutual observation amongst colleagues and listening to the views of learners can be a powerful means of challenging thinking and provoking experimentation (Ainscow, Booth and Dyson 2006). Again, here, there is potential for schools to support one another in collecting and engaging with such evidence in a way that has the potential to make the familiar unfamiliar.

Led by headteachers, the Families of Schools proved to be successful in strengthening collaborative processes within the city region. So, for example, primary schools in one Family worked together to strengthen leadership in each school. This included headteachers visiting one another to carry out *learning walks*, during which colleagues had opportunities to reflect upon and debate noticeable differences in practices. Eight schools in another primary Family identified a shared desire to build stronger relationships with the children's homes – for example, parents of children with English as an additional language where there were communication issues or groups of students with lower attendance.

In the secondary sector, schools within one of the Families used a web-based system where students could showcase their work via podcasts, videos and blogs, allowing teachers, parents and students from their own and other schools to view and comment on their efforts. Talking about his school's involvement, a highly experienced secondary headteacher commented, *This is the most powerful strategy for school improvement I have experienced.*

However, involvement of schools in the Families remained patchy, and there were concerns that too often those who might most benefit chose not to do so. Our monitoring of what went on suggested certain conditions that lead to higher involvement and a greater impact on student achievement. These are a collective commitment to improve the learning of every student, in every school in the group; an analysis of statistical data, using professional insights in order to identify areas that need addressing; pinpointing expertise within the schools that can be used to address these concerns; collaborative activities involving people at different levels, including, in some instances, children and young people; and a small number of headteachers taking on the role of leading these collaborative activities

In moving collaboration forward in a way that supports development within a Family of Schools, we found that shared leadership was a central driver. This required the development of leadership practices that involve many stakeholders in sharing responsibility. Often this necessitated significant changes in beliefs and attitudes, and new relationships, as well as improvements in practice. The goal was to ensure that collaboration was between school communities, and not restricted to headteachers, since arrangements that rely on one person are unlikely to survive the departure of those individuals who brokered them.

In terms of schools *working* in the most disadvantaged contexts, more intensive school partnerships were found to be the most powerful means of fostering improvements (Hutchings et al. 2012). Most notably, the *Keys to Success* programme led to striking improvements in the performance of some 200 Greater Manchester schools facing the most challenging circumstances. A common feature of almost all of these interventions was that progress was achieved through carefully matched pairings (or, sometimes, trios) of schools that, once again, cut across social *boundaries* of various kinds, including those that separate schools that are in different local authorities (Ainscow 2013). In this way, expertise that was previously trapped in particular contexts became more widely available.

Whilst increased collaboration of this sort proved to be vital as a strategy for developing more effective ways of working, the experience of Greater Manchester shows that it was not enough. The essential additional ingredient was an engagement with evidence that can bring an element of mutual challenge to such collaborative processes. We found that evidence was at its most powerful where partner schools were carefully matched and knew what they were trying to achieve. Evidence also helped schools go beyond cosy relationships that have no impact on outcomes. Consequently, schools need to base their relationships on evidence about each other's strengths and weaknesses, so that they can challenge each other to improve.

Another effective strategy to facilitate the movement of expertise was the creation of various types of hub schools. For example, some of the hubs provided support for other schools about ways to engage students with English as an additional language. Similarly, so-called teaching schools[3] providing professional development programmes focused on bringing about improvements in classroom practice.

A key factor in the success of both the London and Greater Manchester Challenge programmes was the involvement of teams of expert advisers. Chosen because of their track records of leading successful school improvement, they were given the mandate and resources to intervene in schools, helping them to develop, implement and monitor the impact of their own improvement plans.

An independent evaluation of the City Challenge programme concluded that it had been largely successful in achieving its objectives (Hutchings et al. 2012). Commenting on this, the authors of the report argue:

> *Clearly a great many factors contributed to these improvements, including national policies and strategies and the considerable efforts of head teachers and staff. However, these factors apply everywhere in the country. The most plausible explanation for the greater improvement in Challenge areas is that the City Challenge programme was responsible. The vast majority of stakeholders at all levels who contributed to this evaluation attributed the additional improvements that have been made in these areas to the work of City Challenge.*
>
> *(p. vi)*

The evaluators also concluded that the strategic factors contributing to its success were the timescale; the focus on specific urban areas; the flexibility of approach; the use of expert advisers and bespoke solutions; school staff learning from practice in other schools; and the programme ethos of trust, support and encouragement. These factors were to inform another system-change development, across the border in Wales.

A national initiative in Wales

In 2014 I was invited by the Welsh Government to lead Schools Challenge Cymru, a national initiative to promote equity across the country, the design of which was much influenced by what had happened in City Challenge. Wales shares a close political and social history with the rest of Great Britain, and almost everyone speaks English. However, the country has retained a distinct cultural identity and is officially bilingual, with Welsh being spoken by about 20% of the population, mostly in the north and west of the country. Although it is part of the United Kingdom, Wales has a form of self-government created in 1998 following a referendum and has its own education policies. There are 22 local authorities responsible for a range of public services, including education.

Wales is small, with about 3.1 million inhabitants. The performance of its school system has long been a cause for concern, particularly in terms of outcomes for learners from low-income families, as noted in an OECD country review (2014). Most significantly, the review argued that whilst the pace of reform in recent years had been high, it has lacked a long-term vision, an adequate school improvement infrastructure and a clear implementation strategy that all stakeholders share.

The review noted that the system has many strengths but suggested a number of concrete policy options that would strengthen it over the longer term. It advocated the development of a long-term vision which could be translated into measurable objectives. In response to this the Welsh government instigated a five-year reform plan for the education of 3- to 19-year-old learners. The plan, entitled *Qualified for Life*, provided a timeline for key activities and identified immediate measures to be taken. One of these was the introduction of Schools Challenge Cymru.

Launched in 2014, the purpose of the initiative was to accelerate progress across the education system. In particular, it aimed to bring about rapid improvements in the performance of schools serving the more disadvantaged communities and use lessons from these developments to strengthen the capacity of the education system to improve itself. The budget was approximately 20 million pounds per year.

Building on the earlier experiences in London and Greater Manchester, the Welsh initiative worked with 40 secondary schools serving disadvantaged communities (designated as the *Pathways to Success*) and their local primary school partners. Similar to City Challenge, a team of advisers were involved in supporting these schools. In addition, a small group of champions advised on the overall strategic direction of the initiative.

The advisers and champions were directly accountable to the Minister for Education and Skills. As was the case in City Challenge, the Minister was closely associated with the initiative, visiting each of the schools at least twice over the first 18 months. This provided the political mandate that Claeys et al. (2014) argue is essential to improvement strategies that mainly emphasise bottom-up action.

The results over the first two years showed that overall attainment in examinations taken by almost all students at the age of 16, across the Pathways to Success schools, improved by 7.0 percentage points, with 87% of the schools securing improvements in this measure. This rate of improvement was faster than the overall progress made across Wales over the same period. Meanwhile, the attainment of students entitled to free school meals[4] across the schools improved by 8.2 percentage points, with 74% of the schools securing improvements.

In making sense of these trends, it is important to remember that the participating schools were chosen because of the challenges they face and the fact that they had, to varying degrees, performed poorly over many years. Some of them became striking examples of what is possible when the expertise and energy within schools are mobilised. However, these gains were hard-won and likely to remain fragile without continuing support.

Beyond the 40 schools, there was evidence, too, that Schools Challenge Cymru began to have a ripple effect across the education system in ways that raised expectations about how rapidly improvements can be achieved (Hadfield and Ainscow 2018). This has implications for efforts to improve outcomes for learners from economically disadvantaged families, where low expectations can be a factor in preventing their progress (Kerr and West 2010).

An independent evaluation of Schools Challenge Cymru concluded that the quality of leadership and management had improved in the majority of Pathways to Success schools (Carr, Brown and Morris 2017). In two-fifths of the schools, involvement in the programme was considered to be largely, or wholly, responsible for the changes in student engagement. Some schools were optimistic about sustaining perceived improvements in student attendance, hoping that good attendance becomes the norm. The report also concluded that the programme had strengthened professional development within the schools.

Barriers to implementation

Common to the system-wide improvement initiatives I have described was an emphasis on bottom-up leadership within a context of top-down political mandate, and the use of evidence to inform to stimulate innovation and collaboration within and between schools, and with community partners. However, we found that the implementation of such thinking was sometimes difficult because of a series of interconnected contextual barriers (Ainscow, Chapman and Hadfield 2020). Broadly stated, these relate to the following:

- **Social factors**, including the extent to which relationships exist that encourage the sharing of expertise through mutual support and challenge;
- **Political factors**, due to the impact of the attitudes and preferences of key partners; and
- **Cultural factors**, created by local traditions and the expectations of those involved as to what is possible.

In what follows I reflect on my involvement in these earlier projects, plus more recent experiences of the Scottish Attainment Challenge and a number of other smaller place-based developments in England, in order to make sense of these barriers (see Ainscow, Chapman and Hadfield 2020, for accounts of these initiatives).

Social factors. It does seem that size is an important factor, as illustrated by this example.

VIGNETTE 7.1   Size matters

I contributed to planning in a small rural district, where there were concerns about poor standards in the schools. To an outsider with lots of urban experience, the closeness of the links between headteachers in this community seemed to be a positive feature in terms of the encouragement of greater collaboration.

In line with the thinking developed in this book, I encouraged a restructuring that would enable existing good practices within local schools to be made available to more students and encourage joint practice developments. This was to be achieved through the strengthening of various forms of cooperation between the schools. It required new roles for headteachers, some of whom volunteered to take on the task of leading these developments. With this in mind, I consulted with all the heads within the authority. As a result, a new momentum for change quickly emerged in the primary sector, where a group of five relatively successful headteachers took on responsibility for moving things forward.

In discussing their roles, these heads commented on the social complexities they faced in getting colleagues to cooperate. In particular, they commented on the implications of the fact that amongst schools in a small community, *everybody knows one another*. They explained that relationships were usually warm and cordial, something that I certainly experienced. However, it was also apparent that this closeness between colleagues had the potential to create subtle barriers to genuine collaboration between schools. One headteacher summed this up when she said, '*we don't bare our souls around here*'. In other words, if you have a problem in your school, you keep it to yourself. Clearly, such a social climate can make it difficult for colleagues to support one another. It also means that the external researcher – there to support and advise – faces what may well be hidden barriers to an understanding of the dynamics of the local school system.

It follows that the involvement of an *outsider*, acting in the role of adviser, requires constructive relationships with key partners. I have found that maintaining such relationships creates many dilemmas that usually have to be addressed when and where they occur. For example, a meeting was held with senior officers in one local authority where we were concerned about the poor quality of support provided for primary schools. At times the meeting became heated, as authority staff attempted to challenge our analysis, and one colleague in particular was clearly distressed. Indeed, at one point he explained that he had never felt so personally humiliated during his long professional career. This particular meeting did not lead to an immediate outcome that could be described as being positive. Nevertheless, I felt that it was necessary to intervene in a context where thinking and practices were limiting opportunities for children. Subsequently, a series of further meetings did lead to an agreement as to necessary actions to strengthen the work of this particular local authority in supporting its schools.

In reflecting on incidents such as this one, I am occasionally reminded of Robert Bales' theory of group systems that we had used in earlier research (see Ainscow, Hargreaves and Hopkins 1995). As Bales predicts, attempts to get different stakeholders to pull together lead to tensions between the need to establish cohesion amongst groups and taking actions to achieve our goals. It is relatively easy to maintain cooperation until the moments when hard decisions have to be made, most particularly regarding the setting of priorities and the allocation of resources.

Political factors. The most striking evidence of the political nature of large-scale system change projects occurred following two national elections. This led to new ministers being appointed and, as a result, the Challenge projects losing much of their political mandate. The projects did continue, however, although with less power to make things happen. Having said that, in the case of one of the initiatives, we have recent empirical evidence of the continuing impact of its legacy six years later, most strikingly in terms of partnerships and networks (Armstrong and Ainscow 2018).

The programmes emerged during an unprecedented period of change within their education systems, not least in terms of decision-making regarding education policy. The ways in which decisions were made regarding changes varied across the countries. England was in the process of giving schools much greater autonomy, especially in the use of financial resources and the appointment of staff members. This also lead to a much greater role for headteachers as system leaders, working together to coordinate collaborative improvement efforts. In all of the contexts, the role of the local authority in the management of the school system was being questioned and, in the case of England, massively reduced over the past three decades (Salokangas and Ainscow 2017).

Meanwhile, Wales and Scotland continued in a much more centralised way, with decisions mainly shared between the national government and local authorities. In both countries there are continuing tensions between these two levels regarding policies, the determination of priorities and the use of resources.

During the setting up phases of the Challenge programmes, much use was made by government officials of the term *partnership* in describing what was to happen. I sensed that for some local authority colleagues, this was a source of irritation, in that the decisions to have the initiatives were largely imposed by national governments as processes of intervention in areas of concern.

One factor behind these tensions were different views as to what needed to happen in order to improve education systems: put bluntly, a difference between those who believe in locally led development and others who continue to adopt a centralising perspective. For example, the latter view was starkly expressed in an email sent to colleagues within the DfES in London during the City Challenge period, which stated that, as far as improving attainment amongst disadvantaged students was concerned, *the strategy must be exactly the same, whether it is in Plymouth (in the south west of England), or in Sunderland (in the far north east).* The implication is that we know what to do: it therefore needs to be done irrespective of context.

VIGNETTE 7.2   Imposed priorities

An instinct to direct from the centre kept surfacing at meetings of the challenge advisers when civil servant colleagues took opportunities to brief the groups on the latest proposals from the central government and the necessity for reporting back to the central government through complex mechanisms. In general, the teams found these inputs helpful in that they made them feel ahead of the game regarding policy decisions, although the bureaucratic reporting and accountability systems were perceived to be frustrating and heavy-handed. In these cases, my concern was that, too often, the meetings gave the wrong message with respect to the theory of change we had adopted.

A striking example of this, that created a significant distraction, was as a result of the publication of a White Paper about the reform of the English system. The civil servant who led on this initiative as far as primary schools was concerned became particularly dogged in her efforts to impose a centrally determined strategy on the schools. With this in mind, for some months she guided the agenda of the team of primary school advisers in a direction that represented a significant deviation from the rationale we had developed together. During this phase, my own involvement in decision-making was clearly marginalised.

Sustainability was a major concern in all of the initiatives. The history of large-scale, heavily funded improvement projects is that, even when they are seen to be initially successful, the impact gradually fades once the additional resources are taken away (Ainscow 2015). One way of addressing this problem is to strengthen the so-called middle tier, the administrative arrangements that are intended to coordinate the development of education provision within a local area. In Wales, for example, this meant the 22 local authorities, which are grouped together in four regional consortia that are intended to support school improvement efforts. There are, however, potential barriers to making such regional partnerships work, including the large geographical areas that they sometimes cover, competing philosophies and educational agendas and the struggles they can create regarding decision-making across political boundaries.

Within national systems such as Scotland that continue to emphasise top-down accountability, the responses of local authorities can also act as a barrier to school-level innovation. For example, one very experienced headteacher, appointed to improve a school in difficulty, talked about local authority officers frequently commenting negatively regarding the ways he dealt with minor administrative matters.

Cultural factors. Efforts to inject greater pace into the improvement of schools within the Challenge programmes drew attention to the untapped potential that exists within schools. They also threw light on the factors that had limited the impact of earlier improvement efforts. Our monitoring suggested that these barriers mainly relate to existing ways of working, which, although well intended, consume time and resources and delay action in the field. A Welsh headteacher echoed the views of many others when he commented that, in his part of the world, *school improvement is like trying to drive more quickly down a road with speed bumps every few yards.*

The experience of the Challenge programmes suggests that many of the *bumps* relate to existing ways of working, which reflect taken-for-granted assumptions as to what is possible. Although well intended, these traditions often consume time and resources and delay action. They include, for example, the overemphasis placed by some local authorities on putting schools, particularly those facing challenging circumstances, under unnecessary pressure. This tends to demoralise the key agents of change, i.e. the staff in the schools. It can also lead to considerable time being wasted on debating and disputing plans and targets. My experience is that, whilst plans and target setting can be helpful, without powerful support strategies they are unlikely to lead to sustainable change.

Linked to this are actions by some local authority staff that limit the freedom of school leaders to take responsibility for their own improvement. In particular, we found that there were often multiple reporting arrangements, leading school leaders to spend too much time preparing reports for different audiences, attending various review and scrutiny meetings, and being given different (and at times conflicting) advice on the improvements required and how they can be achieved. Despite calls for the empowerment of schools and headteachers, this limited freedom can foster a sense of dependency on outsiders to lead improvement efforts, rather than empowering those in schools to take responsibility and be accountable for improved outcomes. In such situations, school leaders can feel undermined and disenfranchised. As a result, they tend to make poor decisions, and therefore find it more difficult to prioritise their improvement strategies.

In addressing these contextual barriers, efforts are needed to clarify the roles of local authorities. Specifically, this requires local authority staff to know, trust and support school personnel and provide appropriate encouragement to improve. These changes in roles and responsibilities are challenging during periods of transition, as locally led improvement strategies are developing, but they are precursors to achieving rapid progress.

There are also barriers related to the uncertainty that exists within governments about how to support the development of locally driven collaborative improvement. One step to reduce that uncertainty is to recognise that using the power of collaboration as a means of achieving equity in schools requires an approach to national policy implementation that fosters greater flexibility at the local level and gives practitioners the space to analyse their particular circumstances and determine priorities accordingly.

So, when thinking about system change, we must not ignore the impact of cultural factors. To take the example of Wales, almost all schools are part of a local authority and most children attend a school near to their home. In these senses the Welsh context seems to offer promising opportunities for the sorts of collaboration that seems so important for promoting inclusion and educational equity. However, this is more complicated than it might seem.

VIGNETTE 7.3 Cultural factors

I was told a story by the Welsh Government Minister I worked with on Schools Challenge Cymru about a tourist looking at a newly landed bucketful of lobsters on the quayside. As the lobsters writhed around, she asked a fisherman: *Don't you need to put a lid on the bucket? One of them could easily climb out. Don't you worry about that*, came the reply. *They are Welsh lobsters, the others will pull it back down.*

The Minister used this story to explain how the country's tightly knit educational community is both supportive and, at the same time, restrictive. It is restrictive in the sense that there is a reluctance amongst practitioners to put themselves or their innovatory practices forward for fear that they will be seen as *getting above themselves*. The solidarity of this tightly knit community can make it difficult for those within it to break with certain traditions or challenge existing norms without their actions being seen at least, in part, as a criticism or rejection of that community.

The significance of the lobster story is that it illustrates how existing local cultures, into which policies emerge, influence not only the nature of the existing system's response to the *new* but, crucially, also how they will continue to effect its development even after it has become established.

The story is a parable of how shared professional identities and collective agency influence developments within an education system over the longer term, way beyond the tenure of a particular government. This throws further light on the complexities involved in attempts to build research knowledge and processes into system change strategies.

Drawing lessons

In thinking about the complexities experienced in the contexts referred to in these accounts of system change initiatives, I am occasionally reminded of Karl Weick's argument that educational organisations should be understood as being *loosely coupled*. That is to say, they consist of units, processes, actions and individuals that tend to operate in isolation from one another. Weick illustrates this by describing an unconventional soccer match in which the field is round, with several goals scattered haphazardly around. He explains that players enter and leave the game whenever they want, saying *that's my goal*, as many times as they want. He adds that the entire game takes place on a sloped field and is played as if it makes sense (Weick 1985).

Bearing this complexity in mind, with colleagues, I proposed a way of thinking about system change in order to promote equity (Ainscow, Chapman and Hadfield 2020). This involves a series of interconnected propositions that point to a need for the following:

- **A shared understanding of overall purposes.** Many of the difficulties in implementing the initiatives described in this chapter originated from a lack of agreement about the intended outcomes. Given that change requires coordinated efforts across the different levels of an education system, an agreed and clear purpose is an essential condition. Reaching the required degree of clarity is both a cultural and political process in which there is a risk that certain voices might be overlooked, whilst others are over-privileged, and in which underpinning assumptions need to be challenged.
- **Ongoing contextual analysis of a system's existing capacity for collaborative improvement.** This has to be capable of providing a deeper analysis of the barriers that are limiting progress. At the same time, it should identify areas of promising practice, drawing out key learning and applying this to the development of the necessary human and social capital to support system-level improvement efforts. It is important that this analysis continues across different levels of the system.
- **Brokerage that crosses professional and social boundaries, within schools and across networks.** This is in order to increase exposure to various sources of expertise and innovative practice. It requires the orchestration of different forms of individual and organisational networks into integrated sub-systems capable of fostering system-level improvements, even in challenging circumstances.
- **The development of capacity for leadership at all levels of a system.** Leaders must be capable of initiating and steering collaborative learning within and between schools and within the wider community. This requires the micro-mobilisation of successful senior staff members to take on system leadership roles, in combination with the macro-mobilisation of enough school leaders at all levels to create a professional movement with sufficient momentum to overcome internal and external resistance.
- **The creation and maintenance of a strong political mandate at the national and local levels.** This is necessary to create the conditions within the system that support collaborative local action. It requires new thinking, attitudes and relationships across education systems. It also means that inequalities of power between elements of the system are addressed.

What connects these design principles is the way that they focus attention on the importance of managing and interconnecting individual, organisational and system-level learning, within complex transitional dynamics. These learning processes help to make the familiar unfamiliar in ways that challenge expectations as to what is possible, while drawing attention to examples of different ways of working that can act as the focus of joint practice development. In such contexts, the presence of researchers – acting as critical friends, drawing attention to relevant research evidence from elsewhere, and advising about how processes of inquiry can be built into strategies that are trialled – can make significant contributions (Chapman and Ainscow 2019).

Since effective change requires coordinated efforts at all levels of an education system, the use of these propositions has implications for the various key stakeholders within education systems. It requires teachers, especially those in senior positions, to see themselves as having a wider responsibility for all children and young people, not just those who attend their own schools. For those who administer district school systems, it means adjusting their priorities and ways of working in response to improvement efforts that are led from within schools. And for schools it means aligning what they do with the efforts of other local players – employers, community groups, universities, public services and so on – so that there is a coherent strategy focused on improving the lives of young people.

Finally, this has significant implications for national policy makers. In order to create the conditions within which this form of research-based change can occur, they need to foster greater flexibility at the local level so that practitioners, community partners and researchers have the space to work together. This means that policy makers must recognise that the details of policy implementation are not amenable to central regulation. Rather, they have to be dealt with by those who are close to and, therefore, in a better position to understand local contexts.

A postscript

The thinking summarised in this chapter proved to be particularly relevant during the recent COVID-19 period, which revealed and exacerbated pre-existing societal and educational inequalities. For example, it was at the forefront of thinking within Greater Manchester during the development of Pathways to Success, the city region's post-pandemic educational recovery strategy.[5]

The Pathways to Success strategy involved the creation of action learning groups made up of three schools that encouraged the sharing of experiences. So, for example, some schools shared ideas about how they have put in place a support structure for home learning, including training children on how to access online lessons via platforms. Equipment and resources were also provided for students to enable them to access these resources.

Over 200 schools participated in this process. Working in trios, practitioners in these schools held online meetings and then provided a summary of what had emerged from their discussions. This led to a rich resource of information relating to how schools had responded to the crisis and the ongoing challenges they faced. At the same time, it further demonstrated the potential benefits of school-to-school support.

The recovery strategy showed how, during the period of the pandemic, schools demonstrated remarkable flexibility in response to unprecedented challenges. This meant that they had to find different ways of carrying out their core business of teaching and learning. At the same time, many schools developed new ways of supporting families and local communities.

The logical implication of these developments is that most of the best expertise regarding ways of providing support in the new context lies amongst practitioners. I argue that, in moving forward with the continuing recovery of education systems, use must be made of this largely untapped knowledge. This points to the importance of schools working together, a strategy that builds on the evidence presented in this book of the potential of networking and collaboration as a means of making schools inclusive.

Conclusion

My involvement in the sorts of government-sponsored projects described in this chapter, with their focus on narrow views of learning outcomes, led to many dilemmas. Indeed, at times I felt that I was dancing with the devil. At the same time, they offered a political mandate and financial resources to explore ways of using the ideas presented in this book at a system level. In this way, they led to a greater understanding of how school developments can be supported or hindered.

These approaches to system change involve processes of social learning: the bringing together of different types of expertise to address challenges faced in particular contexts. It is important to note that this approach is contrary to the pervasive what works approach to educational change that is becoming dominant in an increasing number of countries, including my own.

The what works approach is based on very different assumptions regarding how to use research knowledge to inform improvement efforts. It assumes that the task of researchers is to convince practitioners to change their behaviour in light of evidence from elsewhere. The implication is that teachers are there to *deliver* practices that have been designed and evaluated by researchers – this means that practitioners are constructed as users of expert knowledge, not as knowledge creators.

In an earlier era, this approach involved systematic reviews of research findings that were expected to facilitate evidence-based policy-making and practice. Institutional moves were made to increase the production of such reviews; for example, the Evidence for Policy and Practice Information Coordinating Centre established at the Institute for Education, University of London. Hammersley (2001) expresses concerns about the rather instrumental model the reviews present of the relationship between research and practice. Furthermore, he argues, it involves a search for technical solutions to what may well be political or social problems.

Notes

1　There are 152 English local authorities. They are democratically accountable for providing a range of services for their local communities, including education.
2　https://www.london.gov.uk/press-releases/assembly/the-link-between-school-exclusions-violent-crime
3　The idea of teaching schools, which act as professional development hubs, subsequently became part of national policy in England.
4　An indication of economic disadvantage.
5　https://www.gmlp.org.uk/The-Greater-Manchester-educational-recovery-strate/

8 Addressing barriers

A few years ago I visited a primary school in a small town in the eastern part of Austria. In one classroom there were 17 children sitting mainly in pairs at tables arranged informally, some pointing to the front of the room, others directed towards the centre of the room. Meanwhile, one boy was sitting alone at a desk towards the rear of the room. There was thick snow outside and all the children wore slippers. The lesson was about Christmas celebrations and all the children had on their desks in front of them a worksheet that had been prepared by the class teacher.

After a short introductory presentation by the teacher, the children carried out the tasks on the worksheet, chatting to one another as they worked. Meanwhile, the boy sitting at the back of the room was being addressed by another teacher in a way that suggests that she perceived him as experiencing significant difficulties in understanding the spoken word. It seems that she was there to provide support to two students who are seen as having special needs, one of whom was absent. This support teacher had her own desk, also located at the rear of the room. On this occasion she had designed a separate worksheet for the children she supports, one that deals with similar content but in a less demanding way.

This experience raises many questions. Certainly, the boy in question is present in a regular classroom and, given his apparent difficulties in learning, this would possibly not be the case in some European countries. He also has the advantage of a large amount of individual attention of the sort for which parents in other countries have to fight. On the other hand, his physical location at the back of the room suggests that he remains somewhat marginalised, not least because the support teacher tends to stand between him and the rest of the class as she addresses him. So, is he included or not? Can we take lessons from this encounter that might inform the development of more inclusive practices in other parts of the world?

Engaging with evidence

As I have explained, the approach to educational improvement that I am suggesting involves *a process of increasing the participation of students in, and reducing their exclusion from, school curricula, cultures and communities.* In this

DOI: 10.4324/9781003438014-8

way notions of inclusion and exclusion are linked together because the process of increasing participation of students entails the reduction of pressures to exclude. This link also encourages us to look at the various constellations of pressures acting on different groups of students and acting on the same learners from different sources.

For these reasons, I have suggested that a starting point for the development of practice within a school has to be with a close scrutiny of how existing practices may be acting as barriers. This means that attention has to be given to helping practitioners develop a reflective attitude to their work such that they are continually encouraged to explore ways of overcoming such barriers. With this in mind, the approaches discussed in this book place considerable emphasis on the need to observe the process of schooling and to listen carefully to those involved. Illustrations of what form this can take place have been provided, as well as examples of techniques that have been found to be helpful.

This chapter looks more closely at the concerns raised in the previous chapter about the contextual barriers that can obstruct efforts for promoting inclusion and equity within education systems. The examples I describe, which come from a variety of countries, show that there are many sources of inequity in education, related to political, economic, social, cultural and institutional factors, and that these factors may vary both within and across countries. This means that whilst lessons can undoubtedly be learned from the accounts I provide, they must be interpreted and applied with care.

Context matters

The idea that system change strategies have to be contextually sensitive is one of the pervading themes of the suggestions I make in this book. To illustrate what this means, I return to a study published over 25 years ago, in which my colleague Tony Booth and I analysed the perspectives on inclusion (and exclusion) revealed by teams of researchers in their accounts of schools in eight countries (Booth and Ainscow 1998).

The study arose from our dissatisfaction with much of the existing comparative education research, which seeks findings that will have global significance by oversimplifying educational processes and practices, and by ignoring problems of interpretation and translation. We were also concerned about studies that assumed the existence of a single national perspective, rather than reporting the conflicts of interest and points of view that arise in all countries. In these ways, we argued that important differences between and within countries are too often omitted from study and debate.

Given these concerns, Tony and I intended that our study of developments in the eight countries would enhance interest in the shaping effect of national and local policies, as well as cultural and linguistic histories, on educational practice. It would do this, we hoped, by extending existing comparative reviews of inclusion through making their viewpoints explicit and illustrating practice in all its messiness. We also set out to challenge the way notions of inclusive education are often interpreted through the narrow, deficit lens of traditional special education thinking.

We went on to argue that an awareness of viewpoint diversity would avoid two pitfalls of comparative research: the idea that, in any country, there is a single national perspective on inclusion; and the notion that practice can be generalised across countries without attention to local contexts and meanings. The tendency to present single national perspectives, we explained, is often matched by a failure to describe the way practice is to be understood in its local and national context. This is part of a positivist view of social science, in which research carried out in one country can be amalgamated with that of others in order to support generalisable conclusions.

All of this is in marked contrast to the examples I present in this chapter and, indeed, elsewhere in this book. These accounts attempt to draw out nuances of the meaning of policy and practice in particular places. In most cases, this means listening directly to the voices of those involved, not least those of children and young people, and their families. Rather than reducing the potential contribution of research conducted in unfamiliar contexts, I suggest that a careful analysis of these differences in perspective, context and meaning enhances their value.

Understanding contextual barriers

In the accounts of practice that follow, I present a series of accounts that throw light on the nature of the contextual barriers I have experienced. These examples relate to events in a diverse range of contexts. The first of these is set in England.

> **Account 8.1. Responding to learner voices.** With a colleague, Ian Kaplan, I collaborated with a small group of sixteen year old students to record their views of five years in their secondary school, using a 'photovoice' approach (Ainscow and Kaplan, 2005). We hoped that their perspectives would give us deeper insights into what had happened in the school, which had a strong commitment to inclusion. We also intended that their views could be used to stimulate further developments amongst members of staff.
>
> Working in pairs the students took photographs around the school of areas they saw as welcoming and supportive, and areas that were less so. The pairs then produced posters based on their photographs. As they worked we recorded their conversations and probed them further about their experiences and opinions.
>
> The students made many positive comments about the school and its inclusiveness, confirming impressions we had gained from staff. They also explained that the school had a good reputation in the local community. However, they highlighted several things they felt made the school a 'less welcoming' place. For example, students pointed out some

inconsistencies in the school's application of its rules. There was, they argued, a sense that the best and worst students were exempt from certain rules, leaving those in the middle, sometimes feeling unfairly penalized.

One student explained. *If you're a good student you get away with a lot more, but if you're a bad student you can't get away with nothing.* Another elaborated, *But if you're really bad you can get away with things because the teachers can't be bothered to keep telling you.*

Students also used the project to highlight what they saw as some of the worst aspects of decay in the school buildings. They acknowledged that some of this was because some students vandalise the school. This apparent contradiction, in which students find the results of vandalism to be unwelcoming and unpleasant but are sometimes involved with the perpetration of the very vandalism they decry, generates a sort of ambivalence, which can seem irresolvable and quickly lead to apathy.

One of the few places in the school that students have almost entirely to themselves are the toilets. However, these are some of students' least favourite spaces, since they are often dirty and vandalized. Students expressed their despair at what they felt was the futility of trying to prevent vandalism of the toilets. For example: *They're just going to do it anyway, day after day, so there's no point stopping them. It's just going to get worse. The toilets are the main part where you just wouldn't want to go whatsoever.* The school's reaction to this had been to lock the toilets during lesson times but this response, perhaps necessary in the short term, did not seem to students to be a good long-term solution.

The importance of having their own spaces in the school were important to the students and they illustrated this by contrasting the staff room, which they understood to be a special place, only for teachers, to the toilets, which they saw as being one of the equivalent places for students. The students understood this to be a somewhat overdramatic distinction, but used it to highlight the point. They expressed the desire for different sort of space for older students in the school, one student saying: *We thought, if there's a staff room there should be a year 11 room...there is the dining room, but it's not one of the most relaxing places to sit down.*

Students also felt it was difficult to outlive a poor reputation in the school, even if the individuals changed their behaviour and academic performance. One student gave a personal example of this: *Sometimes teachers can pick on you. Say you had a bad reputation in year 9, but you've changed when you get to year 11, they're still going to hold a grudge on you.* He went on: *I know for a couple of teachers I can't do nothing right really. I can do stuff right now, but not for them. It's first impressions. If you do something right you know you're not going to get praised and if you do something wrong you know you're not going to get praised so really you just stop caring about it.*

The perspectives of students (as with the perspectives of other members of a school community) need to be understood beyond literal interpretations, to be engaged with and discussed. One student explained what it meant for him to be consulted as part of this project: *It's been different. It's been better than lessons. I think personally it's been a lot different for me. I've enjoyed it really. It's made me feel more involved, being asked what things you prefer about the school and why you prefer it, and what you don't like and why you don't like it…it's really made me think about how it can be changed and things like that.*

Having spent some months collecting views of staff and students about the school's efforts to become more inclusive, Ian and I used our evidence to write an account of what had happened. Our intention was to stimulate *self-questioning, creativity and action.* With this in mind, we shared our account with the headteacher and senior management team of the school. This was then discussed at a meeting we had with them.

Research suggests that using inquiry-based approaches for school improvement can lead to periods of *turbulence* as people struggle to make sense of unfamiliar points of view (Hopkins et al., 1994). Certainly, our meeting with the senior management team was characterised by a sense of turbulence. Whilst there was a range of reactions, some of which were contradictory, there was a general consensus that the students' views were simply wrong.

So, for example, the comments from students about what they saw as the rather token approach to consultation that had taken place about a new school uniform was described as being untrue. Indeed, the senior team saw student involvement in decision making as a strength in the way they were running the school. Many of the group also dismissed the views of students about bullying and the tendency of some staff to stereotype some students.

Reflecting on this account later it struck us that we had probably chosen a bad time to share our findings with these teachers. They were at that time facing a particularly challenging set of circumstances related to school closures. It was, therefore, perhaps understandable that our particular form of interruption was not met with enthusiasm. Nevertheless, the experience suggests that whilst an engagement with evidence can create space for reviewing thinking and practice, it is not in itself a straightforward mechanism for the development of more inclusive practices. The space that is created may be filled according to conflicting agendas. In this way, deeply held beliefs within a school may act as a barrier to the analysis and experimentation that is necessary in order to foster the development of more inclusive ways of working.

School-led change in Cyprus

This second example tells the story of a study carried out by Elena Constantinou, a primary school teacher in Cyprus, a small country which has a relatively centralised education system. I supported Elena as she attempted to promote change within her school (see a full account in Constantinou and Ainscow 2020).

Account 8.2. Working within a centralised system. School improvement initiatives in Cyprus largely serve to achieve standardised outcomes in relation to the national policy agenda. What is even more problematic is that, even though major national reforms are underway that emphasise the idea of democracy in schools, centralisation and policy imposition remain the usual way of doing things.

The project focused on the following questions:

- How can school change be achieved within a centralised education system?
- What are the barriers that need to be overcome?
- What are the implications for leadership practice in schools?

In addressing this agenda, Elena chose to adopt collaborative inquiry as the research strategy, since it can be purposefully designed in order to enable those at the school level to engage actively with the politics of schooling, through school-based research. Such an approach, she argued, can foster a critical edge to practitioner research, since knowledge creation involves struggles regarding purposes and action. At the same time, this can provide deeper insights in relation to the potential of what Fielding (1999) refers to as *radical collegiality* in order to move thinking and practice forward, as a more communal and democratic framework of micro-politics is developed.

The project was carried out over a period of three and a half years. In the context of Cyprus, this timescale proved to be particularly important, since it allowed us to gain insights into the impact of various factors associated with national policies, not least frequent staff changes.

Whilst the methodological approach was conceptualised within the aspirations of radical collegiality, in practice it entailed the development of a form of collaborative inquiry, through which space could be created in order to include and enable the localised complexity of voices (i.e. teachers, parents, students) to assume more active roles and, if possible, bring about change.

Within Cyprus at that time *the usual way* took the form of a model of school change which assumed top-down directives, where the Ministry leads and the profession implements, whilst other stakeholders are viewed, in most respects, as passive recipients of schooling. For example, decisions to do with the curriculum, books, student registration or, even, the selection, recruitment, promotion, transfers and training of staff, were all prescribed and managed centrally. This leads to a narrow educational agenda, according to which each school is expected to achieve similar outcomes, despite their local conditions and communities. In this context, parental choice and involvement are limited.

This approach to educational policy remained dominant in Cyprus despite evidence presented in this book showing how difficult it is to transform schools without a careful consideration of local contexts. Similarly, our research has drawn attention to the importance of schools being able to develop their own change agendas, as a means of ensuring a sense of sustainability.

Further difficulties occurred during the period of the project as a result of increases in the arrival of immigrant families from various parts of the world. This led to a greater emphasis on the identification of vulnerable groups, particularly children of migrant families (9% at the time of the study). In response to this new challenge, the Ministry introduced a policy according to which these students were moved out of the classroom for some hours each week in order to learn the Greek language. This meant that they were expected to be reintegrated into existing structures, even though international research suggests that the inclusion of such vulnerable groups of learners necessitates organisational and pedagogical changes (Opertti, Walker, & Zhang, 2014). Although some new measures were introduced with this in mind (e.g. in-service seminars for teachers; pedagogical material for fast acquisition of the language), these still seemed to focus on the integration of students into the existing system, rather than a restructuring of arrangements to enable their active participation. At the same time, those who hold formal leadership positions within schools have limited space to introduce changes aimed at addressing this agenda.

A related challenge was that, within the Cypriot context, policies on teacher mobility lead to frequent changes in staff. These changes are directed by a national committee appointed by the government and managed by a team of inspectors. Even more significant is the fact that newly appointed teachers, deputy heads and head teachers are expected to work away from their home towns or villages for at least two years. At the same time, the maximum time for staying at a school is up to six years. Staff are then transferred according to a system of points, whereby those with more points are in a better position when selecting or being moved to a school. This means that schools go through significant periods of turbulence every year, as staff are moved around according to the perceived needs of the system. It also creates an impression that schools are simply buildings, rather than social institutions located in particular communities with their own issues and legacies. Meanwhile, staff turnover is routinised to the extent that seems to be quite serendipitous.

As the project developed, it increasingly involved complex processes of meaning-making and decision-making aimed at supporting the development of collaborative inquiry as a model of change. At the same time, the numbers of stakeholders involved gradually increased.

The project took the form of three phases. During the first of these Elena acted as a participant observer, while at the same time maintaining a reflective stance (e.g. keeping a reflective journal, peer-debriefing). At this stage the research was focused on the question: How does school change take place within a centralised education system?

During the second phase stage of the study, the teacher-researcher created space whereby other stakeholders gradually became involved, with separate research groups made up of teachers, parents and students formed through democratic procedures. These groups had regular meetings with the teacher-researcher in order to address the following overall research agenda: *How does change take place in our school and what are the barriers that need to be overcome in order to achieve school change?* In addition to participant observation and reflection, there were interviews with all the teachers, and the technique of photo-elicitation was used with the parent and student research groups in order to generate relevant evidence.

Building on these activities, during the third phase, the three research groups each went on to design, implement and evaluate separate school improvement processes. This opened up possibilities to create a much more challenging inquiry stance which would address wider issues regarding school policies. Whilst these activities were taking place, we continued mapping processes of change using a more traditional research stance that involved participant observation, interviews with teachers and maintaining a reflective stance.

Through these activities, involving different stakeholder groups, we developed and trialled a school-based participatory change model within the overall policy context, which continued to be based on top-down decision making. In so doing, we were able to examine the impact of changes in personnel over time amongst newcomer and established school members. For this purpose, we defined newcomers as those school members who had just arrived at the school, whereas established members were those who had been in the school for more than a year.

This account from Cyprus suggests that, even within a centralised education system, opportunities for school-led improvement can be created when those involved are facilitated to collaborate and shape decision-making towards shared concerns. However, we also found that overcoming barriers to participation and progress requires a particular set of politics, one that promotes voice and active representation. So, for example, we saw how difficult it was for teachers to assume more active roles within a context of externally imposed agendas and frequent changes in staffing membership.

We also saw that parents and students were largely missing from the process of schooling. This meant that spaces for such active participation through school-based research had to be initiated and managed constructively. At the same time, this pointed to the important roles of formal school leaders, especially headteachers, who with their authority and professional status, could legitimate and authorise decisions that could advance active inquiry within their schools. I pick up this theme in the next example.

System-change in Wales

In 2014, I was invited to act as consultant to a new improvement initiative that was to take place in a region of Wales that includes over 400 school in five local authorities. The project was instigated by the Directors of Education of the authorities and received endorsement from local politicians. Additional funding was provided through the Welsh Government.

> **Account 8.2. Building capacity.** Known as the Central South Wales Challenge, the overall purpose was to transform educational outcomes in the region by improving leadership and teaching, and by finding ways of reducing the impact of poverty on student progress. This was to be achieved by building the capacity of schools to be self-improving. Reference was also made to the development of a culture that embraces innovation and enables teachers to work together to improve practice in ways that are informed by research and have a positive impact on students' progress. The espoused aim of having current school leaders co-ordinate the new collaborative system was enacted in practice by the creation of a strategy group, which consisted of head teachers drawn from each of the five authorities and all phases of the system.
>
> At a launch conference for over 400 headteachers, the features of the strategy that had been developed by the group were explained with reference to lessons that could be learnt from research elsewhere, particularly City Challenge in England. At the end of the morning many of the participants expressed their enthusiasm for the rationale presented and the proposed strategies outlined by members of the headteacher strategy group. However, a few commented that they had met in the same conference centre on a number of earlier occasions to hear about what seemed like equally impressive plans. Apparently, none of these had led to significant change.
>
> As if that was insufficient as a source of anxiety, the education reporter of a leading national newspaper wrote about what seemed to him to have been a successful conference. However, in commenting on the suggestion that schools would be expected to cooperate across the borders of the five partner local authorities, he wrote that the *desire to blur the boundaries between schools – as well as bordering local authorities – may be wishful thinking. Breaking down age-old barriers between schools of different hues will be no mean feat and it will be interesting to see whether or not head teachers are willing to play ball.* As things turned out, over the following four years, many heads were willing to play ball, despite the obstacles they faced (see Hadfield & Ainscow, 2018).
>
> Applying strategic lessons from earlier research required a recognition that the histories and politics of competition and collaboration vary across contexts. In particular, there existed in Wales a broad political rejection of more competitive *free market* approaches, combined with a

desire to create a unique *Welsh approach* to challenging the link between social deprivation and under achievement (Evans, 2015).

The strategy was designed to put in place the following features:

- Schools communities where collaborative inquiry is used to improve practice;
- Groupings of schools that engage in joint practice development, drawing on evidence collected by teachers;
- Where necessary, more intensive partnerships supporting schools facing difficulties;
- Families and community organisations supporting the work of schools;
- Coordination of the system provided by school leaders; and
- Local authorities working together to act as the *conscience of the system*.

These features placed the responsibility for the co-ordination of the system on to the shoulders of school leaders, while positioning local authorities as holding them to account. Meanwhile, my role mainly involved working with the group of headteachers, although it sometimes required me to act as a *peace keeper* when tensions occurred between them and senior local authority officers. Whilst this was a rewarding professional learning experience, it presented a number of dilemmas.

As somebody who had worked on a number of earlier system-change projects, it was understandable that the strategy group looked to me to take a lead on strategic decision making. For my part, I was conscious of having limited understanding on the ways in which the Welsh education system worked.

At the inception of the project in 2014, overall student performance in the region, as measured by test and examination results, was below the national average. Three years later, this had improved significantly. This overall trend was driven by improvements in all five authorities, with the two most underperforming improving to the greatest extent and the other three performing above the national average (Hadfield & Ainscow, 2018). At the same time, there were encouraging trends in relation to the average progress of students eligible for free school meals (an indicator of social deprivation) and other students. These positive trends in attainment were matched by similar patterns in the reduction of the numbers of schools categorised as requiring additional support as part of national accountability arrangements.

Over the four years of the project, the dynamics of the relationship within the strategy group also changed, as the headteachers involved became more confident of their capacity to take on the roles of system leaders. In this way, the initiative gradually became much more school-led. However, these developments remained fragile for a variety of reasons. Key amongst these was a political failure to establish clarity around roles and responsibilities between those working at different levels of the system, including the Welsh government. What resulted from this lack of clarity was that, as overlapping and competing interventions played out at different levels of the system, there was no agreement about who was responsible for managing the educational landscape in the longer term.

This experience in Wales also threw light on the barriers experienced when attempting to introduce ideas developed in other settings in a context which is culturally resistant to thinking imported from elsewhere. Significant, too, this was a context in which there were reported to be historically low levels of trust between those leading at different levels of the system (Dixon 2016).

There were also other barriers beyond the political and cultural, including vested interest groups wishing to hold on to existing ways of working, which, although well intended, were seen to consume time and resources, and delay action in the field, as well as different views regarding the goals of the initiative. Nevertheless, there is anecdotal evidence that the programme has continued to influence thinking and practice across the Welsh education system, suggesting that it did, to some degree at least, act as a catalyst for change.

Developing networks in Uruguay

Over recent years I have been a member of a group of researchers working to promote inclusion and equity in various Latin American countries (see Calderón-Almendros et al. 2020). This region is particularly challenging in that it has the greatest imbalance in income distribution in the world, even though in the first decade of the current century poverty decreased (UNESCO 2015). The account that follows is set within Uruguay, a country with a population of 3.4 million that is relatively advanced in relation to educational development within the region.

> **Account 8.3. Identifying resources.** A report published by the OECD as a result of a review in 2016 explained that universal access has been reached in primary education within Uruguay.[1] In addition, access to pre-primary education is good for children aged 4 and 5, with coverage rates considerably above the average for the Latin America region. However, the report notes that the completion rates of lower and upper secondary education remain unsatisfactory and have increased slowly over the past decades compared to other countries of the Latin American region. Furthermore, levels of student achievement in international assessments have decreased even though they remain above the regional average. A major concern is the significant proportion of students underperforming in and, in many instances, dropping out of secondary education.
>
> The recognition of these equity challenges led Uruguay to invest considerably in targeted programmes aimed at improving equity in education. Nevertheless, there remain marked educational inequities based on

students' socio-economic status. Furthermore, U ruguay had the fifth strongest association between socio-economic status and student performance among all PISA 2012 participating countries.

Working within this challenging context, I recently collaborated with a locally-based colleague, Mercedes Viola, on a collaborative project, *Towards Inclusive Schools*. Building on the findings of the research programme described in earlier chapters, the initiative set out to address the following questions:

- How can schools be developed in order to respond positively to student diversity?
- How can classroom practices be developed that will ensure that lessons are inclusive?
- How can schools engage families, partner schools and the wider community in their efforts to become inclusive and equitable?

This relevance of this agenda became even more crucial as schools sought to find ways of ensuring quality education for all their students within the context of the COVID-19 pandemic.

Using a specially adapted set of the professional development materials I developed for UNESCO,[2] six schools were supported over a school year in using collaborative inquiry to make better use of the existing expertise of their teachers. The schools were diverse in terms of their location in the country, as well as the nature of the populations they served. They included two secondary schools, two technical education centres and two teachers´ training centres.

A deliberate decision was made to focus on a small group of schools in order that their efforts could be monitored closely. In this way, it was hoped to learn from their experiences, so as to draw lessons that could inform later, larger scale developments within the country. Given the particular concerns about school drop-out amongst teenagers, it was decided to focus attention on various types of secondary schools.

Schools were chosen and invited to take part in the project by government colleagues and were varied in terms of their roles and contexts. Each one created a small staff inquiry group, as suggested in chapter 5. Led by a member of the senior management team, these groups were given responsibility for coordinating a process of school-based collaborative action research. To support their efforts, they took part in an online programme of workshops. These focused on techniques for generating evidence within schools, such as classroom observations, student work scrutiny, lesson study and student voice.

In addition, members of our research team made occasional visits to the schools to support the work of the inquiry groups. Then, towards the end of year, the schools were supported in developing written accounts of their work, plus short video programmes explaining what they had done. These videos were shared at a national conference.[3]

Throughout this process, field notes were kept by our team, including records of meetings and occasional informal interviews with participants. In this context, care was taken to ensure the confidentiality of those who shared information with us.

It is important to underline that the project in Uruguay took place during a period of considerable difficulties for schools as they struggled to respond to the unprecedented challenges created by the Covid pandemic. In this respect, what was achieved is quite remarkable. Although one school experienced particular difficulties in completing the project activities, the other five were able to make considerable progress.

In what follows, I reflect on evidence regarding the collaborative action research carried out by the project schools to address our three research questions.

- **How can schools be developed in order to respond positively to student diversity?**

The work of the project schools demonstrated that there is enormous untapped potential within Uruguayan schools to develop more collaborative and inclusive ways of working. In particular, we saw how teachers enjoyed working together to explore effective ways of reaching all of their students.

The following comments were typical of the views of many teachers when asked about their experience of participating in the project:

The key issue was giving us the opportunity – the opportunity of getting together and reflecting on what inclusion is and how to achieve it.

What enriched us the most was working with other colleagues who could give a different perspective on what we think and do.

Listening to students' voices, working in collaboration – students, teachers, leading team and other educators – and planning with other teachers helped us have a more critical view of how we work, and gave us different perspectives.

However, we also saw how current policies and organisational arrangements sometimes made it difficult to mobilise this potential. In particular, the centralised approach that tends to dominate decision-making within the Uruguayan education system can limit the freedom for such school-led improvement efforts.

Where schools experienced difficulties in implementing the ideas proposed by the project we saw indications of them experiencing barriers resulting from national policies, particularly the frequent changes of staff that occur. This includes changes in the leadership of schools, a factor that we had seen as creating a barrier to developments during the earlier project in Cyprus.

Meanwhile, the system in Uruguay is fragmented, being made up of four education councils that act more or less independently of each other. Finally, there is high centralization, since decisions are made from the country's capital, which reduces flexibility and initiative capacity at the departmental or local level, and frequently generates slowness in different types of initiatives and in solving problems (Castro et al., 2019).

Consistent with this overall policy emphasis, the process of identifying and selecting the schools for the project was decided centrally, in collaboration with regional inspectors. Schools were not given the choice to join the project, nor informed on why there were chosen to take part. In one case, this led to a noticeable reluctance amongst senior members of staff to get involved.

The insider knowledge of key players at different levels of an education system is an essential means of carrying out a contextual analysis. In the context of Uruguay, teachers found that listening to the voices of students was particularly helpful. For example, in one of the technical schools, many students were not attending the classes they had on Saturdays. These classes are part of the curriculum and being absent affects the students' attendance report and progress. Through having a workshop with the students, where they discussed different issues that were affecting their attendance and performance, the inquiry team learned that many of the students felt tired and needed to relax on Saturdays. Based on this finding they rearranged the schedule so that they could have subjects that were not so academically demanding on Saturdays. Attendance improved considerably due to this simple change.

The inquiry team in one of the teacher training schools found that many of their students felt alone and isolated, and had difficulties in developing relationships and working collaboratively. The team asked the psychologist from another teacher training centre to help them design two experiential workshops in which students could identify their feelings, think about their present and future, set a plan, and talk about their fears regarding their teaching practices. The objective of the workshops was to transform emotional barriers into empathy for others and to provide creative opportunities for collectively planning ways to move forward. It was clear that the students truly valued this opportunity.

All of this requires schools to have greater flexibility to determine how resources are used to address local circumstances. This builds on international research which suggests that when teachers are involved in decision-making this is likely to promote a stronger culture for learning within schools (Schleicher, 2010). The potential of this approach was clearly demonstrated by the progress made in most of the project schools.

- **How can classroom practices be developed that will ensure that lessons are inclusive?**

The work of the project schools provided further evidence of how forms of collaborative inquiry have the potential to draw people together in relation to challenges facing schools, as well as generating evidence that can stimulate innovations aimed at improving thinking and practice. In particular, we saw how the use of evidence collected by practitioners to study teaching within their school can foster the development of practices that are more effective in reaching out to all learners.

So, for example, in one of the high schools, three teachers created a lesson study group, as recommended in the project materials. This required them to plan a lesson together, which each of them implemented while the other two observed the process, focusing specifically on the way students responded. It was a foreign language class.

After the first teacher gave the lesson, the trio got together to share their views. They mentioned that they could observe that some students had not understood exactly what needed to be done. In order to improve that, they decided that during the next lesson, after giving the instructions, they were going to model the activity before asking the students to do it. This simple action helped students understand what was asked of them and all of them participated. This led one of the teachers to comment:

Paying attention to details and fine tuning our practice is crucial to move towards inclusion.

The evidence needed to create this form of stimulation took many forms and involved the use of a variety of techniques. What was common among them, however, was the way they created *interruptions* that helped to make the familiar unfamiliar. It was found that, during the busy school day, this can lead to the sharing of ideas and practices, as well as encouraging collective problem-solving.

In terms of evidence, the obvious starting point was usually with statistical information regarding student attendance, behaviour and progress. In recent years the extent and sophistication of such data have improved, so much so that the progress of groups and individuals can now be tracked in considerable detail, giving a much greater sense of the value that a school is adding to its students.

However, as noted in Chapter 5, statistical information alone tells us very little. We saw that what brings such data to life is when *insiders* scrutinise and ask questions together as to their significance, bringing their detailed experiences and local knowledge to bear on the process of interpretation. In this respect, evidence gathered by classroom observations and through collecting the views of students proved to be particularly powerful in encouraging innovations in practice.

• **How can schools engage families, partner schools and the wider community in their efforts to become inclusive and equitable?**

We saw encouraging examples of what can happen when what schools do is aligned in a coherent strategy with the efforts of other local players within a particular district, especially families. For example, after hearing the views of students and teachers, the inquiry team at a teacher training school decided to create an organic garden space. This was intended to provide a caring context: for the environment and for the mental and physical health of all the stakeholders (i.e. teachers, students, administrative staff, other educators), where not only knowledge but also experiences could be shared.

The school inquiry group went on to work together with the city mayor and representatives of other communities and businesses that are located nearby to create the organic garden space. As a result, many students asked for opportunities to bond with others, sharing experiences in spaces where they could talk and be heard.

The project also demonstrated how school-to-school collaboration can strengthen the capacity of practitioners to respond to learner diversity. Specifically, we saw further examples of how collaboration between schools can help reduce inequalities of provision, to the particular benefit of those students who are marginalised at the edges of a local education system. For example:

We learned a lot listening to the experiences of other schools. We implemented some of their initiatives as well

There was also evidence that when schools develop more collaborative ways of working, this can have an impact on how teachers perceive themselves and their work:

Having the opportunity of being together with other schools during the workshops gave us a lot of insight – food for thought and strategies to implement

We also witnessed examples of how comparisons of practices in different schools can lead teachers to view underachieving students in a new light – in ways that encourages a move away from deficit thinking. As a result, those learners who cannot easily be educated within a school's established routines come to be seen less as *having problems,* but as challenging teachers to re-examine their practices in order to make them more responsive to learner diversity.

Within the project, progress was most evident in those schools where those leading improvement efforts had the backing of key players, particularly senior members of staff. In five of the centres we saw how strong support and involvement of the principals and senior staff led to interesting developments in thinking and practice, whilst the school that did not have that support did not complete the process. In this case, some of the teachers wanted to continue, but without the support of the principal they could not find the way to do it. This suggests that in moving forward there is a need to identify and engage the support of those who can make things happen, as well as those who might block things from happening.

Another key issue that emerged during the project was the difficulty in finding time for reflection and collaborative work – within the team and with the teams in the other project schools. Meanwhile, the occasional rotation of principals and changes in the teaching teams was seen to hinder the continuity of the process of transforming the culture of educational centres towards inclusion. This reminds us that spaces for reflection and collaborative work to take place are crucial in order to sustain cultural transformation.

Like other countries in Latin America, Uruguay faces many challenges as it aims to strengthen its education system. Yet, as we found within this small-scale project, it also has untapped potential within its schools and their communities that can be mobilised to promote policies and practices based on the principles of inclusion and equity. What is needed are strategies that create the conditions within which these resources can be used effectively. This theme is picked up in the next example.

A city-wide strategy in Scotland

Working with my colleagues at the University of Glasgow's Robert Owen Centre for Educational Change, I have been learning much more about the barriers facing those who try to encourage inclusion and equity within a relatively centralised system. Over the previous decade the Glasgow team had worked alongside partners across Scotland to explore how ideas that emerged from City Challenge and Schools Challenge Cymru, described in Chapter 7, could be put into practice. The account that follows focuses on recent developments in one Scottish city.

> **Account 8.4. Creating space for change.** The situation in Scotland indicates many positive features in regard to equity. For example, most students attend local schools that are part of a local authority. However, as in Cyprus and Uruguay, policies are relatively centralised, with local authorities acting as the delivery arms of nationally determined policies. This means that those in schools have limited space to make strategic decisions regarding actions that are needed to address local factors that are limiting the progress of some of their learners. Meanwhile, Kintrea (2021) argues:
>
> *Beneath the calm surface of Scotland's consensual and seemingly inclusive approach lie significant inequalities.*
>
> *(p. X)*
>
> Within this challenging context, I am currently working with members of our University of Glasgow team alongside practitioners to promote

equity across Dundee, a city with particularly high levels of poverty. The strategy, known as *Every Dundee Learner Matters*, involves all the nurseries and schools began in 2021. It is currently in the third year of its implementation and is designed around the ideas presented in this book. However, going to scale across a city is a significant challenge that requires many players to be involved.

The guiding vision is of a high performing education system that is at the forefront of developments to find more effective ways of ensuring the education of all children and young people, particularly those who are most vulnerable to underachievement, marginalisation or exclusion. The strategy is driven by the principle of equity, defined as: *A process of improving the presence, participation and progress of all children and young people in nurseries and schools by identifying and addressing contextual barriers.*

Influenced by the findings of earlier experiences in Wales and England, it is envisioning that the development of a more inclusive system within Dundee will be achieved by building the capacity of schools to be self-improving, developing a culture that embraces innovation and increasing practitioner leadership for work together using inquiry-based approaches to the development of practice.

Despite the centralism that characterises the Scottish education system, the city's strategy sets out to increase the agency of schools regarding decisions about priorities for improvement. With this in mind, the methodology used is *design-based implementation research* (Fishman et al., 2013). This is guided by four principles: a focus on problems of practice from multiple stakeholders' perspectives; a commitment to collaborative design; a concern with developing theory and knowledge related to both classroom learning and implementation through systematic inquiry; and a concern with developing capacity for sustaining change in systems.

The improvement strategy is driven collectively by school leaders and involves practitioners at all phases of the education system – early years, primary and secondary education – in taking shared responsibility for improving the quality of education across the city. An engagement with evidence generated by teachers, through mutual observations and an engagement with the views of students, is a key factor in making this happen. In addition, schools work in improvement partnerships, using peer inquiry visits to stimulate the sharing of practices and mutual professional learning.

As a system-wide strategy, another key element involves the development of leadership capacity in the middle tier, a role that in Scotland is that of local authorities. This involves a significant change in practices, summed up by the following mantra suggested by an education officer during an earlier project: *The job of schools is to improve themselves; our job is to make sure it happens.*

This methodology combines activities linked to both development and research, with the expectations that these two will feed off each other during their implementation, and are adjusted accordingly, as needed. Thus, the approach requires a new set of expectations regarding roles and relationships among stakeholders and researchers.

As the project developed, there have been occasional tensions related to the roles of researchers and developers. Working on the ground, with schools and district partners, demands that we immerse ourselves in the role of developers in critical ways. At the same time, practitioners within the schools and in the local authority have to find time in their hectic schedules to engage with our ideas, as well as carrying out their own research activities.

Within the strategy we are involved in activities to support the strategic vision for change at the district level by meeting with a strategy group that involves headteachers and senior local authority staff to discuss progress, priorities and next steps. This also involved building capacity within establishments by supporting teacher leaders in conducting collaborative action research projects and presenting their findings to other school staff, support services and community members. At the same time, we have supported the professional development of local authority staff as they adjust their contributions to improvement efforts that are led by schools. In addition, we have sought to *interrupt* the structure of interactions within the system, by creating new school partnerships, and coordinating cross-school collaborative activities in an effort to move knowledge around.

A key element of the strategy is for headteachers to contribute to the development of improvement agenda, the importance of which had emerged from the earlier experiences in England and Wales. Meanwhile, as researchers, we are involved in feeding ideas and lessons from earlier experiences elsewhere. Importantly, however, these ideas are sometimes adjusted in relation to local contextual factors explained by the headteachers on the strategy group.

Within these discussions, it was noted that phrases used by members of the research team in explaining these ideas, such, as *an inquiring stance*, *a tight-loose strategy* and *moving knowledge around*, were often adopted by the practitioners. This led to a concern that a degree of unintended brain-washing was taking place.

From our on-going monitoring of the initiative in Dundee, we are encouraged to see promising indications of the implementation of its design features.[4] At the same time, we see frequent evidence of how traditional, top-down patterns of decision-making are acting as barriers to the development of a school-led improvement strategy. For example, having explained to headteachers the government-required targets that schools are expected to achieve, a senior local authority officer commented, *This is what we have been told to do*. All of this reflects what Humes (2020) refers to as a form of *groupthink* that exists within the Scottish education system, leading to the recycling of approved forms of discourse.

Drawing lessons

Underlying these experiences of using forms of collaborative inquiry to promote equity within education systems is a common pattern. Most importantly, they involve an engagement with various forms of evidence collected by practitioners and, sometimes, other stakeholders, with support from university researchers. Usually this begins with a consideration of an established set of practices that are largely taken for granted. School-led inquiry, supported by researchers, then leads to *interruptions* that problematise these ways of working and established norms, provoking a consideration of why current practice is the way it is and how it might be improved.

Fundamental to this approach is the idea that schools, systems and their local communities have untapped potential to improve their capacity for improving the achievement of all of their students, not least those from economically poorer and minority backgrounds. The challenge therefore is to mobilise this potential, although, as I have explained, accountability frameworks and institutional norms are sometimes at odds with so doing.

Relating this to international research on system change (see Chapman and Ainscow 2019), I see these system-level barriers to progress as involving the following factors:

- **National policies that encourage schools to narrow the educational diet**. This tends to involve a focus of attention on ways of improving test scores in relation to a narrowly conceived range of outcomes, for example, as signalled by the emphasis placed by some governments on *raising standards*. Inevitably, this can lead to a tendency to narrow the curriculum and allocate teaching time to those areas of learning that are seen as being most important. My argument is that educational equity assumes that all learners have a right to a broad range of learning experiences, including the expressive arts, humanities, science and physical exercise.
- **Local area administrative structures that limit the freedom of practitioners to experiment**. Where there is a tradition of local authority *line management*, this seems to constrain decision-making amongst school leaders, particularly those who feel under pressure regarding attainment scores. My experience leads me to favour the idea of subsidiarity, i.e. that which individuals can accomplish by their own initiative and efforts should not be taken from them by a higher authority.
- **The tendency to prioritise certain groups of students**. Policy pressures mean that schools sometimes feel that it is necessary to stream students into separate classes, or separate them into different areas of the classroom, on the basis of their perceived abilities. This is despite considerable research

evidence that doubts the effectiveness of such approaches (see, for example, Francis et al. 2016). The commitment to educational equity as a principle leads me to emphasise the importance of young people learning how to live with and learn from one another's differences.

- **Fragmentation within education systems that limit opportunities for sharing expertise**. In some contexts, practitioners continue to work in isolation from one another. Meanwhile, middle managers may see themselves as mainly having a maintenance function, as opposed to being change agents. The best examples in our studies are characterised by a consensus amongst adults around values of respect for differences and a commitment to work together in order to offer all students access to a range of learning opportunities. The implication is that senior staff have to create a climate within which this takes place.
- **Competition between schools that discourages the sharing of expertise across institutions**. As I go on to explain in Chapter 9, this is a particular feature of those education systems where policies are informed by neoliberal perspectives, such as Australia, Chile, England, Sweden and parts of the United States. In these contexts, there may be a reluctance to see other schools as partners that can be used to support development and act as a catalyst for change. The experiences I have documented in this chapter add further evidence of the potential of a more collaborative approach, provided it is well thought through and implemented effectively.
- **Varied levels of practitioner confidence regarding inquiry methods and the use of evidence**. Here again the history of particular organisations is a determining factor, particularly where this has created a culture within which colleagues expect to be alone in addressing challenges. This is why involving teams of practitioners in the design of collaborative inquiry processes is so important. The aim is to demystify methodology, without dumbing it down, and develop a greater capacity to learn from differences.
- **Factors beyond the school gate**. These include geographical isolation, economic pressures and community attitudes. Our work has highlighted the benefit of providing opportunities to minimise isolation through the creation of a forum for tackling wider contextual issues, such as local unemployment, poverty and well-being.

In drawing attention to these factors, as always, I emphasise the importance of considering barriers that may limit progress towards equitable education in particular places. And, of course, these barriers may change over time.

Addressing unexpected barriers

In recent years, further significant barriers to progress have been apparent within education systems across the world in relation to the impact of the coronavirus pandemic. These new challenges pointed to a need for an even greater emphasis on the sorts of approaches I present in this book. This also led many schools to strengthen their involvement with families and communities. For example, the account that follows explains what happened in an English school that serves an urban community with high levels of economic disadvantage.

> **Account 8.5 Responding to crisis.** Westside school has 900 students from ages 2 through to 18. As the country went into lockdown in response to the pandemic, the staff began planning their response to the crisis. This led the school to take a lead in co-ordinating a multi-agency response across their local community.
>
> During the lockdown months, Westside students continued their education online at home. At the primary level (ages 4-11) there was a 98% work completion rate, dropping slightly to 85% at the secondary level (ages 11-18). Senior staff put this down to the strong inclusive school culture and organisation-wide expectations that had been created.
>
> The obvious barrier was a lack of home internet access or a computer amongst some of the families. In those cases where home ICT problems prevailed, students were invited into school to complete their online work individually.
>
> The school had been committed to inclusion since its inception. Forming strong relationships with both students and parents is therefore at the core of the school's culture. This usually involves regular contact with students' families and the COVID-19 response naturally included this.
>
> Every family received at least one contact per week from their class teacher at the nursery and primary levels, or from a familiar member of the secondary staff further up the school. For the most vulnerable parents, this increased to a daily check-in phone call or home visit.
>
> The expectation that students must submit daily work created another point of contact between the school and the families. If a student failed to submit any work on a given day, this triggered a call to make sure that everything was okay and to offer further support if required.
>
> In preparation for the lockdown, the school convened different organisations across the local area for a virtual meeting on how best to support the local community during the crisis. This included charities, churches, local government representatives, schools and youth groups, all of whom completed a survey sent out to highlight the most vulnerable groups of people and where support would be most needed. From this, three working groups were established: food and essentials, mental health and well-being, and financial information and advice.
>
> The food and essentials group response had both a school focus and a community focus. Just over one third of student usually receive a free school lunch because of the low-income of their families. During the lockdown period, this service continued, including during the holiday periods. Fortunately, the school has its own on-site catering facilities and is in charge of providing its own meals to students. This enabled the school to extend its free meal provision beyond its student and family population.

The school caterers produced 400 meals for families every day. This included food for eligible families of three other local schools, as well as 25 vulnerable elderly people who have been asked by the government to self-isolate for 12 weeks. Those who could, picked up their free meals outside the school on a Monday and a Thursday. In addition, a team of staff delivered food to 50 local families who could not get to school due to transport issues, self-isolation or vulnerability.

The mental health and well-being group created a support pack containing a wide range of activities, videos and blogs suggesting strategies for supporting families. The pack also contained the details of where to seek professional help.

The financial information and advice group compiled information on personal and business financial support, and this was made available on the community website. The school anticipated that families would require advice on how to access the government's economic relief support due to a high number of job losses as a result of COVID-19.

Examples similar to this one in different parts of the world led the authors of a UNESCO report to state:

> *The educational response to the COVID-19 crisis has revealed the capacity of educators to draw on their professional knowledge and collaboratively mobilize with a resourcefulness and creativity that could not have been achieved by a public authority simply issuing top down orders. In fact, over the last several months, the education sector which is often unfairly critiqued for its conservatism has shown itself to be among the most robust and adaptable of all social institutions. This is an important lesson from this crisis and one which should lead us to grant teachers greater autonomy and freedom.*

The report concluded:

> *Teachers need to be more recognized and more highly valued; they are essential participants in defining the futures of education.*
>
> *(UNESCO 2020, p. 15)*

As we move forward in the post-COVID era, there can never have been a more important time for people to get together in order to ensure high-quality educational opportunities for all children and young people.

Conclusion

It is sometimes said that educational improvement is technically simple but socially complex. In other words, it is relatively easy to develop a list of recommendations of the sort I present in this book. The big challenge is to get people to understand, accept and act together on the implications of these proposals.

As I have stressed, there is also the challenge of addressing contextual barriers in relation to any recommendations for change. With this in mind, the accounts I provide in this chapter of developments that have occurred in various parts of the world illustrate the shaping effect of national and local policies, and cultural histories, on educational practice. Collective actions are needed to address the barriers that this creates.

The implication is that successful change requires the coming together of different perspectives and experiences in a process of social learning and knowledge creation within particular settings. Researchers who get involved in such processes must expect to face many challenges and dilemmas. Consequently, they have to develop new skills in creating collaborative partnerships that cross borders between actors who have different professional experiences. They also need to mobilise personal support in dealing with the pressures this involves. Hence the importance of the emphasis I place on working in teams. As will have become clear to readers by now, in carrying out my work, I do nothing on my own.

Notes

1 http://dx.doi.org/10.1787/9789264265530-en.
2 http://www.ibe.unesco.org/en/news/reaching-out-all-learners-resource-pack-supporting-inclusion-and-equity-education
3 https://youtube.com/playlist?list=PLAKNeCtmfOGUL_DIIEZmr8dZnxdzf9GK5
4 https://nsee.org.uk/wp-content/uploads/2023/09/EDLMProgressReport-Sept23.pdf

9 Facing new challenges

In the research within the network of schools in Queensland, Australia that I reported in Chapter 4, we saw the impact of policy perspectives that emphasise competition between schools on the efforts of school leaders to promote equity. This led some of them to develop what they saw as *points of difference* from other local schools that would attract parents, particularly those of high achieving students.

So, for example, the strategy adopted in one secondary school was based on the premise that students learn best when their teachers' pedagogical approach is matched with their preferred learning style. While there is limited evidence to support this approach, the school promoted targeted classes to families of prospective students, providing the same teacher for core subject areas and grouping students according to their preferred learning styles.

Descriptions of the targeted classes suggested that greater equity could be encouraged by catering for *individual student needs*. This approach offered one class more opportunities for self-directed learning, whereas another class, recommended for students with gaps in their learning, were offered direct instruction with fewer students.

School leaders assumed that this differentiated approach would better meet students' learning needs, although some of the teachers tended to see it as a way of streaming students. Meanwhile, despite the rhetoric about students being able to select classes to suit their learning styles, many indicated that they believed that they were placed in *lower* or *higher* classes on the basis of their previous performance. So, for example, when asked, a teenage girl explained that she and her friends were in a particular class '*because we are stupid*'.

Conversations amongst leaders of the secondary schools involved in the Queensland network indicated that they were all using some form of ability grouping in an effort to improve average school performance on standardised tests. Limiting the range of students' *ability* within class groups in this way was described by school leaders as a way to assist teachers in differentiating their lessons.

While this strategy may be effective in marketing the school to parents of high achievers, there is clear evidence that ability-based grouping – sometimes referred to as *streaming* – can inhibit a fair and equitable culture of learning.

DOI: 10.4324/9781003438014-9

In particular, it can increase inequity and have negative impacts on students' performance and self-esteem, particularly those in the *lower ability* groups (Francis et al. 2017). The increasing pressure of the school market, however, led these Australian schools to adopt strategies to increase their market share of students who were likely to achieve well on standardised tests 'at all costs' (Klenowski and Wyatt-Smith 2012, pp. 71, 73).

So, what are the implications of such policy trends for efforts to develop inclusive schools? To consider this question I focus on the radical policy changes that have occurred in England over the last 25 years or so.

Lessons from England

As is evident from the examples that I have presented in earlier chapters, England is a particularly interesting case for thinking about ways of promoting inclusion and equity in education. In particular, it is a country where there are worrying differences within the community in relation to economic factors. For example, data for 2019–2020 suggest that 31% of school-aged children were living in poverty.[1] And those eligible for free school meals were the equivalent of 18.1 months behind in their learning than their less disadvantaged peers at age 16.

England is also typical of many countries in having strong spatial concentrations of poverty and poor educational outcomes. These typically occur in places with weak physical, economic and service infrastructures for addressing poor educational outcomes. For one of the wealthiest nations on the planet, such facts are a source of shame. They also serve to remind us that decades of centralised reform, which have weakened local democratic influence and, thereby, have had the effect of fragmenting the school system, have done much more to reinforce rather than address these concerns (Kerr and Ainscow 2022).

With this agenda in mind, in what follows I look more closely at recent developments in England in order to draw lessons for those in other countries who are interested in promoting greater equity within their national education systems. This leads me to argue that whilst school autonomy can be a positive force – particular where it encourages teachers to work together in exploring more inclusive practices – it requires coordination at the local level and the introduction of accountability arrangements that encourage experimentation, as well as resources, to promote the professional development of teachers.

A global trend

The last 30 years have seen efforts by successive governments, of different political persuasions, to improve the English education system. Common to all of these reform efforts is a concern to close the gap in attainment between students from economically disadvantaged students and their peers, although the approaches tried have varied considerably. Most recently, they have involved an increased emphasis on the idea of allowing schools greater autonomy within a policy context based on market forces as the main improvement strategy. This approach to educational development is a growing international trend that has major implications for the promotion of equity (Meyland-Smith and Evans 2009).

The use of this thinking takes a variety of forms, and the schools involved have different titles, such as charter schools in the United States, free schools in Sweden, independent public schools in parts of Australia and academies in England. Implicit in these new types of independent state-funded schools is an assumption that greater autonomy will allow space for the development of organisational arrangements, practices and forms of management and leadership that will be more effective in promoting the learning of all of their students.

This global policy trend is a matter of considerable debate, and there are varied views as to the extent to which it is leading to the desired outcomes. In particular, there is a concern that the development of education systems based on autonomy, coupled with high-stakes accountability and increased competition between schools, will further disadvantage learners from low-income and minority families.

Across countries that have adopted the idea of school autonomy, we also see evidence of a worrying trend towards greater segregation. For example, in Sweden segregation has grown within the education system since the introduction of market-based reforms, including autonomous free schools (Bunar 2010; Wiborg 2010). In the United States this is particularly ironic, since one of the early advocates of charter schools, Albert Shanker, the then president of the American Federation of Teachers, intended that they would address the problem created by community segregation in order to develop schools that bring together children from different backgrounds. He also anticipated that they would facilitate greater involvement of teachers in decision-making (Kahlenberg and Potter 2014).

Meanwhile, there is limited evidence regarding what is actually happening inside these schools in relation to decision-making about policies and practice, and the extent to which this is leading to increased innovation and improved educational outcomes. This lack of evidence arises, in part at least, because these developments are relatively recent. It is also the case that researchers have sometimes found it difficult to get access to the schools in ways that would allow them to dig deeper into what goes on because of the intensive political pressures that are often associated with their existence.

Academies

The major strand in the move towards school autonomy in England has been the rapid expansion of the academies programme. This involves schools being funded directly by national government rather than through a local authority.[2] The foundations for academies were laid well before the programme was launched during the period of the Conservative governments from 1979 to

1997 with the creation of what were called grant-maintained schools. Some of the other key policy changes of that era that had long-term consequences included the following: the creation of a free market approach to education by increasing parental choice and school diversity, the publication of school inspection reports and public league tables of school *performance* in tests, local management of schools, including changes in funding allocations to a per-student basis and the introduction of the national curriculum (West and Bailey 2013).

Academies were launched in the year 2001 with the aim of replacing inner-city secondary schools that were defined as requiring *special measures* as a result of being inspected. What was distinctive about the early academies was that, although they were state-funded, they became autonomous from local authority control, had their own sponsor and were given greater freedom regarding the national curriculum and national agreements on teachers' pay and conditions. Instead of local authority governance, these schools are self-governing non-profit charitable trusts, the terms of which are set out in an individual funding agreement (Tomlinson 2022). However, like all other state-funded schools in England, they are subject to regular inspections and their students sit the same national exams as those in other schools.

Since these earlier initiatives, the academies programme has undergone considerable changes and growth. Following the election of the Conservative-led coalition government in 2010, and then the Conservative government in 2015, it has moved from targeting urban secondary schools seen as *failing* to a system-wide structural change causing seismic shifts in the English education landscape. Writing about this reform, Eyles and Machin (2015) comment:

> *The academies programme that has been undertaken in English education is turning out to be one of the most radical and encompassing programmes of school reform that has been seen in the recent past in advanced countries.*
>
> *(p. 1)*

An independent Commission set up to review these developments pointed out that the original aim of academies was *to address entrenched failure in schools with low performance, most particularly, schools located in the most disadvantaged parts of the country* (Husbands et al. 2013, p. 4). Since then, the focus has changed towards increasing the autonomy of all schools and setting up new academies throughout the country. Meanwhile, all new schools that open must now take the form of free schools, using the academy legislation as their legal framework.

Since 2010, government policies have also encouraged relatively successful schools to convert to academy status, as well as further emphasising the idea of forcing schools in difficulty to become members of an academy chain. Together, these responses have accelerated the pace of change, leading to the years 2010–2013 being referred to as the *Wild West* of academy growth (Ladd and Fiske 2016). Consequently, while there were just 272 academies in England in the 2010–2011 academic year, currently, of the 22,000 state-funded schools in England, just over 10,000 of these are now academies. These are schools run by independent charitable organisations, as opposed to a local authority, and are funded directly by the Department for Education. The current government has in mind that all schools will become academies.

These developments are set within a policy context in which the dominant model has become schools linking together in multi-academy trusts, with oversight coming from national rather than local government (Mansell 2016). This has also brought with it new players, as noted in a report from the House of Commons Education Select Committee, which states:

> *Academy sponsorship has encouraged and facilitated the contribution of individuals not previously involved in education provision and laid down a challenge to maintained schools to improve or face replacement by the insurgent academy model.*
>
> *(HoC Education Committee 2015)*

As a result of this expanding academies programme, the education system in England has become increasingly diverse. Furthermore, the introduction of various other types of schools that operate under the academy legislation – such as free schools, studio schools and university technical colleges – has contributed to the complexity of the scene. Indeed, in a mapping exercise of schools, based on legal status, curricular specialism, student selection, types of academy and school groupings, Courtney (2015) identified as many as 70 or more types of school operating in the English system. All of which suggests that autonomous schools are well on the way to becoming *the* system of English state education, which makes it a particularly interesting case to study.

Taking a closer look

Working with my colleague Maija Salokangas, I was able to take a closer look of the impact of this radical reform agenda within schools through our longitudinal study of *Parkside*,[3] one of the first academies set up (see Salokangas and Ainscow 2017, for a detailed account of this research). Our account was developed as a result of my involvement as a participant observer over a ten-year period. During that time, data were generated in the school and its community in relation to a number of more formal research studies. More in-depth evidence was collected through systematic ethnographic research carried out by Maija, who spent over a year in the school, examining documents, observing practices and decision-making, and carrying out interviews.

Account 9.1. A challenging context. Parkside Academy was seen as something of a flagship of one of the larger academy groups operating in England. When it opened in the early 2000s, it was located in the building of its predecessor school and then moved into purpose-built

accommodation some 24 months later. The principal was appointed before the new school opened, giving her time to assess the situation and
formulate what were to be radical changes in the way it would operate.
For example, I was present when she announced to the staff that teachers, as well as students, would be expected to follow a dress code once
the new school opened. The principal also made a decision to distance
the school from the local authority of which it had previously been part.

The early academies programme was aimed at inner city secondary
schools seen to be 'failing'. The argument supporting this policy was that
closing down a failing school operating in challenging circumstances,
and with a history of poor examination results, and replacing it with an
academy would cut the cycle of underperformance. This was explained
in the 2001 Green paper, 'Schools: Building on success – Raising standards, promoting diversity, achieving results' (DfEE, 2001):

*City Academies offer a radical option to help raise achievement in areas of
historic underperformance …. City Academies are all-ability schools with
the capacity to transform the education of children in areas of disadvantage and need. They will raise standards by innovative approaches to management, governance, teaching and the curriculum, offering a broad and
balanced curriculum with a specialist focus in one area.*

As with all of the first wave of academies, Parkside replaced a secondary school with a bad reputation. It is located in an urban district we call
Green End, an area which is associated with a history of severe financial
and social disadvantage, as well as cultural diversity. In terms of the diverse multicultural nature of the area, according to Census 2001, just
over 50% of the ward's population consisted of ethnic minority groups.
Of these groups, African-Caribbean and Black African are the largest
groups, others include Indian, Pakistani and Chinese.

There were race-riots in the early 1980s, of which a social worker in
the area commented: *The disturbances have to be set aside the background
of young people in the area being denied hope. The local schools' expectations
of them were pretty low.* While those with long connections to the area
feel that it is now safer, more cohesive, and more prosperous than in the
1970s and 1980s, there remain concerns about incidents of gun crime
and gang violence.

Having said that, it is important not to fall into the trap of assum-
ing that everything about the area is a problem. I was part of a team of
researchers that carried out an analysis of the area during the early years
of Parkside's existence. This pointed to the many assets and resources
that could be built on. So, for example, we found that there were many
within the community that had a high regard for what schools have to
offer. Indeed, some families had gone through enormous difficulties to
bring their children to a part of the world that they see as offering many
opportunities to achieve a better life.

Fair access to an appropriate education is seen to be a key equity issue in relation to secondary education in the Green End area. Amongst the secondary schools serving learners from the area, apart from Parkside, there is a faith school and three single sex schools. In addition, there are, within a short bus journey, three independent selective grammar schools, where families are required to pay fees, and a range of special education institutions. This diversity of provision is rather typical of the pattern across England, although the details vary from place to place.

During the period when Parkside was opened, local authority officers reported an established *hierarchy of desirability* based on student attainment, with the faith school at the top and the Academy at the bottom. Data at that time also revealed distinct patterns in school populations, with the faith school catering predominantly for white and Afro-Caribbean learners; the separate girls' and boys' schools, white and Asian learners; while Parkside had a much more ethnically diverse population. One parent explained these patterns as resulting from particular groups of parents choosing to send their children to schools where, in the light of growing inter-ethnic tensions within the district, *they thought they would be safe*.

Government policies to increase parental choice and, with this, diversity in educational provision, were reported to be doing little to change the nature of educational provision in the area, nor was it equitable in terms of access. The view was expressed that *all schools in the area select*, and that this was particularly the case with the higher attaining schools, which attracted more applicants than places.

Meanwhile, some parents were seen to be better able to manoeuvre the admissions system than others, leading to a lack of choice for ill-informed families – who are also often the most vulnerable families. It was suggested to us that these families often assume that their child will go to the nearest school and do not complete admissions procedures, meaning that the local authority is unable to act to facilitate access to schooling.

Parents were also reported to make school choices based on factors such as whether they liked the uniform and local hearsay, with schools' reputations and their actual performance not necessarily matching. Some parents were known to express a negative preference, making comments such as, *I want my child to go anywhere other than the Academy*, with the consequence that their child ended up going to the only schools left open to them as alternatives. In terms of their academic profiles and levels of deprivation, these schools were, at the time, on a par with Parkside, and children who attended them had to travel significant distances and were therefore unlikely to have many peers from their local neighbourhood alongside them in the classroom.

As a result of these historical factors, it is reasonable to assume that, when it was set up, Parkside Academy had a more *challenging* intake than other secondary schools serving the area. Certainly, its student population was drawn almost exclusively from the immediate locality. It also tended to include those whose parents did not look to exercise a choice through local authority admissions procedures, and those children who did not get places at other *more desirable* schools. Compared to the other schools in the area, the Academy's intake was, therefore, skewed towards those experiencing the highest levels of deprivation in the area.

A changing context

Three key issues rose from our study of developments at Parkside: the dynamic nature of improvement, the relationship between school autonomy and teacher autonomy and the role of the sponsor in decision-making. Focusing firstly on the dynamic nature of improvement, during its first five years, Parkside was reshaped into a context characterised by greater optimism, a safer working climate and much higher expectations. This was reflected in the school's massively improved results in national examinations and, eventually, in an inspection report that designated it as being *outstanding* (Salokangas and Ainscow 2017). It is also important to report that I have subsequently heard reports from former students who talk with pride regarding their experience at the school, not least the impact that the principal and staff had on their post-school life chances.

In all these respects, what was achieved at Parkside in its early years was remarkable by any standards. It is also an encouraging example of how the policy of giving schools that are struggling a new start and greater freedom, under different management and governance arrangement, can act as a catalyst for improvement.

However, just a few years later, following a series of changes in leadership and staffing, the examination results declined and a subsequent inspection led Parkside to be designated by inspectors as *requiring improvement* (Salokangas and Ainscow 2017). This suggests that, despite the short-term success of the strategies that were used to improve examination results, they are unlikely to ensure longer term improvements. It also leads me to challenge the assumption embedded in the academy policy rhetoric suggesting that increased autonomy will necessarily lead to greater freedom to innovate amongst teaching staff.

Secondly, our research throws light on the way that teacher autonomy was constrained in this otherwise autonomous school. In particular, we saw how the standards-driven culture and a highly regulated assessment policy limited teachers' pedagogical decision-making, not only framing their assessment practices but also impacting indirectly on their curricular decisions. This became most apparent through the ways in which planning and teaching were designed and conducted to most efficiently prepare students for examinations. Within this context, the overhanging fear of failure in examinations was seen to make staff reluctant to become involved in any form of risk-taking. This is ironic since one of the core arguments supporting early academies was that teachers had more freedom to innovate in their practice.

Thirdly, the evidence we collected portrays an image of an organisation with a heavily centralised approach to governance. In particular, we saw how decision-making regarding leadership recruitment and the membership of the local governing body, plus the existence of a powerful executive board, were symptomatic of an organisation holding significant levels of central power. And, inevitably, this meant that less space is left available for those stakeholders away from the centre.

Meanwhile, Parkside's sponsor did embrace the autonomy to which academies are entitled in dealing with various factors to do with the running of the school. In particular, we heard how staff reported lower pay and longer hours than their colleagues enjoy in the maintained sector. How far these differences were notable and, as such, how significant were the savings the sponsor gained from these contracts and in what ways these possible gains were spent, were questions beyond the scope of our research.

These changes reflect the increased autonomy of academies, particularly when it comes to decisions about major areas of policy. Significantly, they took place in the absence of the involvement of a local authority that might have been in a position to offer constructive advice from a more detached perspective.

Importantly, our account of developments in Parkside also throws light on processes which can lead a school that has been *turned around* to go into decline. The idea that schools regress to the mean is far from new, but, to my knowledge, there are few if any ethnographic accounts of how the process of regression actually happens.

In the case of Parkside, it seems that the erosion of professional autonomy may well have been a factor in the school's regression. Once this was gone, the school had less resilience to deal with the difficulties it faced. In such contexts, schools need to be autonomous only insofar as this means being free (and competent) to follow instructions from above. There may be some real autonomy at different levels, but the autonomy is always prescribed. If the instructions from on high are flawed, or if they fail to deal effectively with local circumstances, there is little else for the system to fall back on.

Wider implications

Linking this analysis of developments at Parkside to other research led us to argue that, although English academies are legally freed from the national curriculum – which arguably gives them space to experiment with educational approaches – this autonomy is largely theoretical. Based on this evidence, we concluded that because an academy's performance is measured against the same national performance indicators as other schools, in reality, examinations and inspections set a tight frame for educational practice in these schools (Kauko and Salokangas 2015; Salokangas and Ainscow 2017). In the case of

Parkside, the pressures this created led the sponsoring organisation to centralise much of the decision-making.

As a result, Parkside's sponsor was seen to have a significant capacity to experiment with matters to do with the school's management, governance and administration, which it utilised actively. The approaches introduced included the following: altering teaching pay and conditions, extending the school day and shortening holidays for senior leaders in comparison to the maintained sector contracts. They also included alternative approaches to principal recruitment, as well as minimising the involvement of local governors.

These ways in which the sponsor actively used the freedoms it had under the legislation to experiment echo developments reported from other sponsored academies in England (see, for example, Kulz 2015; Salokangas and Chapman 2014). They are also in line with the views of one of the key architects of the early academies policy, Andrew Adonis, who was at that time Minister of State for Education. In his book *Education, Education, Education: Reforming England's Schools*, he clarifies how the autonomy associated with academies should be understood:

> *Academies are independent state schools but it is often stated, wrongly, that the magic academy ingredient is independence alone. Rather, it is strong, independent governance and leadership. To be effective, the governors – and the headteachers and management teams they appoint and sustain – need to be unambiguously in control of their schools without managerial interference from local and national bureaucracies .... It is crucial to understand that 'independence' and 'sponsorship' go together and cannot be separated.*
> *(Adonis 2012, pp. 123–124)*

In these senses, Parkside can be seen as an exemplary case of a sponsored academy.

Relating this analysis of what happened at Parkside Academy to more recent international developments confirms my view that such reforms are increasingly shaped by a belief that improvements in schools will be achieved by an intensification of market forces that increase competition. In this context, parental choice is seen to encourage schools to try harder in order to improve their performance within national testing systems, which are focused on a relatively narrow set of learning outcomes. As a result, the innovations taking place tend to mainly involve changes in governance, management and administrative arrangements, often within groupings of schools.

This market-based thinking contrasts with the views of some of the early school autonomy supporters (e.g. Kahlenberg and Potter 2014), whose purpose was to provide greater space for school-level practitioners to explore ways of working that would best suit their particular students. In this way of thinking, independent state schools were seen as laboratories that are intended to generate new ways of working that can be shared with other schools in order to promote a kind of bottom-up system-wide change. Some advocates also stressed the importance of schools having strong links with their local communities and the other schools that serve them (Meyland-Smith and Evans 2009).

There are many individual examples, not least Parkside Academy, which show that greater autonomy can be effective in promoting rapid improvements in the attainment of students as measured by national testing systems, including those from disadvantaged and minority populations. However, the overall evidence from other countries we have considered is less convincing (Salokangas and Ainscow 2017). There are also concerns that where progress has been achieved this has involved the use of standardised, one-size-fits-all responses, within an approach that involves a narrowing of the educational diet. However, the extent to which educational success and failure should be based on the narrow view of education that standardised testing implies is an important question which should be discussed and challenged.

Similarly, there is little international evidence to suggest that independent state schools are promoting greater social integration within school systems, another of the hopes of early advocates. Indeed, there are worrying trends suggesting movement in an opposite direction (e.g. Kahlenberg and Potter 2014; Swanson 2017; Wiborg 2010). In terms of overall improvements, this has to be a concern, since there is increasing evidence that learner diversity can be a catalyst for bringing practitioners together in ways that stimulate professional learning. For example, the progress that has occurred in London and other urban contexts in England over the last 15 years that I report in Chapter 7 illustrates the potential of adopting such an inclusive approach.

Related to all of this, the expectation that these reforms would lead to reductions in bureaucracy as a result of local authorities having little, if any, involvement in the management of schools is another important issue. The worry is that, as with Parkside, the efforts of *new* administrators to centralise policy decisions for their groups of schools have simply replaced one form of top-down control with another. Meanwhile, there are concerns that no one organisation has an overall coordinating role within a local district, such that existing inequities of provision could continue and, possibly, grow.

Having said all of that, it is encouraging to report that there are examples of academies and multi-academy trusts that continue to develop creative and principled ways of working. Whilst they necessarily satisfy narrow national requirements in terms of curriculum and outcomes, people in these schools seem to understand education to be about more than measured attainment and have a broader view of how their students live and what they need to develop into successful adults. This view leads them to address a wider range of factors that disadvantage some of their students than prior attainments. It may also lead some schools to develop a view of education which is about processes rather than outcomes alone, and which therefore sees diversity in terms of respect and recognition rather than as a barrier to achievement.

Drawing out the lessons

Reflecting on these developments in England, Maija Salokangas and I went on to examine the implications of this growing international trend that promotes greater school autonomy as the means of improving state education systems. As I have explained, the assumption is that this will allow space for innovations, leading to new organisational arrangements, practices and forms of management and leadership, that will be more effective in promoting the learning of all students.

This global policy trend remains a matter of considerable debate, and, as I have noted, there are varied views as to the extent to which it is leading to the desired outcomes. Meanwhile, there is limited evidence regarding what is actually happening within these schools in relation to decision-making about policies and practice, and the extent to which this is leading to increased innovation and improved educational outcomes.

Our case study of Parkside began the process of filling this gap. In drawing out lessons from this experience, we adopted a pragmatic view that took account of the fact that the movement towards greater autonomy is picking up speed across the world. In addressing this agenda, we also recognised that there are no simple solutions to what are complex problems. What we can do, however, is to reach out to reformers, and to local actors involved in negotiating reforms, in order to offer them signposts and critical thinking tools that can inform their future actions.

We argued that, in the main, autonomous school reforms in England have not, as yet, successfully delivered on their ambitious promises. A central reason for this is that there have been contradicting forces at play, pulling the reforms in different directions. The coexistence of these forces has created tensions that have blurred the sense of purpose. In so doing, this has hindered autonomous schools from achieving what they were expected to achieve.

In summary, we noted three main contradictory forces that were evident in the story of Parkside. First of all, there is a tension between free market approaches and educational equity. As we have shown, the autonomous school movement is closely aligned with free market approaches in education, i.e. increased choice and competition, deregulation of provision, and opening public school management and governance to new players. The argument put forward to support these moves suggests that they will enhance educational opportunities for all children, since parents will be in a better position to choose what they see as the *best* school. This, in turn, will enhance competition, so that standards in all schools will rise.

However, if we look at evidence from different countries across the world, it becomes evident that market approaches in education have not helped in achieving educational equity and social justice. For example, parental choice and competition between schools have widened the gap between desirable schools and less desirable schools in countries as varied as Chile (Carrasco et al. 2015), Sweden (Wiborg 2010) and Finland (Kosunen 2014). This evidence suggests that divisions between what are seen as *good* and *bad* schools contribute to social injustice in varied ways. What it also tells us is that middle-class, well-educated and wealthier parents tend to be much more capable at making preferable choices in competitive school markets than parents from less advantaged backgrounds (Ball 2003; van Zanten 2009; Waslander, Pater, and van der Weide 2010). In addition, where countries have a private fee-paying tier, these schools mainly serve better off families.

These examples provide a flavour as to how market approaches in education, including autonomous school reforms, have so far failed to create more equitable school systems. They lead me to join the growing ranks of researchers contesting the argument that the education market will fix the system from within and, in so doing, reduce social inequalities to the particular advantage of learners from minority and economically disadvantaged backgrounds (e.g. Reay 2017; Tomlinson 2022). Instead, I argue that if we truly want to see progress towards educational equity, some degree of steering is needed in ensuring that the students in most need receive the support they require.

The second tension arises from the belief in innovation as a fix for many of the ills that are seen to exist in schools. In contrast, Maija Salokangas and I argued that blind belief in innovations *for innovations sake* is incompatible with the nature of work taking place in schools. Let me illustrate what we mean. Innovation has become a buzzword in recent years, which, as a term, carries great promise of a quick fix and a brighter future. However, it is not only education policy and public discourses that have been plagued with innovation hype but also public policy and governance more widely (Hodgson 2012; Russell and Vinsel 2016). This belief in the power of innovation as a solution to many ills can be traced back to technology industry discourses. Indeed, parallels have been drawn between autonomous school innovations and technological developments. So, for example, some promoters of disruptive innovation in education have claimed that charter schools should disrupt the education monopoly (Jacobs 2015), following the direction taken by Uber in developing its taxi empire (Haeffele-Balch and Boettke 2016).

Innovation holds a promise of something better than what was there before, simultaneously discrediting old practices as being poor. However, this kind of innovation hype is particularly problematic in relation to education, as it tends to ignore the unpredictable social nature of what takes place in schools, be it student learning, or staff efforts in academic, pastoral care or administrative work. Take teachers' practices as an example. In reality, their tasks involve a mix of routine and creativity; careful planning and thinking on your feet; tried and tested methods and experimenting with new ones, which sometimes work and sometimes do not. Anybody who has worked as a teacher knows that much of teaching can be repetitive drudgery, as with the learning of certain crucial skills and content, be it irregular verbs in second language, tables in maths or learning to swim, requiring considerable repetitive efforts from the learner to master. However, an experienced teacher also knows that teaching certain content and skills lends themselves to exploration, creativity, problem-solving and Eureka-moments.

In relation to administrative and pastoral care work in schools, the term innovation tends to be an even worse fit, as both should safeguard and ensure the long-term well-being of all students. Quick-fix administrative innovations can, at worst, be risky for students, as they may destabilise the day-to-day work taking place.

The important thing here is to acknowledge this multifaceted and complex nature of work taking place in schools, and the fact that not all *old, or tried and tested* practices are necessarily poor. In line with the argument of Russell and Vinsel (2016), I suggest that instead of focusing on innovations, we should pay more attention to the maintenance of these complex systems and equip practitioners with the skills to improve the system *from within*. That said, as stressed throughout this book, I acknowledge the importance of professional learning, creativity and the continuous development of new ways of working in schools. I also consider it a high priority to offer school staff opportunities to enhance their practices, learn, explore and try out new ways of working.

This is why, instead of blind belief in the power of innovations offering quick-fix solutions for education, Maija Salokangas and I called for more sustainable long-term developments in which teachers and other school staff have the capacity to be creative in their ways of working. This means that we should focus on creating the organisational conditions in which a skilful workforce is able to use professional judgement in the complex social and pedagogical situations they face. It also means that practitioners must be supported by their schools and communities to do so, not least through appropriate professional development opportunities.

Finally, the third tension in the autonomous school reforms is the idea that local autonomy, especially teacher autonomy and high-stakes accountability, can coexist. It is intellectually dishonest to claim that individuals who are subject to high-stakes accountability and control in their work environment are also autonomous in relation to their practice.

Coopetition

Relating all of this to the agenda of this book, a major concern for me about the recent English reforms, particularly the academies programme, is that they are producing more and more losers. Indeed, recent years have seen an increase in the number of children and young people being excluded from schools or placed in segregated provision.[4] Within a policy context that places so much emphasis on competition, there is a sad inevitability about this situation: the creation of winners means that there will inevitably be those who lose out.

Our research team at The University of Manchester has recently carried out a study[5] that points to a possible way forward in relation to this challenge. This involves the creation of area partnerships that combine competition, collaboration and contextually informed accountability.

Account 9.2. Area partnerships. The study drew on the idea of 'coopetition', as defined by Muijs and Rumyantseva (2014), and the following conditions that they suggest are needed in order for it to be effective: partners who see *clear and tangible benefits* from collaboration; *trust between partners*, established through the careful development of relationships between key actors; *clear goals and agreements* between partners; and *forms of leadership that are skilful* in managing tensions.

Muijs and Rumyantseva go on to argue that these conditions are likely to be hard to achieve in competitive situations. Bearing this concern in mind, our research analysed a series of well-established partnerships in different parts of England. All of them involve headteachers taking on system leadership roles. Local authority involvement in the partnerships varies across the sample, with some leading and orchestrating the partnership, others working as joint partners with schools and some having no role whatsoever.

In the most effective of the examples, it was evident that the partnerships were guided by a strong commitment to equity, underpinned by context informed decision making at the local level. These developments build on earlier research which suggests that collaboration between schools has enormous potential for fostering the capacity of education systems to respond to learner diversity. Moreover, such partnerships can help reduce the polarisation of schools within a local area, to the particular benefit of those students who are marginalised at the edges of the system and whose progress is a cause for concern.

This study offers reasons to be optimistic. Despite the competitive atmosphere that permeates the English education system and the fragmentation that this has encouraged, there remains a strong appetite in the field to engage in collaboration. Indeed, several new area partnerships have emerged in recent months.[6] It is significant, too, that many experienced school leaders – including leaders of multi academy trusts – are motivated to take on leadership roles that take them beyond their duties within their own institutions.

That said, although the examples we examined are fulfilling an important means of encouraging mutual support, there is less evidence that they are making direct contributions to changes in practice that address the barriers faced by many young people. Where we saw evidence of this beginning to happen a common set of factors were in place.

Most important of these is the use of available statistical evidence to identify concerns such as poor attendance, increased level of exclusions, and dips in outcomes as determined by results in test and examinations. What made these data more powerful, however, was when, as a result of the partnership structures, local practitioners were able to provide an informed interpretation to guide the actions that were taken.

The findings of this study led my colleagues and I to propose a system of evidence-based professional accountability, coordinated at the local area level. This implies a move away from a heavy reliance on external accountability towards an investment in the professional capital of teachers and school leaders, as suggested by Fullan et al. (2015). However, this has to be challenging and credible. In other words, it must not involve forms of collusion within which partners endorse one another in an acceptance of mediocrity.

Moving forward

Despite the worrying trends that have emerged from the recent reforms in England, greater autonomy for schools still makes sense, particularly if it provides space for practitioners to innovate. The problem is that other policies based on competition between schools have sometimes prevented this from happening. Rather, as we saw in the case of Parkside Academy, they have led to a search for one-size-fits-all strategies for improving examination and test scores that can be imposed on teachers.

This leads me to recommend three actions that are needed in order to make school autonomy more effective in promoting equity within the English education system:

- There needs to be a fundamental rethink of the national accountability systems, not least the ways in which student progress and the outcomes of school inspections are reported, so that there is a focus on progress towards a much broader range of outcomes.
- More resources should be aimed at the improvement of teaching and learning through continuous professional development. This is a recognition that well-educated staff, who are encouraged to upskill their knowledge, are in the best position to respond to the varied needs of their students.
- Incentives need to be provided that encourage greater collaboration within schools and between schools, in order that successful practices are made available to more students. This emphasis on collaboration then needs to move beyond the school gate, with schools drawing on the energy and resources that exist within families and local communities.

Given the dangers associated with school isolation, there also has to be some form of local coordination. Unfortunately, in many areas of England no one organisation has the overall picture that would enable them to orchestrate more collaborative ways of working. With this in mind, I argue that local authorities should be involved in monitoring and challenging schools – including academies – whilst headteachers and their colleagues share responsibility for the overall leadership of improvement efforts.

All of this has significant implications for national policy makers. It suggests that, in order to make use of the potential of autonomy and minimise the risks involved, they need to foster greater flexibility at the local level in order that practitioners have the space to analyse their particular circumstances and determine priorities accordingly. This means that policy makers must recognise that the details of policy implementation are not amenable to central regulation. Rather, these should be dealt with by those who are close to and, therefore, in a better position to understand local contexts: teachers and principals (Ainscow and West 2006).

There is, therefore, a crucial role for governments. They must provide a strong sense of direction regarding the principles that are intended to steer locally led developments. Linked to this, there is a need to ensure that national accountability systems reflect these principles. This involves a recognition that, within education systems, *what gets measured gets done* (Ainscow 2005). So, for example, the education systems mentioned in this chapter now collect far more statistical data on schools than ever before in order to determine their effectiveness. This trend to measure learning through test scores is widely recognised as a double-edged sword precisely because it is such a potent lever for change. On the one hand, data are required in order to monitor the progress of learners, evaluate the teaching and learning, review policies and processes, plan new initiatives and so on.

In these senses, as I noted earlier, data can be seen as the life-blood of educational decision-making. Put simply, in education, what gets measured gets done. On the other hand, if effectiveness is evaluated on the basis of narrow, even inappropriate, performance indicators, then the impact can be deeply damaging. While appearing to promote accountability and transparency, the use of data can, in practice, conceal more than it reveals, invite misinterpretations and, worst of all, have a perverse effect on the behaviour of professionals to teach to the test, such that their efforts to include vulnerable children are not valued and recognised by schools and policy makers.

The challenge, therefore, is to focus on a broader range of data, where progress is determined not just in terms of scores on learning outcomes, but where information on progress regarding equity is incorporated into the analyses. This means that care needs to be exercised in deciding what evidence is collected and, indeed, how it is analysed and used. In other words, we need to measure what we value, rather than is so often the case, valuing what we can measure.

Conclusion

At the heart of the strategies, I have summarised in this book are attempts to develop new, more fruitful working relationships: between national and local government, between administrators and practitioners, within and between schools and between schools and their local communities. A helpful theoretical interpretation that can be made of these strategies is that, together, they can help to strengthen social capital. In this way, they can help establish pathways through which energy, expertise and lessons from innovations can spread.

In recent years, the work of Robert Putnam (2000) has been most influential in making the idea of social capital a focus for research and policy discussion. In so doing, he has demonstrated how it can help to mitigate the insidious effects of socio-economic disadvantage. Writing about the United

States, for example, Putnam states that *what many high-achieving school districts have in abundance is social capital, which is educationally more important than financial capital* (p. 306).

In relation to schools, Mulford (2007) defines social capital in terms of the groups, networks, norms and trust that people have available to them for productive purposes. He goes on to suggest that by treating social relationships as a form of capital, they can be seen as a resource, which people can then draw on to achieve their goals. In a way that echoes the ecology of equity presented earlier in this book, Mulford argues that there are three types of social capital. The first of these is *bonding social capital*, which is what happens amongst work colleagues within a school; *bridging social capital* is what can be developed between schools through various forms of networking and collaboration; and finally, *linking social capital* relates to the formation of stronger relationships between a school and wider community resources.

The evidence I have presented suggests a series of interconnected strategies that can help foster the development of stronger social capital of all three types. As we have seen, these strategies can help to break down social barriers between schools – and between schools and other stakeholders – in order to facilitate the sorts of mutual benefit that we have described when schools learn how to learn from one another. In this sense, the strategies provide the basis for what Hargreaves (2010) describes as a *self-improving school system.*

The implication of all of this is that the search for pathways to inclusion and equity involves an ongoing struggle against forces that are pulling in a very different direction. The good news is that the accounts of developments presented in this book provide reasons for optimism as we continue this struggle.

Notes

1 Child Poverty Action Group. Child Poverty Facts and Figures. 2022. Available online: https://cpag.org.uk/
2 There are 152 local authorities in England. Traditionally they have been responsible for schools in their areas.
3 All names have been changed to avoid identification of the school.
4 https://assets.publishing.service.gov.uk/government/uploads/system/uploads/attachment_data/file/936524/Ofsted_offrolling_report_YouGov_090519.pdf
5 https://thestaffcollege.uk/
6 https://aepa.org.uk/about-us/

10 Reaching out to all learners

Some years ago I visited a village primary school in a rural district of Ghana. There were 50 or so children in each class and the physical resources were noticeably poor. So, e.g., some of the children arrived in the morning carrying stools on their heads. It seems that for these children this is the equivalent of those in my country bringing a pen and a ruler from home. Apparently, each evening the stools are taken home so that they can be used for domestic purposes. It may also be that some families are reluctant to leave them in school where they might be stolen, since the classroom are open, having few walls.

A surprising feature of the school from an English perspective was the presence of a number of students with noticeable impairments. Further inquiries confirmed that the headteacher assumes that it is his responsibility to admit all children in the district. *Where else would they go?* he remarked, adding, *They are all our children*. Further such examples of what Miles (1989) refers to as casual integration can be found in many so-called developing countries, particularly in rural districts.

Addressing dilemmas

As will be clear to readers by now, my focus is on finding ways of reaching out to all learners in schools. Efforts to address this challenge are influenced by the ways in which student differences are perceived. As I explain in Chapter 1, differences may be defined in terms of certain taken-for-granted criteria of normality, against which some come to be seen as being abnormal. Alternatively, perceptions may be guided by a view that every student is unique, with their own experiences, interests and aptitudes.

This argument can be viewed as involving a dilemma.[1] Explaining this concept, Berlak and Berlak (1987) argue that societies are full of interests, incentives and pressures that are loosely held together but which are diverse and, ultimately, work against one another. Such contradictions are embedded in the tasks that education systems are expected to carry out. So, e.g., schools are expected to perform multiple functions that, ultimately, cannot be reconciled one with another, e.g. to enable those with the most advantages to forge ahead, whilst, at the same time, closing the gap between them and their peers

DOI: 10.4324/9781003438014-10

with fewer advantages. At the level of practice, these contradictions present themselves as a series of dilemmas – an obvious one being how to allocate and use resources, particularly human resources. Crucially, such dilemmas can be resolved but not solved.

Keeping in mind this debate, in this concluding chapter I reflect further on what I have learnt over the last 25 years about how to develop schools for all. Remembering the importance of context when thinking about educational developments, I focus on finding local pathways that help identify and address barriers that are limiting the presence, progress and achievement of learners. As I have argued, this requires a collective will amongst stakeholders, using evidence to stimulate and guide their efforts.

This points once again to the importance I place on local contexts. it means that while some challenges can only be addressed at the national government level, there are others that can only be understood and addressed at a local level – by local actors with a deep knowledge of the places where they work who can access local resources (Kerr and Ainscow 2022).

Informed by this argument, the examples presented in this book point to the power of education when stakeholders act on their local knowledge, harnessing local resources to develop coordinated and strategic actions. In doing so, they also diverge markedly from the approach currently being pursued by the current English government as part of its so-called *levelling-up* strategy. As my colleague Kirstin Kerr explained to me recently, this seems to treat high-poverty areas as *containers* into which interventions that *work* can be dropped, rather than as dynamic entities that present both challenges to and opportunities for equitable reforms (Kerr and Ainscow 2022).

Addressing complexity

As illustrated throughout this book, I have been involved in efforts to promote inclusion and equity in many countries. These experiences have thrown light on the complexities involved. To illustrate this, in what follows I focus on developments in the Netherlands and Portugal, two relatively small, economically developed countries, where progress differs significantly.

In considering these accounts, I remind readers about the limitations of the information upon which they are based. In particular, I am conscious that they draw on observations and discussions that occurred during relatively short visits, albeit over many years. At the same time, my engagements were often conducted through interpreters.

> **Account 10.1. The Netherlands.** Recently, Stevenson et al. (2021) argued that the Dutch education system is one of the most decentralised and complex systems in the world, and that the Government has no formal responsibility nor any direct means of control in this policy area.
>
> This diversity of provision is a result of efforts made over many years to provide schools that reflect different views about education within

the community, not least in respect to religious beliefs. This has enabled groups within Dutch society to open their own schools, which are Government funded and part of school boards that vary in size. Furthermore, Stevenson and colleagues note that, since August 2017, the inspectorate no longer holds the direct providers of education (i.e. school leaders) accountable for the educational quality of a school. Instead the responsibility for educational quality and, hence, the focus of the inspectorate, is redirected to school boards.

International comparisons indicate that the Dutch education system grants a high level of autonomy to the school boards (OECD, 2016). Furthermore, Dutch schools (and thus their boards) are more autonomous than schools in many other counties. For example, it is reported that in no other country are so many of the key decisions on education taken at school board level: over 90% compared to an average of 34% (OECD, 2018).

In recent years I have been privileged to spend time learning about the Dutch education system, which has many obvious strengths. It is, for example, highly resourced by international standards and teachers are well paid, although they do work long hours[2]. Classes are relatively small according to international comparisons, and young people feel particularly happy with their lives[3]. And, in terms of the agenda of this book, I have seen examples of good practice and met many teachers who are committed to inclusive education.

On the other hand, recent research suggests that the Dutch education system, which selects at the age of 11, is increasing inequality of opportunity in general[4]. Some experts argue, too, that the government-mandated system of tracking student achievement from the age of six simply increases the amount of testing rather than supporting educational goals. Other studies show that stress levels amongst some of the world's happiest children have increased dramatically in recent years and the Netherlands was judged to have dropped from 4th to 20th place in a worldwide ranking on respecting children's rights[5].

The organisation of the Dutch system is indeed complex, with many different types of schools (Waslander et al. 2016). There is also a relatively high proportion of children taught in various types of special education provision, sometimes away from their homes (Pijl, 2016). For example, talking recently to some students I was shocked to hear that they travel 50 kilometres or more each day to attend a secondary school that has separate arrangements for disabled learners. One young man explained that the director of his local school had refused to take him.

Both public and private providers are eligible for public resources when the funding requirements are met. Consequently, the provision of education is free on the condition that adequate education is provided, which is monitored by the inspectorate. Freedom of education is intended to protect the educational rights of both school organisations, and parents and students, against far reaching government interventions in education (Hooge and Honingh, 2014).

In parallel to these developments there has grown a range of partnerships and networks that, along with local authorities, are involved in the coordination and support of educational developments. Additional resources to support vulnerable groups of learners are distributed through area networks in a way that sometimes seems to create tensions between them and the school boards.

In discussing possible ways forward with Dutch colleagues involved in educational planning, a major question is, what can be done within these complex arrangements to achieve greater inclusion and equity? Thinking about this challenge, I have found the following definitions, proposed in UNESCO guidance (2017), to be useful:

- **Inclusion** is a process that helps overcome barriers limiting the presence, participation and achievement of learners; and
- **Equity** is about ensuring that there is a concern with fairness, such that the education of all learners is seen as having equal importance.

As argued throughout this book, these definitions involve a move away from explanations of educational failure that concentrate on the characteristics of individual children and their families, towards an analysis of contextual barriers experienced by students within schools. In this way, students who do not respond to existing arrangements come to be regarded as *hidden voices* who, under certain conditions, can encourage the improvement of schools. An illustration of what this involves occurred during a conversation with a disabled student in the Netherlands who, talking about the challenges he had faced in getting enrolled in local schools, commented: *People are open minded, the systems are not.*

It seems, then, that movements guided by the principles of inclusion and equity in the Netherlands face deep barriers that reflect history and cultural assumptions. These include systems of assessment that can act as obstacles to the progress of students through the stages of the system. Changing these established arrangements will be difficult. This means that progress will require the involvement of the various key stakeholders within the education system, not least school principals who, as I have indicated, have considerable influence on student admissions.

Some form of local coordination will be needed in order to encourage the forms of evidence-based collaborative developments that will be needed. This is where the situation in the Netherlands is so confusing, particularly to the visitor. For example, which of the various agencies involved have the capacity to provide some form of local coordination? And, which of these are able to drive forward school-led improvement efforts? My impression is that the school boards are in the best position to take on such roles, particularly if they can work together to form area networks.

So, my tentative suggestion is that strategies based on inclusion and equity could be the basis of the next stage of educational development in the Netherlands. This would, I believe, provide the impetus that would move the Dutch education system from good to great. However, as argued by Collins (2001) on the basis of his analysis of approaches used in highly successful businesses, *Good is the enemy of great*. This leads him to suggest that the reason we don't have great schools is principally because we have so many good schools.

Avoiding labels

Moving on, I turn now to the situation in Portugal, where there is evidence that a focus on inclusion and equity over recent years has led to the overall strengthening of the national education system.

> **Account 10.2. Portugal.** Since 2008, Portugal has had in place laws envisioning the provision of education for all students, without exception, in their local mainstream school, in accordance with Article 24 of the United Nations Convention on the Rights of Persons with Disabilities. These laws also create explicit obligations requiring the adjustment of the educational process to include all students.
>
> This reform programme has led to a push for schools *"where each and every student, regardless of their personal and social situation, finds responses to their potential, expectations, and needs, and develops a level of education that creates full participation, a sense of belonging, and equity, contributing to social inclusion and cohesion"* (Decree Law No. 54/2018).
>
> In line with current international thinking regarding educational equity and inclusion, as summarised elsewhere in this book, the Portuguese legislation emphasises the responsibility of schools to identify barriers to individual students' learning and develop strategies to overcome them. It also calls for a change in school cultures to encourage more multilevel and multidisciplinary interventions, a demonstrated commitment to inclusive practices and a move away from categorising students.
>
> Legislation introduced in 2008 led to special schools being transformed into resource centres for inclusion, tasked with supporting their former students, who are now placed in mainstream schools. This pathway continued significantly with the Inclusive Education Act of 2018, Decree-Law 54/2018, which created a further impetus for promoting inclusive education.
>
> With this agenda as the focus, the Government has given priority to the development of education policy that guarantees equal access to public education in ways that are intended to promote educational success and equal opportunities. In so doing, national policies promote the democratisation of education and the other conditions necessary to contribute to equal opportunities; the overcoming of economic, social and cultural inequalities; and the development of personality and the spirit

of tolerance, mutual understanding, solidarity and responsibility, social progress and democratic participation in collective life.

Importantly, the Portuguese legislation has moved away from a view that it is necessary to categorise students in order to intervene. Rather, it supports the idea that all children and young people can achieve a profile of competencies and skills at the end of their compulsory education career, even if they follow different learning pathways. It therefore emphasises flexible curricular models, systematic monitoring of the effectiveness of interventions, and an ongoing dialogue between teachers and parents/caregivers (Alves et al., 2020).

A key feature of the Portuguese education system is the emphasis placed on collaboration. This is facilitated by a well-established pattern of schools working in local clusters – a particular strength in relation to the promotion of inclusive practices and forms of organisation that support the introduction of these ways of working. Indeed, many other countries are seeking to establish similar arrangements, building on the research summarised earlier in this book which suggests that collaboration between schools has an enormous potential for fostering their capacity to respond to student diversity.

A further area of strength in Portugal is the active involvement of community representatives in policy formulation within the school clusters. This includes the appointment of school directors, who are elected for four years. These arrangements provide a sound basis for engaging community partners to support the promotion of inclusion and equity within a local cluster.

I have been occasionally involved in developments in Portugal since 1995. This has included a series of linked initiatives that produced findings that are relevant to the suggestions provided in this book. These developments took the form of collaborative action research projects focusing on the promotion of inclusive practices in schools (Ainscow 2007). I also worked in recent years with schools involved in the development of the Inclusive Inquiry approach, as explained in Chapter 5. Once again, these experiences pointed to how local factors influence the ways in which improvement efforts are interpreted and implemented within particular contexts. They also threw light on the expertise and creativity that exists within Portuguese schools and their communities.

More recently, I was a member of an international team that reviewed progress in Portugal in relation to inclusion and equity (see OECD 2022). A striking feature of our discussions with stakeholders in different parts of the country was the widespread awareness and acceptance of the principles upon which the national education policies are based. Particularly impressive was the way that children and young people talked about their pride at being students in a school that is inclusive. Many also talked of the value they gained from being involved with such a diverse range of classmates.

At the same time, there is a noticeable level of awareness at all levels of the education system of the dangers associated with using labels in referring to potentially vulnerable groups of students. Frequent mention is also made of the political history of the country that has influenced the concern to see education as a basis for fostering democracy.

What is most significant, however, is that as the Portuguese education system has moved forward in relation to inclusion over the last two decades, the country has also seen impressive developments in terms of equity. Indeed, it is one of the few countries with a positive trajectory of improvement in all of the subjects assessed by OECD's Programme for International Student Assessment (PISA). In addition, the rate of early leavers from education has reduced significantly, although there are significant variations between regions.

A paradigm shift?

As we see, the approach taken in Portugal is in stark contrast to that taken in the Netherlands and, indeed, many other countries, where recent years have led to an expansion of labels that situate problems of educational progress within the child. For example, in England, this emphasis on labelling has led to a massive expansion in the number of learners placed in separate provision of various forms and I was disappointed to see that the current Government plans to open more special schools. At the same time, there has been a worrying increase in those who are out of school altogether (Kerr and Ainscow 2022).

Meanwhile, the experience of Portugal suggests that seeing inclusion as a principle for educational reform can provide a pathway to equity. This points to the urgent need for a new direction in education policies across the world.

As I argued earlier in this book, as countries formulate policies for education reform, it is time to take *an inclusive turn*. Moving in this radically new direction will take time, as is evident in the account of developments in Portugal, where, of course, there are still more challenges to be addressed. It will also require that the resources and expertise that exist within special education provision should be redirected towards the development of schools where children and young people learn how to learn together and live together.

Comparing developments in the Netherlands and Portugal, I am also conscious of the impact of local histories, not least in the way that they influence the way policies are developed and implemented. I am certainly not qualified to analyse this factor but it cannot be overlooked.

In the case of Portugal, it is evident that the major political changes that occurred in the 1970s have continued to shape developments. Meanwhile, the history of attempts to address differences within the Netherlands, as reflected in the tradition of coalition governments, appears to make policy change difficult. Commenting on these differences recently, a senior Dutch educator, having visiting schools in Portugal, said, 'We think of problems, they think of solutions'.

The two accounts also throw light on an ongoing debate within the field regarding what inclusive education means and how best it can be addressed. For example, a distinguished academic, known to be positive towards inclusive education, was heard to comment recently that the problem with the Index for Inclusion is that it does not take account of *children with PMLD* (i.e. profound and multiple learning disabilities).

Remarks such as this indicate that the perspective adopted in this book involves a paradigm shift. That is to say, it requires a fundamental change in the way the idea of inclusive education is understood and addressed. Writing about this some 30 years ago, I suggested that it involves a move away from *an individual gaze*, where educational difficulties are explained in terms of the characteristics of children, towards what I called a *curriculum perspective*, where difficulties experienced by learners are defined in relation to tasks and activities, and classroom conditions (Ainscow 1993).

The idea of paradigm shifts was brought into use by the physicist and philosopher Thomas Kuhn (1970). Even though he restricted the use of the term to the natural sciences, the concept has been used in numerous social contexts to describe a profound change in a fundamental model or perception of events. As explained by Burrell and Morgan (1979), paradigms represent different views of social realities. However, a problem that has been identified is that, unlike in the hard sciences, where new paradigms replace previous ways of thinking, within the social world, earlier and new paradigms may well continue to operate at the same time (Skrtic 1991). This perhaps explains why competing definitions of inclusive education lead to misunderstandings and, sometimes, disputes in the field.

Discussing such debates, Clark et al. (1999) make reference to what they refer to as the *dilemma of commonality versus difference*, i.e. how do we respond to what it is that learners have in common yet at the same time respond to what it is that is different about each of them? And, as noted earlier in this chapter, whilst such dilemmas can be *resolved* they cannot be *solved*.

A framework for inclusive development

Kurt Lewin, often called *the father of action research*, famously argued that *the best way to understand an organization is by trying to change it*. The projects described in this book have demonstrated the truth of this statement, not least in the way they have exposed the barriers that can limit progress in relation to the principles of inclusion and equity. This leads me to repeat the argument of the OECD (2012) when it states:

> *The evidence is conclusive: equity in education pays off. The highest performing education systems across OECD countries are those that combine high quality and equity. In such education systems, the vast majority of students can attain high level skills and knowledge that depend on their ability and drive, more than on their socio-economic background.*
>
> *(p. 17)*

Through my involvement as a consultant to UNESCO over the last 30 years or so, I have had the privilege of working with colleagues in many countries, including politicians and senior government officials, in attempts to foster greater inclusion and equity within their education systems. During this period, I have also contributed to various international events and publications designed to influence thinking, policy and practice.

These experiences led me to formulate a framework for identifying pathways that can help promote inclusion and equity within education systems (see Figure 10.1). Amended from earlier versions (Ainscow 2005, 2020), the framework has emerged from efforts to move education systems in a more inclusive and equitable direction. These experiences have also thrown light on the factors that can facilitate or limit the progress of such initiatives.

As can be seen, the framework places schools at the centre of the analysis. This reinforces the point that moves towards inclusion must be focused on increasing the capacity of local neighbourhood schools to support the participation and learning of an increasingly diverse range of learners. This is the change of direction I have referred to in this book as an *inclusive turn*. A radical move, it argues that a focus on inclusion should be about the development of schools, rather than attempts to integrate vulnerable groups of students into existing arrangements.

At the same time, the framework draws attention to a range of contextual factors that bear on the way schools carry out their work. As I will explain, these are influences that may provide support and encouragement to those in schools who are wishing to move in an inclusive direction. However, the same

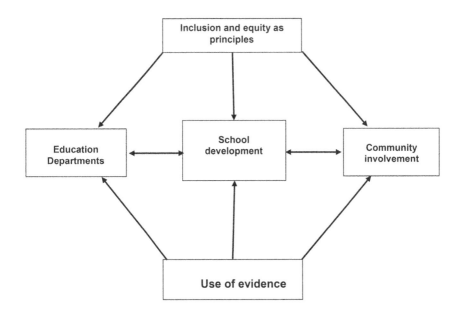

Figure 10.1 A framework for contextual analysis in relation to inclusion and equity.

factors can also help identify barriers to progress and pathways to follow in order to overcome these difficulties.

In what follows, each of these five factors is explained, leading to a series of key ideas that need to be considered when analysing a particular context in order to develop future policies. These ideas are guided by a belief that **inclusion and equity should not be seen a separate policy**. Rather, they should be viewed as principles that inform all national policies, particularly those that deal with the curriculum, assessment, school evaluation, teacher education and budgets. They must also inform all stages of education, from early years through to higher education.

Inclusion and equity as principles

Terms such as *equity* and *inclusion* can be confusing since they may mean different things to different people. This is a particular problem when trying to move forward with others – particularly in schools, where everybody is so busy. If there is not a shared understanding of the intended direction of travel, progress will be more difficult. There is, therefore, a need to agree definitions of these concepts.

As explained in Chapter 1, in establishing a definition for strategic purposes, our earlier research (i.e. Ainscow et al. 2006) led us to suggest that inclusion in education should be as follows:

- **Seen as a process**. That is to say, inclusion has to be seen as a never-ending search to find better ways of responding to diversity. It is about learning how to live with and learn from difference. In this way differences come to be seen more positively as a stimulus for fostering learning, amongst children and adults.
- **Concerned with the identification and removal of barriers.** Consequently, it involves collecting, collating and evaluating information from a wide variety of sources within particular contexts in order to plan for improvements in policy and practice. It is also about using evidence of various kinds to stimulate creativity and problem-solving.
- **Focused on improving the presence, participation and achievement of all students.** Here, *presence* is concerned with where children are educated, and how reliably and punctually they attend; *participation* relates to the quality of their experiences whilst they are there and, therefore, must incorporate the views of the learners themselves; and *achievement* is about the outcomes of learning across the curriculum, not merely test or examination results.
- **Involve a particular emphasis on those groups of learners who may be at risk of marginalisation, exclusion or underachievement**. This indicates the moral responsibility to ensure that those groups that are statistically most at risk are carefully monitored, and that, where necessary, steps are taken to ensure their presence, participation and achievement within the

education system. At the same time, there is a need to keep an eye out for learners who may be overlooked.

Our experience is that a well-orchestrated debate about these elements can lead to a wider understanding of the principle of inclusion. Furthermore, such a debate, though by its nature slow and, possibly, never ending, can help to foster the conditions within which schools can feel encouraged to move in a more inclusive direction. Crucially, this must seek to involve all stakeholders, including families, communities, political and religious leaders, and the media. It must also involve those within national and local education district offices.

The use of evidence. As I argue in Chapter 2, in order to address concerns about inclusion and equity in education systems, it is important to know who is included, who is segregated, who feels marginalised and who is excluded from schooling. Without such evidence, there can be no accountability. However, when data collection efforts are only focused on particular categories of learner, there is a risk of promoting deficit views of those students who share certain characteristics or come from similar backgrounds.

Engaging with evidence, including the views of children and their families, regarding these challenging questions has the potential to stimulate efforts to find more effective ways of promoting the participation and progress of all learners (Ainscow and Messiou 2017). Data on contextual factors are also needed, including resources and facilities, as well as attitudes, beliefs and social relationships.

With the growing technological capacity to handle large amounts of different types of data, it is increasingly possible to generate information about the many influences that effect the marginalisation, segregation and exclusion of students within education systems. As I have argued throughout this book, focusing on these factors can help to create the conditions for promoting inclusion and equity.

With this in mind, I have presented a different way of responding to learner diversity, one that is viewed in relation to barriers that exist within a given context, and opportunities to enhance and democratise learning opportunities, processes and outcomes. This leads me to argue that the extent to which students' experiences are inclusive and equitable is not dependent only on the educational practices of their schools. Instead, it depends on a whole range of interacting processes that reach into the school from outside. These include the demographics of the areas served by schools, the histories and cultures of the populations who send (or fail to send) their children to a school, and the economic and social realities faced by those populations.

As explained in Chapter 3, it is therefore helpful to generate evidence that addresses three interlinked sets of factors that impact on the participation and learning of students. These relate to: *within-school factors* to do with existing policies and practices; *between-school factors* that arise from the characteristics of local school systems; and *beyond-school factors*, including the demographics, economics, cultures and histories of local areas with a focus on reducing inequalities.

School development. There is not one single model of what an inclusive school looks like. What is common to highly inclusive schools, however, is that they are welcoming and supportive places for all of their students, not least those with impairments and others who sometimes find learning difficult. This does not prevent these schools from being committed to improving the achievements of all of their students. Indeed, they tend to have a range of strategies for strengthening achievement that are typical of those employed by all effective schools, and the emphasis on supporting vulnerable students does not appear to inhibit these strategies (Dyson, Howes and Roberts 2004). A key factor is the emphasis placed on tracking and supporting the progress of all students.

The implication is that schools need to be reformed and practices need to be improved in ways that will lead them to respond positively to student diversity – seeing individual differences not as problems to be fixed but as opportunities for enriching learning. Within such a conceptualisation, a consideration of difficulties experienced by students can provide an agenda for change and insights as to how such changes might be brought about. As I have explained in earlier chapters, this kind of approach is more likely to be successful in contexts where there is a culture of collaboration that encourages and supports problem-solving. According to this view, the development of inclusive practices is seen as involving those within a particular context in working together to address barriers to education experienced by some learners.

This means that attempts to develop inclusive schools should pay attention to the building of consensus around inclusive values within school communities. It implies that school leaders should be selected in the light of their commitment to inclusive values and their capacity to lead in a participatory manner (Riehl 2000). Finally, the external policy environment should be compatible with inclusive developments in order to support rather than to undermine schools' efforts.

Involving the wider community. In order to foster inclusion and equity in education, governments need to mobilise human and financial resources, some of which may not be under their direct control. Forming partnerships among key stakeholders who can support the process of change is therefore essential. These include the following: parents/caregivers; teacher trainers and researchers; national-, local- and school-level administrators and managers; policy makers and service providers in other sectors (e.g. health, child protection and social services); civic groups in the community; and members of minority groups that are at risk of exclusion.

Family involvement is particularly crucial. In some countries, parents and education authorities already cooperate closely in developing community-based programmes for certain groups of learners, such as those who are excluded because of their gender, social status or impairments (OECD 2018). A logical next step is for families to become involved in supporting change for developing inclusion in schools.

Where parents lack the confidence and skills to participate in such developments, it might be necessary to engage and build capacity and networks. This could include the creation of parent support groups, training parents to work with their children or building the advocacy skills of parents to negotiate with schools and authorities. Here, it is worth adding that there is evidence that the views of families, including children themselves, can be helpful in bringing new thinking to the efforts of schools to develop more inclusive ways of working.

All of this means changing how families and communities work and enriching what they offer to children. In this respect, there are many encouraging examples of what can happen when what schools do is aligned in a coherent strategy with the efforts of other local players – employers, community groups, universities and public services (Kerr et al. 2014). This does not necessarily mean schools doing more, but it does imply partnerships beyond the school, where partners multiply the impacts of each other's efforts.

With this argument in mind, two of my Manchester colleagues have explored the idea of area-based initiatives modelled on the principles underpinning the highly acclaimed Harlem Children's Zone in the United States (Dyson and Kerr 2013). This work involves attempts to improve outcomes for children and young people in areas of disadvantage through an approach characterised as being *doubly holistic*. That is to say, it seeks to develop coordinated efforts to tackle the factors that disadvantage children and enhance the factors which support them, across all aspects of their lives, and across their life spans, from conception through to adulthood. This approach was further explored through the Children's Neighbourhoods Scotland initiative (Drever, McLean and Lowden 2021).

All of this has implications for the various key stakeholders within education systems. In particular, teachers, especially those in senior positions, have to see themselves as having a wider responsibility for all children, not just those who attend their own schools. They also have to develop patterns of internal organisation that enable them to have the flexibility to cooperate with other schools and with stakeholders beyond the school gate. It means, too, that those who administer school systems have to adjust their priorities and ways of working in response to improvement efforts that are led from within schools.

Education departments. Policy is made at all levels of an education system, not least at the school and classroom levels. Furthermore, the promotion of equity is not simply a technical or organisational change – it is a movement in a clear philosophical direction. Moving to more inclusive ways of working therefore requires changes across an education system. These span from shifts in policy makers' values and ways of thinking, which enable them to provide a vision shaping a culture of inclusion, to significant changes within schools and the communities they serve.

A culture of inclusion within an education system requires a shared set of assumptions and beliefs among senior administrative staff at the national, district and school level that value differences, believe in collaboration and are committed to offering educational opportunities to all students. However, changing the cultural norms that exist within an education system is difficult to achieve, particularly within a context that is faced with so many competing pressures and where practitioners tend to work alone in addressing the problems they face. Therefore, leaders at all levels, including those in civil society and other sectors, have to be prepared to analyse their own situations, identify local barriers and facilitators, plan an appropriate development process and provide support for inclusive practices and effective strategies for monitoring equity in education.

National and district administrators have particularly important roles in promoting inclusive ways of managing schools and education processes. In particular, they need to establish the conditions for challenging non-inclusive, discriminatory educational practices. They also need to build consensus and commitment towards putting the principle of inclusion into practice.

As I explained in Chapter 3, there is also evidence that school-to-school collaboration can strengthen the capacity of individual organisations to respond to learner diversity. Specifically, collaboration between schools can help to reduce the polarisation of schools, to the particular benefit of those students who are marginalised at the edges of the system. In addition, there is evidence that when schools seek to develop more collaborative ways of working, this can have an impact on how teachers perceive themselves and their work. We have seen many examples of where comparisons of practices in different schools can lead teachers to view underachieving students in a new light. In this way, learners who cannot easily be educated within the school's established routines are not seen as *having problems*, but as challenging teachers to re-examine their practices in order to make them more responsive and flexible.

Local coordination is therefore needed in order to encourage this form of area-based collaboration. Here, it is significant that a recent study found that four of the most successful national education systems – Estonia, Finland, Ontario (Canada) and Singapore – all have well-developed systems for coordinating local school districts, regardless of their differing extents of school autonomy or devolution of decision-making (Bubb et al. 2019). In particular, they all have district-level structures that seek to ensure equity as well as excellence.

All of this points to the importance of the ways financial resources are allocated within education systems. This can be crucial in creating the flexibility within schools to encourage the sorts of experimentation I have described. Alternatively, it can lead to further segregation, with resources used to provide separate attention for some students – within the school, or in separate special schools or classes. In this sense, finance is another powerful lever for change (Meijer and Watkins 2019).

There are also important implications here for the future roles of special provision. If I think of the best special education contexts I have known, including some special schools that I have worked with, they always seem to involve a particular way of working. In essence this means the creation of a problem-solving culture within which those involved learn how to use one another's experiences and resources in order to invent better ways of overcoming barriers to learning. My view is that this is the most important gift that the special education community can offer to the movement towards more inclusive forms of education.

With this in mind, I worked on a collaborative inquiry project with a network of special school headteachers that led to the production of another series of *accounts of practice* (Ainscow 2006). These focused on ways in which special schools in different parts of England were attempting to work in partnership with mainstream schools in order to foster the development of inclusive practices.

Reflecting on the accounts that were produced, it was noticeable that the schools were working in a variety of ways. These included the following:

- The development of enclaves within mainstreams schools, so that special school students could experience mainstream curriculum;
- Strategies to provide direct support for individual students in the mainstream who were seen as being likely for possible transfer to special provision, or vulnerable to exclusion; and
- The development of new roles for the special school in strengthening inclusive practices more generally within the mainstream.

The first two of these approaches focus on individual students in ways that reflect the traditions of special education practice, whereas the third approach reflects a perspective that is more in keeping with the argument I present in this book. Each has potential to improve services for vulnerable groups of students and each presents difficulties and strategic dilemmas. And, of course, there is potential for the three approaches to be linked.

The work of the special school headteachers involved in this project suggested that they were prepared to think and act in new ways that might make significant new contributions to the development of a more inclusive education system. That said, my involvement in similar attempts to develop the roles of special schools over the last 40 years lead me to have serious doubts as to how likely it is that this will lead to radical change (see, e.g., Ainscow and Tweddle 1979). This suggests that the sorts of radical policies introduced in Italy, New Brunswick and Portugal may be the only way forward. That said, there is likely to be strong opposition to such moves from those in the field who have a vested interest in the status quo.

The roles of research and researchers

The challenging agenda I address in this book has particularly important implications for those of us in the research community. With this in mind, the book is intended to contribute to ongoing debates about finding ways of ensuring that educational research has an impact on thinking and practice in the field.

The idea that educational research can simply be applied to practice and have direct effects in the field has now largely been abandoned, even though it may still be held by some researchers, who, it has been suggested, '*seem surprised or even dismayed that their work is not immediately adopted into policy or practice*' (Levin 2011, p. 17). Meanwhile, there have been numerous efforts to bring research, policy and practice closer together. In so doing, this has often involved *research and development*, a tradition across a wide range of disciplines in which research sets out to solve problems generated by practice. The assumption, then, is that practitioners will implement the findings and that implementation will itself be researched, so that solutions might be refined. The implication being that educational research does speak to issues of practice, if only the right people will listen.

The studies reported in this book adopt a different perspective, defined broadly as *development and research*. Although they varied in terms of their contexts and the way they were formulated, the projects all:

- Set out to influence changes in thinking and practice;
- Formulated action with reference to the overarching principle of equity;
- Involved a research strand that invites stakeholders to inquire into their own practices;
- Assumed that such inquiries will impact on the values on which they act; and
- Positioned university researchers as supporters and critical friends of practitioners and policy makers.

At this stage, it is important to say something more about the evolution of this stance. As explained in Chapter 3, in 2004 my colleague Alan Dyson and I founded the Centre for Equity in Education at the University of Manchester. Shortly afterwards we were joined by Sue Goldrick and Kirstin Kerr, who both made significant contributions to the ideas presented in this book. Gradually, as our research programme developed, other university colleagues became involved.

The Centre was established with a remit to work in high-poverty places, with schools, communities and policy makers, in response to the challenges and opportunities arising in particular complex localised contexts (Ainscow et al. 2009). The overall direction of the Centre's programme of work was monitored and guided by a *thinktank* that met termly. This was made up of well-connected players in the education field, including a local authority officer, headteachers, representatives of other disciples within the university, a retired Ofsted inspector and various eminent academics from other universities. Regular reports were published, including manifestos prior to elections that were designed to have an impact on community debates.[6]

What made the Centre's approach particularly distinctive was its explicit intention to blend together research and development. It set out to do this not through some top-down, linear pathways, where those working and living in particular places would be expected to implement recommendations arising from university-led research. Rather, it involved us in working alongside those leading local efforts to develop more equitable arrangements.

A distinctive methodological approach evolved through the Centre's work, which we recently termed *design-based equity research* (Kerr and Ainscow 2023). In summary we define this as a principled approach, characterised by the following:

- A values framework that facilitates the discussion of equity;
- The use of evidence (locally generated and from existing research) to drive change;
- A process of synthesis, accommodation and mediation between different stakeholders' knowledge and perspectives (e.g. practitioners, policy makers, researchers, students, parents, community groups); and
- A strong iterative relationship between the values of equity, research evidence and the process of intervening in local education systems, with values emerging, being refined and given meaning in context.

Over time, we came to understand the process of acting on these elements as one in which researcher and practitioner knowledge meet in particular contexts to produce new understandings of ways in which broad values of equity might be better realised in practice. This has included developing our use of the idea of theory of change in ways that make values of equity central to thinking about how interventions will work (Kerr and Dyson 2020). Thus, while our approach owes much to established action-oriented approaches, these emphases, we believe, make a distinctive contribution to the wider field.

This central tenet of *working with, rather than working on* has been explored in detail throughout this book. In summary, it can be characterised by a sustained working relationship between researchers and practitioners, founded on a shared purpose and values stance. In these contexts, practitioners own and lead developments, and researchers, as *critical friends*, elucidate and support ongoing development processes, bringing their knowledge and expertise to this. As expressed in one of our Centre's working maxims, our aim is to work in ways that allow us to be *at the table* when policy decisions are debated, even if others at the table do not always like what we have to say.

We have found that this way of working to sometimes has an uncomfortable relationship with the wider community of academic peers. We have, e.g., struggled at times even to have our work recognised as *research*, finding ourselves categorised either as consultants, as doing *development work* – seen as a non-research activity, or, more simply, in the words of one colleague, *messing around in schools*.

Within the approach I have explained, academic researchers count as secondary actors; i.e. they can act on that situation but only through the mediation of practitioners, who are the primary actors. However, researchers can make two distinctive contributions. First of all, by providing access to resources (e.g. research skills, relevant literature, experience in other contexts) that practitioners might, in principle, have access to, but which, in practice, are often denied them. And second, researchers are defined by their distance from practice and therefore from the assumptions on which practice is based. In other words, we belong to a socio-cultural group that is not that of practitioners, and which is therefore able to draw on different sets of assumptions and open up further possibilities for action.

The different roles and socio-cultural contexts of practitioners and academics create a complex set of power relations that have to be factored into the process explicitly. Practitioners derive their power from being primary actors: they can cause things to happen, or to cease to happen, in a way that is denied to academics. Meanwhile, academic researchers derive their power from standing at a distance: they can problematise the actions of practitioners (Chapman and Ainscow 2019).

At their most productive, these power relationships lead to dialogue in which the academics' views are informed by the realities of practice, and practitioners' views change in response to *outsider* critique. At the least productive, academics mistake their distant position for superiority and claim moral and intellectual authority over practitioners, while practitioners dismiss academics as ignorant and resist their critiques. Managing these relationships is crucial to any successful process of collaboration between practitioners and researchers.

Research-practice partnerships

Reflecting further on these experiences in the field, I connect my work to the growing movement towards building research-practice partnerships, both in the United Kingdom (see, e.g.: Armstrong et al. 2021; Sharples, Maxwell and Coldwell 2023) and internationally (see Sjölund et al. 2022). This momentum has largely been fuelled by the recognition that educational change and the construction of more equitable education structures require different educational actors to be active participants in the process, in order to create new forms of knowledge and feed these into systems through social learning approaches (Ishimaru 2020; Spillane et al. 2019).

As a result of their analysis of recent developments in the field, Farrell et al. (2021) define a research-practice partnership in education as:

> *A long-term collaboration aimed at educational improvement or equitable transformation through engagement with research. These partnerships are intentionally organized to connect diverse forms of expertise and shift power relations in the research endeavor to ensure that all partners have a say in the joint work.*
>
> *(p. iv)*

Using this definition, Farrell and colleagues go on to highlight the differences between research-practice partnerships and other kinds of collaboration in education in that they: are long term; work towards educational improvement, or equitable transformation; feature engagement with research as a leading activity; are intentionally organised to bring together a diversity of expertise;

and employ strategies to shift power relations in research in order to ensure that all participants have a say.

For university researchers, the prolonged contact that such partnerships involve enables them to gain a detailed knowledge of the locality, as well as the institutions and systems – and the assumptions inherent within these – that structure local activity. This time spent in the field allows the researcher to identify and explore problems of practice, as well as test out and refine potential solutions, in ways that create knowledge and understanding as to *why, how, and under what conditions programs and policies work* (Gutiérrez and Penuel 2014, p. 1).

Meanwhile, for practitioners this prolonged contact not only enables them to understand better aspects of their local context in confronting their own professional assumptions, but they are also likely to have a greater understanding of research findings generated where they have been actively involved in this process. Furthermore, they will have ready access to guidance and support in terms of applying these research-informed solutions to their local development strategies.

In this regard, such partnerships are well positioned to develop research that directly relates to local issues and to do so in ways that take account of particular contexts, as well as local educational experiences and outcomes. Underpinning all this, for all the groups involved, the prolonged contact of working alongside each other enables all those taking part in the partnership to develop strong, long-lasting relationships, mutuality and trust, founded on shared values, and a shared commitment to key outcomes (see Penuel et al, 2013).

Within such contexts, I see my role as providing support to practitioners in developing the best possible propositions about what will promote inclusion and equity within a given situation. Moreover, what emerges from practitioners' attempts to act on these propositions is not a finely tuned and context-independent set of practices which can be transferred wholesale to other sites. Rather, the practices developed in one site, together with their underpinning rationale, become an elaborated set of propositions to be put forward in other contexts.

Challenges

Despite international acknowledgement of the potential importance of such research-practice partnerships as a catalyst for strengthening systems and promoting equity, there are a number of challenges that make building and sustaining these collaborations difficult. One particular challenge is the misalignment of close-to-practice research with established academic timeframes, norms and structures, given the extensive time it takes to build a partnership and generate research findings. In this regard, Penuel et al. (2013, p. 13) suggest that, in the United States, researchers are actively *steered away* from close-to-practice research. In many cases, this is due to the small-scale, local nature of such studies, resulting in them not being eligible for submission in promotion or tenure applications due to concerns about scale and generalisability. Yet, they suggest that even where it might be counted towards institutional promotion criteria, the time taken to develop high-quality research outputs within a close–to-practice project may severely limit an academic's career progression. A similar situation exists in the United Kingdom, where the Research Excellence Framework (REF), which seeks to measure research quality across institutions and disciplines, appears to promote narrow perceptions as to what constitutes high-quality research.

Meanwhile, as I explain in Chapter 7, a different approach to the use of research knowledge in education is becoming dominant in an increasing number of countries, not least within the United Kingdom. Sometimes referred to as *what works*, the approach is based on different assumptions regarding how to use research knowledge to inform improvement efforts. In this way of thinking, the task of researchers is to convince practitioners to change their practices in the light of evidence from elsewhere.

Such a research stance precludes the collaborative nature of knowledge creation within the context of social learning (Ishimaru 2022) – what I have referred to as *working with, rather than working on* – that is so essential to address real-world wicked challenges. This results in a narrowing of what constitutes robust research across the field and presents a two-fold threat to the quality and originality of educational research as broadly conceived.

First, in privileging a positivist, unidirectional standpoint, the notion of researcher values, positionality and stance is stripped out of research. This places emphasis on arms-length, top-down studies, rather than the messiness of working in the field and on studies that identify, explore and seek to solve complex and often intersectional real-world issues, generating theory from the ground up.

Second, if we are not co-creating research with practitioners and policy makers in response to the wicked challenges that they are confronted with in their work, this may result in practitioners and policy makers turning away from university-led research and relying on decontextualised, narrowly conceived evidence from other sources, or indeed no evidence at all. This runs the risk of intensifying the challenges and inequities that already play out within education systems.

All of this leads me to be concerned that the future of the educational research community could be in peril. After all, for what and for whom is educational research knowledge generated? Based on a narrowing expectation of what constitutes research, it might well be argued that it is being created simply to read by other academics, rather than be of and for the education system, with the ultimate aim of improving young people's educational experiences and outcomes.

Final thoughts

In January 2023 I gave a keynote presentation at the International Congress for School Effectiveness and Improvement held in Vina del Mar, Chile. Titled *Promoting inclusion and equity in education: lessons from international experience*, my talk was based around the arguments developed in this book.

In my introduction to the talk I explained how 25 years earlier I had spoken at the conference of the same association in Manchester. I recalled that on that occasion I seemed to be the only voice stressing the need to focus improvement efforts on all children and young people, particularly those vulnerable to marginalisation and exclusion. Looking through the 2023 conference programme, I saw that equity had now become its main theme.

Reflecting on this striking change, it occurred to me that the efforts of global organisations to promote inclusion and equity have had a significant influence. In particular, it seems that the aim of Sustainable Development Goal 4 to ensure inclusive and equitable quality education and promote lifelong learning opportunities for all is influencing thinking across the world. This is reassuring for me in that I have often had doubts as to whether the time I have spent encouraging this global trend, particularly my close involvement with UNESCO since 1990, has been worth all the effort.

That said, I am conscious of the many challenges remain, both in economically poorer and richer countries. My own country is a particular concern in this respect, not least because its educational policies tend to be so influential internationally.

As I have explained, the emphasis in England on using market forces as an improvement strategy has created winners and losers, as reflected in the growing numbers of children and young people who are placed in segregated provision. Even more concerning is the increase in the number of students who are out of school altogether.

Another worrying development in England is the expansion of labels that situate problems of educational progress within children, not least through the adoption of the term *special educational needs and disability*. This has led to the widespread use of the shorthand label 'SEND', which is explained on the government's website as follows:

> *Special educational needs and disabilities (SEND) can affect a child or young person's ability to learn. They can affect their: behaviour or ability to socialise, for example they struggle to make friends; reading and writing, for example because they have dyslexia; ability to understand things; concentration levels, for example because they have attention deficit hyperactivity disorder (ADHD); and physical ability.*[7]

Alongside the pressures on schools created by market forces, this unquestioned emphasis on student deficits has led to a massive expansion in the number of learners being labelled in order to attract additional resources to support their education. This, in turn, is placing additional pressures on local authority budgets that are already stretched. And, of course, it is creating further barriers to the promotion of inclusive schools.

All of this reminds me of the ground-breaking research of Gillian Fulcher (1989) who described how, in Victoria, Australia, during the 1980s, some pupils in regular schools came to be labelled as *integration children*. She notes that over 3,000 children came to be seen as being in this category, which had not existed prior to 1984, and that often schools would argue that these pupils, who were already there in local mainstream schools, could not be taught unless extra resources were made available. The implication is that policies for integration can lead to more segregation.

So, despite the strong lead of international organisations, the struggle to achieve inclusion in schools and equity across education systems must continue. My hope is that, in a small way, the experiences and suggestions presented in this book will encourage such efforts, which, I argue, should be guided by the UNESCO principle that *every learner matters and matters equally.*

Notes

1 I am grateful for Alan Dyson for suggesting this argument to me
2 https://gpseducation.oecd.org/CountryProfile?primaryCountry=NLD&treshold=10&topic=EO
3 https://dutchreview.com/news/dutch-kids-grow-up-happiest/
4 buff.ly/3O5slEd
5 https://www.kidsrights.org/research/kidsrights-index/?gclid=Cj0KCQjw2eilBhCCARIsAG0Pf8vDtNFXL_7WcDhPFCebVlpvE9Bf3zsxje-dvx8VL6QSsTSfxYxy580aAoO5EALw_wcB
6 https://camdenlearning.org.uk/wp-content/uploads/2018/07/Equity-in-Education-Report-2017.pdf
7 https://www.gov.uk/children-with-special-educational-needs

References

Adonis, A. (2012) *Education, education, education: Reforming England's schools.* London: Biteback Publishing.

Ainscow, M. (1993) *Towards Effective Schools for All.* London: NASEN.

Ainscow, M. (1994) *Special needs in the classroom: A teacher education guide.* London: Jessica Kingsley Publishers Ltd and UNESCO.

Ainscow, M. (1995) Education for all: Making it happen. *Support for Learning* 10(2), 147–157.

Ainscow, M. (1999) *Understanding the development of inclusive schools.* London: Routledge.

Ainscow, M. (2005) Developing inclusive education systems: What are the levers for change? *Journal of Educational Change* 6(2), 109–124.

Ainscow, M. (2006) From special education to effective schools for all: A review of progress so far. In L. Florian (Ed) *The handbook of special education.* London: Sage.

Ainscow, M. (2007) Taking an inclusive turn. *Journal of Research in Special Educational Needs* 7(1), 3–7.

Ainscow, M. (2012) Moving knowledge around: Strategies for fostering equity within educational systems. *Journal of Educational Change* 13(3), 289–310.

Ainscow, M. (2013) Developing more equitable education systems: Reflections on a three-year improvement initiative. In V. Farnsworth and Y. Solomon (Eds) *What works in education? Bridging theory and practice in research.* London: Routledge.

Ainscow, M. (2015) *Towards self-improving school systems: Lessons from a city challenge.* London: Routledge.

Ainscow, M. (2016a) *Struggles for equity in education: The selected works of Mel Ainscow.* London: Routledge World Library of Educationalists series.

Ainscow, M. (2016b) Collaboration as a strategy for promoting equity in education: Possibilities and barriers. *Journal of Professional Capital and Community* 1(2), 159–172.

Ainscow, M. (2020a) Promoting inclusion and equity in education: Lessons from international experiences. *The Nordic Journal of Studies on Educational Policy* 6(1), 7–16.

Ainscow, M. (2020b) Promoting equity in education through system change: Lessons from the United Kingdom. In C. McLaughlin and A. Ruby (Eds) *Implementing educational reform: Cases and challenges.* Cambridge: Cambridge University Press, 2012.

Ainscow, M. (2023) Collaboration as a strategy for improvement. In *The International Encyclopedia of Education*, 4th Edition. London: Elsevier

Ainscow, M., Booth, T., Dyson, A., Farrell, P., Frankham, J., Gallannaugh, F., Howes, A., and Smith, R. (2006) *Improving schools, developing inclusion*. London: Routledge.

Ainscow, M., Booth, T., and Dyson, A. (2004) Understanding and developing inclusive practices in schools: A collaborative action research network. *International Journal of Inclusive Education* 8(2), 125–140.

Ainscow, M., Chapman, C., and Hadfield, M. (2020) *Changing education systems: A research-based approach*. London: Routledge.

Ainscow, M., Dyson, A., Goldrick, S., and Kerr, K. (2009) Using research to foster equity and inclusion within the context of new labour educational reforms. In C. Chapman and G. M. Gunter (Eds) *Radical reforms: Perspectives on an era of educational change*. London: Routledge.

Ainscow, M., Dyson, A., Goldrick, S., and West, M. (2012) *Developing equitable education systems*. London: Routledge.

Ainscow, M., Dyson, A., Goldrick, S. and West, M. (2016) Using collaborative inquiry to foster equity within school systems: opportunities and barriers. *School Effectiveness and School Improvement* 27(1), 7–23

Ainscow, M. and Fox, S. (2000) Leadership, behaviour and learning: The development of practice. *Sparks* 3(1), 6–14.

Ainscow, M., Gallannaugh, F., and Kerr, K. (2012) *An evaluation of the communication trust's 'Talk of the Town' project*. Manchester: Centre for Equity in Education, University of Manchester.

Ainscow, M., Hargreaves, D. H., and Hopkins, D. (1995) Mapping the process of change in schools: The development of six new research techniques. *Evaluation and Research in Education* 9(2), 75–89.

Ainscow, M. and Hopkins, D. (1992) Aboard the 'Moving School'. *Educational Leadership* 50(3), 79–81.

Ainscow, M. and Howes, A. (2007) Working together to improve urban secondary schools: A study of practice in one city. *School Leadership and Management* 27, 285–300.

Ainscow, M. and Kaplan, I. (2005) Using evidence to encourage inclusive school development: Possibilities and challenges. *Australasian Journal of Special Education* 29(2), 12–21.

Ainscow, M. and Messiou, K. (2017) Engaging with the views of students to promote inclusion in education. *Journal of Educational Change* 19(1), 1–17.

Ainscow, M. and Muncey, J. (1989) *Meeting individual needs in the primary school*. London: Fulton.

Ainscow, M., Nicolaidou, M., and West, M. (2003) Supporting schools in difficulties: The role of school-to-school cooperation. *NFER Topic* 30, 1–4.

Ainscow, M. and Sandill, A. (2010) Developing inclusive education systems: The role of organisational cultures and leadership. *International Journal of Inclusive Education* 14(1), 1–16.

Ainscow, M. and Southworth, G. (1996) School improvement: A study of the roles of leaders and external consultants. *School Effectiveness and School Improvement* 7, 229–251.

Ainscow, M. and Tweddle, D. A. (1979) *Preventing classroom failure*. London: Fulton.

Ainscow, M. and Tweddle, D. A. (1984) *Early learning skills analysis*. London: Fulton.

Ainscow, M. and West, M. (eds) (2006) *Improvement Urban Schools: Leadership and Collaboration*. New York: Open University Press

Alves, I., Campos Pinto, P., and Pinto, T. J. (2020) Developing inclusive education in Portugal: Evidence and challenges. *Prospects* https://doi.org/10.1007

Argyris, C. and Schön, D. (1996) *Organisational learning II: Theory, method and practice*. Reading, MA: Addison Wesley.

Armstrong, P. and Ainscow, M. (2018) School-to-school support within a competitive education system: Views from the inside. *School Effectiveness, School Improvement* 29(4), 614–633.

Armstrong, P., Rayner, S., and Ainscow, M. (2021) Bridging the digital divide: Greater Manchester schools creating pathways to success. In *On digital inequalities: Analysis and ideas on addressing digital inequalities* (pp. 37–41). Manchester: University of Manchester.

AuCoin, A., Porter, G. L., and Baker-Korotkov, K. (2020) New Brunswick's journey to inclusive education. *Prospects*. https://doi.org/10.1007/s11125-020-09508-8

Avalos, B. (2011) Teacher professional development in teaching and teacher education over ten years. *Teaching and Teacher Education* 27, 10–20.

Ball, S. J. (2003) *Class strategies and the education market*. London: Routledge.

Ballard, K. (1997) Researching disability and inclusive education: Participation, construction and interpretation. *International Journal of Inclusive Education* 1(3), 243–256.

Bartolome, L. I. (1994) Beyond the methods fetish: Towards a humanising pedagogy. *Harvard Education Review* 54(2), 173–194.

Benn, M. and Millar, F. (2006) *A comprehensive future: Quality and equality for all of our children*. London: Compass.

Berlak, A. and Berlak, H. (1987) Teachers working with teachers to transform schools. In J. Smyth (Ed) *Educating teachers: Changing the nature of pedagogical knowledge*. London: Falmer.

Black-Hawkins, K. and Florian, L. (2012) Classroom teachers craft knowledge of their inclusive practice. *Teachers and Teaching: Theory and Practice* 18(5), 567–584.

Bleicher, R. E. (2014) A collaborative action research approach to professional learning. *Professional Development in Education* 40(5), 802e821.

Booth, T. (1995) Mapping inclusion and exclusion: Concepts for all? In C. Clark, A. Dyson, and A. Millward (Eds) *Towards inclusive schools?* London: David Fulton.

Booth, T. and Ainscow, M. (Eds) (1998) *From them to us: An international study of inclusion in education*. London: Routledge.

Borgatti, S. P., Everett, M. G., and Johnson, J. C. (2018) *Analyzing social networks*. London: Sage.

Bubb, S., Crossley-Holland, J., Cordiner, J., Cousin, S., and Earley, P. (2019) *Understanding the middle tier: Comparative costs of academy and LA-maintained school systems*. London: Sara Bubb Associates.

Bunar, N. (2010) Choosing for quality or inequality—Current perspectives on the implementation of school choice policy in Sweden. *Journal of Education Policy* 25(1), 1–18.

Burgess, S. (2014) *Understanding the success of London's schools*. Bristol: CMPO, Working Paper No.14/333.

Burrell, G. and Morgan, G. (1979) *Sociological paradigms and organisational analysis*. London: Heinemann.

Butler, D. L. and Schnellert, L. (2012) Collaborative inquiry in teacher professional development. *Teaching and Teacher Education* 28, 1206e1220.

Cain, T. and Milovic, S. (2010) Action research as a tool of professional development of advisers and teachers in Croatia. *European Journal of Teacher Education* 33(1), 19e30.

Calderón-Almendros, I., Ainscow, M., Bersanelli, S., and Molina-Toledo, P. (2020) Educational inclusion and equity in Latin America: An analysis of the challenges. *Prospects* 49, 169–186.

Campbell, A. and Groundwater-Smith, S. (Eds) (2007) *An ethical approach to practitioner research: Dealing with issues and dilemmas in action research*. London: Routledge.

Carrasco, A., Falabella, A., and Mendoza, P. (2015) School choice in Chile as a sociocultural practice. In P. Seppänen, A. Carrasco, M. Kalalahti, R. Rinne, and H. Simola (Eds) *Contrasting dynamics in education politics of extremes. School choice in Finland and Chile* (pp. 245–266). Rotterdam: Sense Publishers.

Carr, W. and Kemmis, S. (1986). *Becoming critical: Education, knowledge and action research* (3rd edition). London: Falmer Press

Carr, C., Brown, S., and Morris, M. (2017) *Assessing the contribution of schools challenge Cymru to outcomes achieved by Pathways to success schools*. Cardiff: Welsh Government.

Castro, L., Hernández, M., and Oreiro, C. (2019) Mecanismos de elaboración, aprobación y asignación del presupuesto para la ANEP y la asignación a los centros escolares en Uruguay https://www.redalyc.org/journal/4030/403062991009/

Chapman, C. and Ainscow, M. (2019) Using research to promote equity within education systems: Possibilities and barriers. *British Education Research Journal* 45(3), 899–917.

Claeys, A., Kempton, J., and Paterson, C. (2014) *Regional challenges: A collaborative approach to improving education*. London: Centre Forum.

Clandinin, D. J. (2019) *Journeys in narrative inquiry: The selected works of D. Jean Clandinin*. London: Taylor & Francis.

Clark, C., Dyson, A., Millward, A., and Robson, S. (1999) Theories of inclusion, theories of schools: Deconstructing and reconstructing the 'inclusive school'. *British Educational Research Journal* 25(2), 157–177.

Clarke, P., Ainscow, M., and West, M. (2006) Learning from difference: Some reflections on school improvement projects in three countries. In A. Harris and J. H. Crispeels (Eds.) *Improving schools and education systems* (pp. 77–89). London: Routledge.

Coburn, C. E. and Penuel, W. R. (2016) Research–practice partnerships in education: Outcomes, dynamics, and open questions. *Educational Researcher* 45(1), 48–54.

Cochran-Smith, M. and Lytle, S. L. (2009) *Inquiry as stance: Practitioner research for the next generation*. New York, NY: Teachers College Press.

Coleman, M. and Earley, P. (2005) *Leadership and management in education: Culture, change and context*. Oxford: Oxford University Press.

Collins, J. (2001) *Good to great*. New York: Random House.

Constantinou, E. and Ainscow, M. (2020) Using action research to achieve school-led change within a centralised education system: Perspectives from the inside. *Educational Action Research* 28(1), 4–21.

Copland, M. A. (2003) Leadership of inquiry: Building and sustaining capacity for school improvement. *Educational Evaluation and Policy Analysis* 25(4), 375–395.

Corbett, J. (2001). *Supporting Inclusive Education: a connective pedagogy*. London: Routledge Falmer.

Cordingley, P., Bell, M., Evans, D., and Firth, A. (2005). The impact of collaborative CPD on classroom teaching and learning. In *Research evidence in education library*. London: EPPI-Centre, Social Science Research Unit, Institute of Education, University of London.

Courtney, S. (2015) Corporatised leadership in English schools. *Journal of Educational Administration and History* 47(3), 214–231.

Delamont, S. (1992) *Fieldwork in educational settings*. London: Falmer.

Deppeler, J. (2013) Developing equitable practices in schools: Professional collaboration in research. In P. Jones (Ed) *Bringing insider perspectives into inclusive teacher learning: Potentials and challenges for educational professionals* (pp. 178–188). New York, NY: Routledge.

Deppeler, J. and Ainscow, M. (2016) Using inquiry-based approaches for equitable school improvement. *School Effectiveness and School Improvement* 27(1), 1–6.

DfEE (2001) *Schools: Building on success - Raising standards, promoting diversity, achieving results (Green Paper)*. London: DfEE

Dixon, P. (2016) *Testing Times: Success, Failure and Fiasco in Welsh Education Policy Since Devolution*. Cardiff: Welsh Academic Press

Dobbie, W. and Fryer, R. G. (2009) *Are high-quality schools enough to close the achievement gap? Evidence from a bold social experiment in Harlem*. Cambridge: Harvard University.

Drever, A., McLean, J., and Lowden, K. (2021) Focusing on place: Working beyond the school gate. In C. Chapman and M. Ainscow (Eds) *Educational equity: Pathways to success*. London: Routledge.

Dyson, A. (1990) Special educational needs and the concept of change. *Oxford Review of Education* 16(1), 55–66.

Dyson, A. (2006) Beyond the school gates: context, disadvantage and "urban schools". In M. Ainscow and M. West (Eds.) *Improving urban school: leadership and collaboration*. Maidenhead: Open University Press.

Dyson, A., Gallannaugh, F., and Millward, A. (2003) Making space in the standards agenda: Developing inclusive practices in schools. *European Educational Research Journal* 2, 228–244.

Dyson, A., Howes, A., and Roberts, B. (2004) What do we really know about inclusive schools? A systematic review of the research evidence. In D. Mitchell (Ed) *Special educational needs and inclusive education: Major themes in education*. London: Routledge.

Dyson, A. and Kerr, K. (2013) *Developing children's zones for England: What's the evidence?* London: Save the Children.

Dyson, A. and Millward, A. (2000) *Schools and special needs: Issues of innovation and inclusion*. London: Paul Chapman.

Ehrich, L. S., Harris, J., Klenowski, V., Smeed, J., and Ainscow, M. (2015) Ethical leadership in a time of increasing accountability. *Leading & Managing* 21(1), 22–35.

Elliott, J. (1991) *Action research for educational change*. Buckingham: Open University Press.

Elmore, R. F. (2004) *School reform from the inside out*. Cambridge: Harvard Education Press.

Elmore, R. F., Peterson, P. L., and McCarthy, S. J. (1996) *Restructuring in the classroom: Teaching, learning and school organisation*. San Francisco, CA: Jossey-Bass.

Evans, G. (2015) *A class apart; Learning the lessons of education in post-devolution Wales*. Cardiff: Ashley Drake.

Eyles, A. and Machin, S. (2015) *Academy schools and their introduction to English education*. London: Centre for Education Economics.

Farrell, C. C., Wentworth, L., and Nayfack, M. (2021) What are the conditions under which research-practice partnerships succeed? *Phi Delta Kappan* 102(7), 38–41.

Fielding, M. (1999) Radical collegiality: Affirming teaching as an inclusive professional practice. *Australian Educational Researcher* 26(2), 1–34.

Fielding, M., Bragg, S., Craig, J., Cunningham, I., Eraut, M., Gillinson, S., Horne, M., Robinson, C., and Thorp, J. (2005) *Factors influencing the transfer of good practice*. Nottingham: DfES Publications.

Fishman, B. J., Penuel, W. R., Allen, A. R., Cheng, B. H., and Sabelli, N. O. R. A. (2013) Design-based implementation research: An emerging model for transforming the relationship of research and practice. *Teachers College Record* 115(14), 136–156.

Florian, L. and Black-Hawkins, K. (2011) Exploring inclusive pedagogy. *British Educational Research Journal* 37(5), 813–828.

Fox, S. and Ainscow, M. (2006) Moving leadership practice in schools forward. In M. Ainscow and M. West (Eds) *Improving urban schools: Leadership and collaboration*. Maidenhead: Open University Press.

Francis, B., Archer, L., Hodgen, J., Pepper, D., Taylor, B. and Travers, M. (2017) Exploring the relative lack of impact of research on 'ability grouping' in England: a discourse analytic account. *Cambridge Journal of Education* 47 (1), 1–17.

Francis, B., Archer, L., Hodgen, J., Pepper, D., Taylor, B., and Travers, M. (2016) Exploring the relative lack of impact of research on 'ability grouping' in England: A discourse analytic account. *Cambridge Journal of Education* 47(1), 1–17.

Fulcher, G. (1989). *Disabling policies? A comparative approach to education policy and disability*. London: Falmer.

Fullan, M. (2007) *The new meaning of educational change* (4th Ed.). New York, NY: Teachers College Press.

Fullan, M. and Gallagher, M. J. (2020) *The devil is in the details: System solutions for equity, excellence, & student well-being*. Thousand Oaks, CA: Corwin.

Fullan, M., Rincon-Gallardo, S., and Hargreaves, A. (2015) Professional capital as accountability. *Education Policy Analysis Archives*, 23(15) http://dx.doi.org/10.14507/epaa.v23.1998

Fuller, B. and Clark, P. (1994) Raising school effects while ignoring culture? Local conditions and the influence of classroom tools, rules and pedagogy. *Review of Educational Research* 64(1), 119–157.

Gross, S. J., Shaw, K. M. and Shapiro, J. P. (2003) Deconstructing accountability through the lens of democratic philosophies: Towards a new analytic framework. *Journal of Research for Educational Leaders* 1(3), 5–27.

Groundwater-Smith, S. (2011) Concerning equity: The voice of young people. *Leading and Managing* 17(2), 52–65.

Gutierrez, R. and Lipman, P. (2016) Toward social movement activist research. *International Journal of Qualitative Studies in Education* 29(10), 1241–1254.

Gutiérrez, K. D. and Penuel, W. R. (2014) Relevance to practice as a criterion for rigor. *Educational Researcher* 43(1), 19–23.

Hadfield, M. and Ainscow, M. (2018) Inside a self-improving school system: Collaboration, competition and transition. *Journal of Educational Change* 19(4), 441–462.

Hadfield, M. and Ainscow, M. (2020) Layering' peer enquiry as a system change strategy: Some lessons from Wales. In D. Godfrey (Ed) *School peer review for educational improvement and accountability: Theory, practice and policy implications*. London: Springer.

Hadfield, M. and Jopling, M. (2018) Case study as a means of evaluating the impact of early years leaders: Steps, paths and routes. *Evaluation and Program Planning* 67, 167–176.

Haeffele-Balch, S. and Boettke, P. (2016) Disrupt the Education Industry: Charter Schools and private schools can do for education what Uber is doing for transportation. US News, 01/11/2016. Available from: http://www.usnews.com/opinion/economic-intelligence/articles/2016-01-11/the-education-industry-needs-to-be-disrupted-by-an-uber

Hall, G. E., Loucks, S. F., and Rutherford, B. W. (1975) Levels of use of the innovation: A framework for analyzing innovation adoption. *Journal of Teacher Education* 26(1), 52–56.

Hammersley, M. (2001) On 'systematic' reviews of research literatures: A 'narrative' response to Evans & Bene. *British Educational Research Journal* 27(5), 543–554.

Hargreaves, A. (2000). Contrived collegiality: The micropolitics of teacher collaboration. In S. J. Ball (Ed) *Sociology of education: Major themes* (vol. 3; pp. 1481–1503). London: Psychology Press.

Hargreaves, D. H. (1995) School culture, school effectiveness and school improvement. *School Effectiveness and School Improvement* 6(1), 23–27.

Hargreaves, D. H. (2003). *Leadership for transformation within the London Challenge*. Annual lecture at the London Leadership Centre, May 19. London.

Hargreaves, D. H. (2010) *Creating a self-improving school system*. Nottingham: National College for School Leadership.

Hargreaves, A. and Ainscow, M. (2015) The top and bottom of leadership and change. *Phi Delta Kappa*, November, 2015.

Harris, J., Carrington, S., Ainscow, M., with Comber, B., Ehrich, L., Klenowski, V., Smeed, J., and Spina, J. (2017) *Promoting equity in schools: Collaboration, inquiry and ethical leadership*. London: Routledge.

Hart, S. (1992) Differentiation – Way forward or retreat? *British Journal of Special Education* 19(1), 10–12.

Hart, S. (2003) Learning without limits. In M. Nind, K. Sheehy, and K. Simmons (Eds) *Inclusive education: Learners and learning contexts*. London: Fulton.

Hart, S., Dixon, A., Drummond, M. J., and McIntyre (2004) *Learning without limits*. Maidenhead: Open University.

Hawes, H. (1988) *Child-to-child: Another path to learning*. Hamburg: UNESCO Institute for Education.

Hayes, D. (2000) Cascade training and teacher professional development. *English Language Teaching Journal* 54(2), 135e145.

Heshusius, L. (1989) The Newtonian mechanistic paradigm, special education and contours of alternatives: An overview. *Journal of Learning Disabilities* 22(7), 403–421.

Hiebert, J., Gallimore, R., and Stigler, J. W. (2002) A knowledge base for the teaching profession: What would it look like and how can we get one? *Educational Researcher* 31(5), 3–15.

Hill, H. C., Beisiegel, M., and Jacob, R. (2013) Professional development research: Consensus, crossroads, and challenges. *Educational Researcher* 42(9), 476e487.

Hodgson, N. (2012) The only answer is innovation…' Europe, policy and the big society. *Journal of Philosophy of Education* 46(4), 537–545.

Hooge, E. and Honingh, M. (2014) Are school boards aware of the educational quality of their schools? *Educational Management Administration and Leadership* 42(4S), 139–154.

Hopkins, D. (2007) *Every school a great school: Realizing the potential of system leadership*. Maidenhead: Open University Press.

Hopkins, D., Ainscow, M., and West, M. (1994) *School improvement in an era of change*. London: Cassell.

Horn, I. S. and Little, J. W. (2010) Attending to problems of practice: Routines and resources for professional learning in teachers' workplace interactions. *American Educational Research Journal* 47(1), 181e217.

HoC Education Committee (2015). *Academies and Free Schools: Fourth Report of Session 2014*. London: House of Commons Education Committee

Howes, A., Frankham, J., Ainscow, M. and Farrell, P. (2004) The action in action research: mediating and developing inclusive intentions. *Educational Action Research* 12(2), 239–258.

Howes, A., Booth, T., Dyson, A. and Frankham, J. (2005) Teacher learning and the development of inclusive practices and policies: Framing and context. *Research Papers in Education* 20, 133–148.

Huberman, M. (1993) The model of the independent artisan in teachers' professional relationships. In J. W. Little and M. W. McLaughlin (Eds) *Teachers' work: Individuals, colleagues and contexts*. New York, NY: Teachers College Press.

Humes, W. (2020) Re-shaping the policy landscape in Scottish education, 2016–20: The limitations of structural reform. *Scottish Educational Review* 52(2), 89–111.

Husbands, C., Gilbert, C., Francis, B., and Wigdortz, B. (2013) *Unleashing greatness: Getting the best from an academised system. The report of the academies commission*. London: RSA/Pearson.

Hutchings, M., Hollingworth, S., Mansaray, A., Rose, R., and Greenwood, C. (2012) *Research report DFE-RR215: Evaluation of the city challenge programme*. London: Department for Education.

Ianes, D., Demo, H., and Dell'Anna, S. (2020) Inclusive education in Italy: Historical steps, positive developments, and challenges. *Prospects* https://doi.org/10.1007/s11125-020-09509-7

Iano, R. P. (1986) The study and development of teaching: With implications for the advancement of special education. *Remedial and Special Education* 7(5), 50–61.

Innocenti Centre (2018) *An unfair start: Inequality in children's education in rich countries', innocenti report card 15*. Florence: UNICEF Office of Research – Innocenti.

Ishimaru, A. M. (2020) *Just schools: Building equitable collaborations with families and communities*. New York, NY: Teachers College Press.

Ishimaru, A., et al., (2022) Transforming the role of RPPs in remaking educational systems. *Educational Researcher* 51 (7), 1–9.

Jacobs, J. (2015). Disrupting the education monopoly: A conversations with reed Hastings, *Education Next* 15(1). Available from: http://educationnext.org/disrupting-the-education-monopolyreed-hastings J -interview/

Jaipal, K. and Figg, C. (2011) Collaborative action research approaches promoting professional development for elementary school teachers. *Educational Action Research* 19(1), 59–72.

Johnson, D. W. and Johnson, R. (1989) *Learning together and alone: Cooperative, competitive, and individualistic learning*. Boston, MA: Allyn & Bacon.

Johnston, K. and Hayes, D. (2007) Supporting student success at school through teacher professional learning: The pedagogy of disrupting the default modes of schooling. *International Journal of Inclusive Education* 11(3), 371–381.

Kahlenberg, R. D. and Potter, H. (2014) *A smarter charter: Finding what works for charter schools and public education*. New York: Teachers College Press.

Kauko, J. and Salokangas, M. (2015) The evaluation and steering of English academy schools through inspection and examinations: National visions and local practices. *British Educational Research Journal* 41(6), 1108–1124.

Kemmis, S. (2010) Research for praxis: Knowing doing. *Pedagogy, Culture and Society* 18, 9–27.

Kemmis, S. and McTaggart, R. (1988). *The action research planner* (3rd Ed.). Geelong: Deakin University Press.

Kerr, K. and Ainscow, M. (2022) Promoting equity in market-driven education systems: Lessons from England. *Education Science* 12, 495.

Kerr, K. and Ainscow, M. (2023) The development of a methodology for enhancing equity within education systems. *International Journal of Research & Method in Education*. DOI:10.1080/1743727X.2023.2231862

Kerr, K. and Dyson, A. (2020) Researching complex extended education initiatives in England: A design-based approach using theory of change. In S. H. Bae et al. (Eds) *International developments in research on extended education* (pp. 115–134). Leverkusen: Barbara Budrich Publishers.

Kerr, K., Dyson, A., and Gallannaugh, F. (2016) Conceptualising school-community relations in disadvantaged neighbourhoods: Mapping the literature. *Educational Research* 58(3), 265–282.

Kerr, K., Dyson, A., and Raffo, C. (2014) *Education, disadvantage and place: Making the local matter*. Bristol: Policy Press.

Kerr, K. and West, M. (Eds.) (2010) *Insight 2:* Social inequality: can schools narrow the gap? Macclesfield: British Education Research Association.

Kidson, M. and Norris, E. (2014) *Implementing the London challenge*. London: Joseph Rowntree Foundation.

Kintrea, K. (2021) Is there a place for place in educational attainment policy? *Oxford Review of Education* 47(2), 207–223.

Klenowski, V. and Wyatt-Smith, C. (2012) The impact of high stakes testing: The Australian story. *Assessment in Education: Principles, Policy & Practice* 19(1), 65–79.

Kools, M. and Stoll, L. (2016) What makes a school a learning organisation?, OECD Education Working Papers, No. 137, OECD Publishing, Paris.

Kosunen, S. (2014) Reputation and parental logics of action in local school choice space in Finland. *Journal of Education Policy* 29(4), 443–466.

Kugelmass, J. (2001) Collaboration and compromise in creating and sustaining an inclusive school. *Journal of Inclusive Education* 5(1), 47–65.

Kuhn, T. (1970) *The structure of scientific revolutions*. Chicago, IL: University of Chicago Press.

Kulz, C. (2015) Heroic heads, mobility mythologies and the power of ambiguity. *British Journal of Sociology of Education* 38(2), 85–104.

Ladd, H. F. and Fiske, E. B. (2016). *England Confronts the Limits of School Autonomy*. Working Paper 232: National Center for the Study of Privatization in Education, Teachers College, Columbia University.

Lambert, L. (2005) Constructivist leadership. In B. Davies (Ed) *The essentials of school leadership* (pp. 93–109). London: Paul Chapman Publishing and Corwin Press.

Lamote, C. and Engels, N. (2010) The development of student teachers' professional identity. *European Journal of Teacher Education* 33(1), 3e18.

Lawson, H. and Van Veen, D. (eds) (2015) *Developing community schools, community learning centers, multi-service schools and extended-service schools: International exemplars for practice, policy and research*. The Hague: Springer International.

Leithwood, K., Jantzi, D., and Steinbach, R. (1999) *Changing leadership for changing times*. Buckingham: Open University Press.

Leithwood, K. A. and Reihl, C. (2003), *What we know about successful leadership*. National College for Educational Leadership. Chicago: AERA. http://olms.ctejhu. org/data/ck/file/What_we_know_about_SchoolLeadership.pdf

Leo, E. and Barton, L. (2006) Inclusion, diversity and leadership: Perspectives, possibilities and contradictions. *Educational Management Administration and Leadership* 34(2), 167–180.

Levin, B. (2011) Mobilising research knowledge in education. *London Review of Education* 9(1), 15–26.

Lewin, K. (1946) Action research and minority problems. *Journal of Social Issues* 2(4), 34–46.

Lewis, C., Perry, R., and Murata, A. (2006) How should research contribute to instructional improvement? The case of lesson study. *Educational Researcher* 35(3), 3–14.

Lipman, P. (1997) Restructuring in context: A case study of teacher participation and the dynamics of ideology, race and power. *American Educational Research Journal* 34(1), 3–37.

Lipman, P. (2004) *High stakes education: Inequality, globalisation and urban school reform*. New York, NY: Routledge.

Lipsky, D. K. and Gartner, A. (1998) Factors for successful inclusion: Learning from the past, looking forward to the future. In S. V. Vitello and D. E. Mithaug (Eds) *Inclusive schooling: National and international perspectives*. Mahwah, NJ: Lawrence Erlbaum Associates.

Locke, T., Alcorn, N., and O'Neill, J. (2013) Ethical issues in collaborative action research. *Educational Action Research* 21, 107–123.

Lowe, J. (2015) The London schools revolution: Something remarkable has happened in the capital's schools. *Prospect*, February 2015.

Lo, M. L., Yan, P. W., and Pakey, C. P. M. (Eds) (2005) *For each and everyone: Catering for individual differences through learning studies*. Hong Kong: Hong Kong University Press.

Mansell, W. (2016) *Academies: Autonomy, accountability, quality and evidence*. York: Cambridge Primary Review Trust.

Meijer, C. J. W. and Watkins, A. (2019) Financing special needs and inclusive education: From Salamanca to the present. *International Journal of Inclusive Education* 23(7/8), 705–721.

Messiou, K. (2019) The missing voices: Students as a catalyst for promoting inclusive education. *International Journal of Inclusive Education* 23(7/8), 768–781.

Messiou, K. and Ainscow, M. (2015) Engaging with the views of pupils: A catalyst for powerful teacher development? *Teacher and Teacher Education Teaching and Teacher Education* 51, 246–255.

Messiou, K. and Ainscow, M. (2020) Inclusive inquiry: Student-teacher dialogue as a means of promoting inclusion in schools. *British Journal of Educational Research* 46(3), 670–687.

Messiou, K., Ainscow, M., Echeita, G., Goldrick, S., et al. (2016) Learning from differences: A strategy for teacher development in respect to student diversity. *School Effectiveness and School Improvement* 27 (1), 45–61. DOI:10.1080/09243453. 2014.966726

Meyland-Smith, D. and Evans, N. (2009) *A guide to school choice reforms.* London: Policy Exchange.

Miles, M. (1989) The role of special education in information-based rehabilitation. *International Journal of Special Education* 4(2), 111–118.

Ministry of Education (2019) *Supporting all schools to succeed.* Wellington: Ministry of Education.

Muijs, D., Ainscow, M., Chapman, C., and West, M. (2011) *Collaboration and networking in education.* London: Springer.

Muijs, D., Ainscow, M., Dyson, A., Raffo, C., Goldrick, S., Kerr, K., Lennie, C., and Miles, S. (2010) Leading under pressure: Leadership for social inclusion. *School Leadership & Management* 30(2), 143–157.

Muijs, D. and Rumyantseva, N. (2014) Coopetition in education: Collaborating in a competitive environment. *Journal of Educational Change* 15, 1–18.

Muijs, D., West, M., and Ainscow, M. (2010) Why network? Theoretical perspectives on networking. *School Effectiveness and School Improvement* 21(1), 5–26.

Mulford, B. (2007). Building social capital in professional learning communities: Importance, challenges and a way forward. In L. Stoll and K. Seashore Louis (Eds) *Professional learning communities: Divergence, depth and dilemmas* (pp. 166–188). London: Open University Press.

Nias, J. (1989) *Primary teachers talking: A study of teaching as work.* London: Routledge.

OECD (2012) *Equity and quality in education: Supporting disadvantaged students and schools.* Paris: OECD Publishing.

OECD (2016) *PISA Low-performing students: Why they fall behind and how to help them succeed.* OECD Publishing, Paris. http://dx.doi.org/10.1787/9789264250246-en

OECD (2018) *Education at a glance 2018: OECD indicators.* Paris: OECD Publishing.

OECD (2021) *Education at a glance 2021: OECD indicators.* Paris: OECD Publishing.

OECD (2022) *Review of inclusive education in Portugal.* Paris: OECD Publishing.

Oliver, M. (1988) The political context of educational decision making: The use of special needs. In L. Barton (Ed) *The politics of special educational needs.* Lewes: Falmer.

Opertti, R., Walker, Z., and Zhang, Y. (2014) Inclusive education: From targeting groups and schools to achieving quality education as the core of EFA. In L. Florian (Ed) *The SAGE handbook of special education* (2nd Revised Ed.). London: SAGE.

Opfer, V. D. and Pedder, D. (2010) Benefits, status and effectiveness of continuous professional development for teachers in England. *Curriculum Journal* 21(4), 413c431.

Penuel, W., Coburn, C., and Gallagher, D. (2013) Negotiating problems of practice in research-practice design partnerships. *Yearbook of the National Society for the Study of Education* 112(2), 237–255

Pijl, S. J. (2016) Fighting segregation in special needs education in the Netherlands: The effects of different funding models. *Discourse: Studies in the Cultural Politics of Education* 37(4), 553–562.

Putnam, R. D. (2000) *Bowling alone.* New York: Simon & Schuster.

Reason, P. and Bradbury, H. (Eds) (2001) *Handbook of action research: Participative inquiry and practice.* London: Sage.

Reay, D. (2017) *Miseducation: Inequality, education and the working classes*. Bristol: Bristol University Press.

Revans, R. (1972) Action learning – A management development programme. *Personnel Review* 1(4), 36–44.

Rickinson, M. and Edwards, A. (2021) The relational features of evidence use. *Cambridge Journal of Education* 51, 509–526.

Riehl, C. J. (2000) The principal's role in creating inclusive schools for diverse students: A review of normative, empirical, and critical literature on the practice of educational administration. *Review of Educational Research* 70(1), 55.

Robinson, V., Lloyd, C., and Rowe, K. (2008) The impact of leadership on student outcomes: An analysis of the differential effects of leadership types. *Educational Administration Quarterly* 44(5), 635–674.

Rosenholtz, S. J. (1989) *Teachers' workplace: The social organization of schools*. New York, NY: Longman.

Russell, A. and Vinsel, L. (2016). *Hail the maintainers, AEON*. Published 07/04/2016. Available from: https://aeon.co/essays/innovation-is-overvalued-maintenance-often-matters-more

Sabel, C., Saxenian, A., Miettinen, R., Kristenson, P. H., and Hautamaki, J. (2011) *Individualized service provision in the new welfare state: Lessons from special education in Finland*. Helsinki: SITRA.

Sadker, D. M., Sadker, M., Zittleman, K. R., and Sadker, M. (2009) *Still failing at fairness: How gender bias cheats girls and boys in school and what we can do about it*. New York: Scribner.

Salokangas, M. and Ainscow, M. (2017) *Inside the autonomous school: Making sense of a global educational trend*. London: Routledge.

Salokangas, M. and Chapman, C. (2014) Exploring governance in two chains of academy schools: A comparative case study. *Educational Management Administration & Leadership* 42(3), 372–386.

Schein, E. (1985) *Organisational culture and leadership*. San Francisco, CA: Jossey-Bass.

Schleicher, A. (2010) International comparisons of student learning outcomes. In A. Hargreaves, A. Lieberman, M. Fullan, and D. Hopkins (Eds) *Second handbook of educational change*. London: Springer.

Schön, D. (1983) *The reflective practitioner: How professionals think in action*. New York, NY: Basic Books.

Schön, D. A. (1987) *Educating the reflective practitioner*. San Francisco, CA: Jossey Bass.

Seashore-Louis, K. (2020) Preface. In M. Ainscow, C. Chapman, and M. Hadfield (Eds) *Changing education systems: A research-based approach*. London: Routledge.

Senge, P. M. (1989) *The fifth discipline: The art and practice of the learning organisation*. London: Century.

Sergiovanni, J. T. (1992) *Moral leadership: Getting to the heart of school improvement*. San Francisco, CA: Jossey-Bass.

Shah, S. (2006) Leading multiethnic schools: A new understanding of Muslim youth identity. *Educational Management Administration and Leadership* 34(2), 215–237.

Sharples, J., Maxwell, B., and Coldwell, M. (2023) Developing a systems-based approach to research use in education. *BERA Blog*, 13 February 2023. Available at https://www.bera.ac.uk/blog/developing-a-systems-based-approach-to-research-use-in-education

Simon, H. (1978) Rationality as process and as product of thought. *The American Economic Review* 68(2), 1–16.

Sjölund, S., Lindvall, J., Larsson, M., & Ryve, A. (2022). Mapping roles in research-practice partnerships–a systematic literature review. *Educational Review* 75(7), 1–29.

Skrtic, T. M. (1991) The special education paradox: Equity as the way to excellence. *Harvard Educational Review* 61(2), 148–206.

Slee, R. (1996) Inclusive schooling in Australia? Not yet. *Cambridge Journal of Education* 26(1), 19–32

Spillane, J. P., Seelig, J. L., Blaushild, N. L., Cohen, D. K., and Peurach, D. J. (2019) Educational system building in a changing educational sector: Environment, organization, and the technical core. *Educational Policy* 33(6), 846–881.

Spina, N., Harris, J., Carrington, S., and Ainscow, M. (2019) Resisting governance by numbers. In S. Riddle and M. W. Apple (Eds) *Re-imagining education for democracy*. London: Routledge.

Stenhouse, L. (1975) *An introduction to curriculum research and development*. London: Heinemann.

Stevenson, L., Honingh, M., and Neeleman, A. (2021) Dutch boards governing multiple schools: Navigating between autonomy and expectations. *School Leadership & Management* 41, 370–386.

Swanson, E. (2017) Can we have it all? A review of the impacts of school choice on racial integration. *Journal of School Choice* 11(4), 507–526.

Talbert, J. E. and McLaughlin, M. (2002) Professional communities and the artisan model of teaching. *Teachers and Teaching: Theory and Practice* 8(3/4), 325–343.

Termeer, C., Dewulf, A., and Biesbroek, R. (2019) A critical assessment of the wicked problem concept: Relevance and usefulness for policy science and practice. *Policy and Society* 38(2), 167–179.

Tomlinson, S. (2012): The irresistible rise of the SEN industry. *Oxford Review of Education*. DOI:10.1080/03054985.2012.692055

Tomlinson, S. (2017) *A sociology of special and inclusive education. exploring the manufacture of inability*. Abingdon: Routledge.

Tomlinson, S. (2022) *Ignorance: Demolishing a Beveridge giant*. Newcastle-on-Tyne: Agenda Publishing.

Trent, S. C., Artiles, A. J., and Englert, C. S. (1998) From deficit thinking to social constructivism: A review of theory, research and practice in special education. *Review of Research in Education* 23, 277–307.

UIS (2019) *Fact sheet no. 56*. Paris: UNESCO. http://uis.unesco.org/sites/default/files/documents/new-methodology-shows-258-million-children-adolescents-and-youth-are-out-school.pdf

UNESCO (1990) *World declaration on education for all*. Paris: UNESCO.

UNESCO (1994) *Final report: World conference on special needs education: Access and quality*. Paris: UNESCO.

UNESCO (2000) *World education forum, Dakar, Senegal, 26–28 April 2000: Final report*. Paris: UNESCO.

UNESCO (2015) *Incheon Declaration and framework for action for the implementation of sustainable development goal 4*. Paris: UNESCO.

UNESCO (2017) *A guide for ensuring inclusion and equity in education*. Paris: UNESCO.

UNESCO (2019) *Cali commitment to equity and inclusion in education*. Paris: UNESCO.

UNESCO (2020) *Education in a post-COVID world: Nine ideas for public action*. Paris: UNESCO.

UNGEI (2012) *Gender analysis in education: A conceptual overview*. Paris: United Nations Girls' Education Initiative.

UNICEF (2019) *Fast facts: 10 facts illustrating why we must EndChildMarriage* New York: UNICEF. Available at: https://www.unicef.org/press-releases/fast-facts-10-facts-illustrating-why-we-mustendchildmarriage

United Nations (2008) *Convention on the rights of persons with disabilities*. New York: United Nations.

Vaino, K., Holbrook, J. and Rannikmae, M. (2013) A case study examining change in teacher beliefs through collaborative action research. *International Journal of Science Education* 35(1), 1e30.

Valli, L., Stefanski, A. and Jacobson, R. (2018) School-community partnership models: Implications for leadership. *International Journal of Leadership in Education* 21, 31–49.

van Zanten, A. (2009) Competitive arenas and schools' logics of action: A European comparison. *Compare: A Journal of Comparative and International Education* 39(1), 85–98.

Warren, M., Calderón, J., and Su, C. (2018) Is collaborative, community-engaged scholarship more rigorous than traditional scholarship? On advocacy, bias, and social science research. *Urban Education* 53(4), 445–472.

Warren, M., Park, S., and Tieken, M. (2016) The formation of community engaged scholars: A collaborative approach to doctoral training in education research. *Harvard Educational Review* 86(2), 233–260.

Waslander, S. Pater, C., & van der Weide, M. (2010). *Markets in education: an analytical review of empirical resercah on market mechanisms in education*. OECD Education working papers, 52.

Wasser, J. D. and Bresler, L. (1996) Working in the collaborative zone: Conceptualising collaboration in qualitative research teams. *Educational Researcher* 25(5), 5–15.

Weick, K. E. (1985) Sources of order in under organised systems: Themes in recent organisational theory. In Y. S. Lincoln (Ed) *Organisational theory and inquiry*. Beverly Hills, CA: Sage.

Wenger, E. (1998) *Communities of practice: Learning, meaning and identity*. Cambridge: Cambridge University Press.

West, M. and Ainscow, M. (2010) Improving schools in Hong Kong: A description of the improvement model and some reflections on its impact on schools, teachers and school principals. In S. Huber (Ed) *School leadership – International perspectives*. London: Springer.

West, M., Ainscow, M., and Nottman, H. (2003) *What leaders read: Key texts from education and beyond*. Nottingham: National College for School Leadership.

West, M., Ainscow, M., and Stanford, J. (2005) Sustaining improvement in schools in challenging circumstances: A study of successful practice. *School Leadership and Management* 25(1), 77–93.

West, A. & Bailey, W. (2013) The development of the academies programme: 'privatising' school-based education in England 1986–2013, *British Journal of Educational Studies* 61(2), 137–159.

Whitehurst, G. J. and Croft, M. (2010) *The Harlem Children's Zone, promise neighborhoods, and the broader, bolder approach to education*. Washington, DC: The Brookings Institution.

Wiborg, S. (2010) Learning lessons from the Swedish model. *Forum* 52(2), 279–284.

Wilkinson, R. and Pickett, K. (2009) *The spirit level*. London: Allen Lane.

Yost, D. S., Sentner, S. M., and Forlenza-Bailey, A. (2000) An examination of the construct of critical reflection: Implications for teacher education programming in the 21st century. *Journal of Teacher Education* 51(1), 39e49.

Yurkofsky, M. M., Peterson, A. J., Mehta, J. D., Horwitz-Willis, R., and Frumin, K. M. (2020) Research on continuous improvement: Exploring the complexities of managing educational change. *Review of Research in Education* 44, 403–433.

Zollers, N. J., Ramanathan, A. K., and Yu, M. (1999) The relationship between school culture and inclusion: How an inclusive culture supports inclusive education. *Qualitative Studies in Education* 12(2), 157–174.

Index

Note: Pages in *italics* represent figures.